Siegel's
CIVIL
PROCEDURE

Essay and Multiple-Choice Questions and Answers

Fifth Edition

BRIAN N. SIEGEL
J.D., Columbia Law School

LAZAR EMANUEL
J.D., Harvard Law School

Revised by

Allan Ides
Christopher N. May Professor of Law
Loyola Law School, Los Angeles

Wolters Kluwer
Law & Business

Published by Wolters Kluwer Law & Business in New York.

Wolters Kluwer Law & Business serves customers worldwide with CCH, Aspen Publishers, and Kluwer Law International products. (www.wolterskluwerlb.com)

To contact Customer Service, e-mail customer.service@wolterskluwer.com, call 1-800-234-1660, fax 1-800-901-9075, or mail correspondence to:

> Wolters Kluwer Law & Business
> Attn: Order Department
> PO Box 990
> Frederick, MD 21705

The authors gratefully acknowledge the assistance of the California Committee of Bar Examiners, which provided access to questions on which many of the essay questions in this book are based. Essay questions 18 and 34-35 are reproduced with the permission of CCH Incorporated from Allan Ides and Christopher N. May, chapters 6 and 7, Civil Procedure Cases and Problems, Fourth Edition, © 2012.

Printed in the United States of America.

1 2 3 4 5 6 7 8 9 0

ISBN 978-1-4548-0924-1

About Wolters Kluwer Law & Business

Wolters Kluwer Law & Business is a leading global provider of intelligent information and digital solutions for legal and business professionals in key specialty areas, and respected educational resources for professors and law students. Wolters Kluwer Law & Business connects legal and business professionals as well as those in the education market with timely, specialized authoritative content and information-enabled solutions to support success through productivity, accuracy, and mobility.

Serving customers worldwide, Wolters Kluwer Law & Business products include those under the Aspen Publishers, CCH, Kluwer Law International, Loislaw, Best Case, ftwilliam.com, and MediRegs family of products.

CCH products have been a trusted resource since 1913, and are highly regarded resources for legal, securities, antitrust and trade regulation, government contracting, banking, pension, payroll, employment and labor, and healthcare reimbursement and compliance professionals.

Aspen Publishers products provide essential information to attorneys, business professionals and law students. Written by preeminent authorities, the product line offers analytical and practical information in a range of specialty practice areas from securities law and intellectual property to mergers and acquisitions and pension/benefits. Aspen's trusted legal education resources provide professors and students with high-quality, up-to-date and effective resources for successful instruction and study in all areas of the law.

Kluwer Law International products provide the global business community with reliable international legal information in English. Legal practitioners, corporate counsel and business executives around the world rely on Kluwer Law journals, looseleafs, books, and electronic products for comprehensive information in many areas of international legal practice.

Loislaw is a comprehensive online legal research product providing legal content to law firm practitioners of various specializations. Loislaw provides attorneys with the ability to quickly and efficiently find the necessary legal information they need, when and where they need it, by facilitating access to primary law as well as state-specific law, records, forms and treatises.

Best Case Solutions is the leading bankruptcy software product to the bankruptcy industry. It provides software and workflow tools to flawlessly streamline petition preparation and the electronic filing process, while timely incorporating ever-changing court requirements.

ftwilliam.com offers employee benefits professionals the highest quality plan documents (retirement, welfare and non-qualified) and government forms (5500/PBGC, 1099 and IRS) software at highly competitive prices.

MediRegs products provide integrated health care compliance content and software solutions for professionals in healthcare, higher education and life sciences, including professionals in accounting, law and consulting.

Wolters Kluwer Law & Business, a division of Wolters Kluwer, is headquartered in New York. Wolters Kluwer is a market-leading global information services company focused on professionals.

Introduction

Although law school grades are a significant factor in obtaining a summer internship or entry position at a law firm, no formalized preparation for finals is offered at most law schools. For the most part, students are expected to fend for themselves in learning how to take a law school exam. Ironically, law school exams may bear little correspondence to the teaching methods used by professors during the school year. At least in the first year, professors require you to spend most of your time briefing cases. This is probably not great preparation for issue-spotting on exams. In briefing cases, you are made to focus on one or two principles of law at a time; thus, you don't get practice in relating one issue to another or in developing a picture of an entire problem or the entire course. When exams finally come, you're forced to make an abrupt 180-degree turn. Suddenly, you are asked to recognize, define, and discuss a variety of issues buried within a single multi-issue fact pattern. Alternatively, you may be asked to select among a number of possible answers, all of which look inviting but only one of which is right.

The comprehensive course outline you've created so diligently, and with such pain, means little if you're unable to apply its contents on your final exams. There is a vast difference between reading opinions in which the legal principles are clearly stated and applying those same principles to hypothetical essay exams and multiple-choice questions.

The purpose of this book is to help you bridge the gap between memorizing a rule of law and *understanding how to use it* in an exam. After an initial overview describing the exam-writing process, you see a large number of hypotheticals that test your ability to write analytical essays and to pick the right answers to multiple-choice questions. *Read them—all of them!* Then review the suggested answers that follow. You'll find that the key to superior grades lies in applying your knowledge through questions and answers, not through rote memory.

GOOD LUCK!

Table of Contents

Essay Answers

Multiple-Choice Questions

Multiple-Choice Answers

Tables and Index

Preparing Effectively for Essay Examinations

To achieve superior scores on essay exams, a law student must (1) learn and understand "blackletter" principles and rules of law for each subject; (2) analyze how those principles of law arise within a test fact pattern; and (3) clearly and succinctly discuss each principle and how it relates to the facts. One of the most common misconceptions about law school is that you must memorize each word on every page of your casebooks or outlines to do well on exams. The reality is that you can commit an entire casebook to memory and still do poorly on an exam. Our review of hundreds of student answers has shown us that students know most of the rules. Students who do *best* on exams are able to analyze how the rules relate to the facts in the questions, and they are able to communicate their analysis to the grader. The following pages cover what you need to know to achieve superior scores on your law school essay exams.

The "ERC" Process

To study effectively for law school exams you must be able to "ERC" (*E*lementize, *R*ecognize, and *C*onceptualize) each legal principle covered in your casebooks, class discussions, and course outlines. *Elementizing* means reducing each legal theory and rule you learn to a concise, straightforward statement of its essential elements. Without knowledge of these elements, it's difficult to see all the issues as they arise.

The "minimum contacts" test provides a good example. While the basic principle of personal jurisdiction can be stated at a very general level as involving the reasonableness of a court's exercise of power over a nonresident defendant, application of the minimum contacts test is more precise and requires the consideration of several specific and interconnected questions: (1) Has the nonresident defendant engaged in purposeful activities in the forum or directed toward the forum? (2) Are the purposeful contracts identified in step (1) related to the plaintiff's claim or, if not, are those contacts so substantial as to permit the exercise of personal jurisdiction over unrelated claims? (3) Assuming an affirmative response to both (1) and (2), would the exercise of personal jurisdiction over the nonresident defendant be unreasonable under the circumstances? In other words, the application of the minimum contacts test, which you may well be asked to do on a Civil Procedure exam, requires something more than a generalized inquiry in reasonableness or fairness. In fact, it requires a very structured examination of the facts.

1

Recognizing means perceiving or anticipating which words or ideas within a legal principle are likely to be the source of issues and how those issues are likely to arise in a hypothetical fact pattern. With respect to the first element of the minimum contacts test, key facts would be those reflective of a relationship between the nonresident defendant and the forum state, such as her activities in the state, any contractual relationships with residents of the state, the shipment of products into state, or the causing of effects in the state by activities occurring outside of the state.

Conceptualizing means imagining situations in which each element of a rule of law can give rise to factual issues. ***When you can imagine or construct an application of each element of a rule, you will truly understand the rule!*** If you can't imagine hypothetical fact patterns or stories involving particular rules of law, you will probably miss issues involving those rules on an exam. It's *crucial* (1) to *recognize* that issues result from the interaction of facts with rules of law and (2) to develop the ability to *conceptualize* or *imagine* fact patterns using the words or concepts within the rule.

For example, a set of facts illustrating the purposeful contacts element of the minimum contacts test might be the following:

> A, a State X corporation, manufactures shoes in State X. It sells its shoes in several other states, including State Z, where it employs 13 salespersons who solicit orders for shoes from residents of that state. The contracts for the sales are finalized in State X, after which the shoes are shipped to the purchaser in State Z. Has A engaged in purposeful activities in State Z? Yes, even though A manufactures its shoes in State X and even though the contracts for all sales are finalized there as well, A has engaged in purposeful activities in State Z by using in-state employees to solicit orders for A's shoes.

An illustration of how the word "related" might generate an issue is the following:

> Hotel, Inc., a Hong Kong corporation, operates a major hotel in Hong Kong. Toy Buyer is a State X business that imports toys made in Asia. Toy Buyer employees often make business trips to Hong Kong. Hotel sent an e-mail to Toy Buyer offering a special "new client" rate to Toy Buyer employees on their next visit to Hong Kong. The e-mail included an attached brochure that described the hotel's facilities, including the hotel's indoor pool. Immediately after receiving the e-mail, Toy Buyer booked a room for Bob, the company's chief buyer. On the evening of his first night at the hotel, Bob drowned in the hotel pool. His wife has brought a wrongful death action against Hotel in a State X court. Assuming the e-mail from Hotel to Toy Buyer constitutes a purposeful contact with State X, is that contact "related" to the wife's wrongful death action? Arguably, yes. The e-mail

is certainly not the proximate cause of the death—the strongest form of relatedness—since the e-mail would not be relevant to determining responsibility for Bob's death. But the e-mail is at least the cause in fact of the drowning—but for the e-mail, Bob would not have used the pool. The e-mail may even be more closely related to the claim in the sense that the drowning was a foreseeable consequence of the solicitation of business.

Notice how the above example takes the discussion beyond the basic relatedness element by using the facts to explore different ways of thinking about relatedness.

Issue-Spotting

One of the keys to doing well on an essay examination is issue-spotting. In fact, issue-spotting is *the* most important skill you will learn in law school. If you recognize a legal issue, you can find the applicable rule of law (if there is one) by researching the issue. But if you fail to see the issues, you won't learn the steps that lead to success or failure on exams or, for that matter, in the practice of law. It is important to remember that (1) an issue is a question to be decided by the judge or jury and (2) a question is "in issue" when it can be disputed or argued about at trial. The bottom line is that *if you don't spot an issue, you can't raise it or discuss it.*

The key to issue-spotting is to learn to approach a problem in the same way an attorney does. Let's assume you've been admitted to practice and a client enters your office with a legal problem involving a dispute. He or she will recite his facts to you and give you any documents that may be pertinent. The client will then want to know if he or she can sue (or be sued, if your client seeks to avoid liability). To answer your client's questions intelligently, you will have to decide the following: (1) what procedural or substantive principles or rules can possibly be asserted by your client, (2) what defense or defenses can possibly be raised to these principles, (3) what issues may arise if these defenses are asserted, (4) what arguments each side can make to persuade the fact finder to resolve the issue in the client's favor, and finally, (5) what the *likely* outcome of each issue will be. *All the issues that can possibly arise at trial will be relevant to your answers.*

How to Discuss an Issue

Keep in mind that *rules of law are the guides to issues* (i.e., an issue arises where there is a question whether the facts do, or do not, satisfy an element of a rule); a rule of law *cannot dispose of an issue* unless the rule can reasonably be *applied to the facts.*

A good way to learn how to discuss an issue is to study the following mini-hypothetical and the two student responses that follow it.

Mini-Hypothetical

Alex, a resident of State X, is the creator of More Hair, a useful hair-growth elixir for which Alex has a federal patent. More Hair is marketed by E-Market, Inc., a State X corporation, under a contract that requires E-Market to make the "best effort" to promote sales of the More Hair. Alex believes that E-Market's sales performance has fallen far short of its contractual obligations. Accordingly, he has sued E-Market in a U.S. federal district court sitting in State Y claiming that E-Market's breach of contract has diminished the value of the More Hair patent. He seeks $75,000 in damages. Defendant has filed a motion to dismiss for lack of subject matter jurisdiction. How should the court rule on that motion?

Pertinent Principles of Law:

1. A U.S. district court may exercise subject matter jurisdiction over (1) claims arising under federal law—federal question jurisdiction—and (2) controversies between citizens of different states when the amount in controversy exceeds $75,000—diversity jurisdiction.

2. Federal question jurisdiction may be exercised only if the plaintiff's claim is either created by federal law or includes an essential federal ingredient. There is no amount in controversy requirement in federal question cases.

3. Diversity jurisdiction may be exercised only if no plaintiff is a citizen of the same State as any defendant and only if the amount in controversy exceeds $75,000.

First Student Answer

Did the U.S. district court have jurisdiction over E-Market?

A U.S. district court may exercise personal jurisdiction over a nonresident defendant to the same extent as a court of the forum state. This requires an application of the minimum contacts test. There are insufficient facts to determine whether E-Market has purposeful contacts with State Y. There may also be some issues regarding proper venue.

As to subject matter jurisdiction, Alex's claim appears to be a state-created breach of contract claim. Hence, the creation test would not be satisfied. However, if federal law did create Alex's claim the creation test would be satisfied. But it probably does not. Even if the creation test is not satisfied, however, it appears that Alex's claim includes an essential federal ingredient, namely, the diminished value of his federal patent. Unfortunately, jurisdiction will not be permitted since the amount in controversy, which is $75,000, does not "exceed" the required minimum.

The district court does not have subject matter jurisdiction (and possibly personal jurisdiction), so the case should be dismissed.

Second Student Answer

Federal Question Jurisdiction:

Alex's claim does not arise under federal law for purposes of §1331 (federal question jurisdiction). Section 1331 can be satisfied in one of two ways: (1) the plaintiff asserts a federally created claim, or (2) the plaintiff asserts a state-created claim that includes an essential federal ingredient. Neither of these standards is satisfied.

Alex's claim is premised on E-Market's failure to meet its contractual obligation. That is a breach of contract claim and classically one that is created by state law. Nothing in these facts suggests otherwise. Hence, the creation is not satisfied. Nor is the essential federal ingredient test satisfied. Although Alex might argue that this case involves a patent (i.e., the marketing of a patented product), the defendant will convincingly argue by that nothing in Alex's claim suggests any need to construe federal patent law or to examine the patent in any manner. Quite likely the court will agree that the "federal issue" plays no part in his claim.

Diversity of Citizenship:

A federal court may exercise jurisdiction over a state law claim between citizens of different states if the amount in controversy exceeds $75,000. Neither standard is satisfied. Both Alex and E-Market are citizens of State X and the amount in controversy, which is "exactly $75,000, fails to meet the statutory minimum.

The district court must dismiss the suit.

Critique

Let's start by examining the First Student Answer. There are many problems with this answer, beginning with the very first sentence. The clear call of the question is whether the district court may exercise subject matter jurisdiction over Alex's lawsuit—"Does the district court have subject matter jurisdiction over Alex's claim?" Yet the First Student answer opens with a discussion of personal jurisdiction. It's true that there might be a personal jurisdiction or venue problem lurking in these facts, but the question clearly does not ask for an assessment of that issue. Moreover, the fact that were no facts on which to assess E-Market's contacts with State Y (or venue in State Y) should have provided a clue that these topics were non-starters.

When the question moves to the call of the question—subject matter jurisdiction—it seems that the answer is heading in a good direction. It notes that Alex's claim appears to be a state-created claim but then equivocates and rambles between the two possibilities (i.e., state created or federally created). This type of chatty answer is not likely to impress your professor. Commit to a position and explain it. If you then must argue the other side, commit to that side as well. "It could be this and it could be that" will not take you far.

As to the essential federal ingredient test, the answer simply assumes that the diminished value of the patent presents a federal issue. This is incorrect, however, and had the writer attempted to explain the contrary conclusion, he or she might have seen that there was nothing to the argument.

Finally, instead of discussing diversity separately, the first answer skips that very simple discussion and erroneously imports the amount in controversy standard into §1331, where it has no function whatsoever.

The Second Student Answer is much better than the First Student Answer. To begin with, it is well organized in the sense that the organization (and helpful labels) reflect the two separate jurisdictional statutes that must be considered—§1331 and §1332. Each section also begins with a succinct and correct statement of the legal standard to be applied. Also, unlike the first answer, the second answer is the opposite of chatty (and meandering); rather, it is direct and to the point.

The second answer also applies the law to the facts in a way that lets the reader know that the writer understands the material and how to apply that material to the facts presented.

Notice that both answers arrive at the correct conclusion, somewhat underscoring the relative unimportance of the conclusion.

Structuring Your Answer

Graders will give high marks to a clearly written, well-structured answer. Each issue you discuss should follow a specific and consistent structure that a grader can easily follow.

The Second Student Answer utilizes the *I-R-A-A-O format* with respect to the essential federal ingredient issue. In this format, the *I* stands for *Issue*, the *R* for *Rule of law*, the first *A* for *one side's Argument*, the second *A* for *the other party's rebuttal Argument*, and the *O* for your *Opinion as to how the issue would be resolved*. The *I-R-A-A-O* format emphasizes the importance of (1) discussing *both* sides of an issue (if there are two sides) and (2) communicating to the grader that, where an issue arises, an attorney can only advise his or her client as to the *probable* decision on that issue. Notice that the First Student Answer also uses I-R-A-A-O, albeit very poorly, in discussion the creation test.

A somewhat different format for analyzing each issue is the *I-R-A-C format*, which the Second Student Answer utilizes for the creation test and diversity. Here, the *I* stands for *Issue*, the *R* for *Rule of law*, the *A* for *Application of the facts to the rule of law*, and the *C* for *Conclusion*. *I-R-A-C* is a legitimate approach to the discussion of a particular issue, within the time constraints imposed by the question. The *I-R-A-C format* must be applied to each issue in the question; it is not the solution to the entire answer. If there are six issues in a question, for example, you should offer six separate, independent *I-R-A-C* analyses.

Whether to use the *I-R-A-C* approach or the *I-R-A-A-O* formula will depend on the nature of the issue presented as it relates to the underlying facts. Can you see how the Second Student Answer correctly navigated between the two? Whatever format you choose, however, remember the following rules:

First, *analyze all of the relevant facts*. Facts have significance in a particular case *only as they come under the applicable rules of law*. The facts presented must be analyzed and examined to see if they do or do not satisfy one element or another of the applicable rules, and the essential facts and rules must be stated and argued in your analysis.

Second, you must communicate to the grader the *precise rule of law* controlling the facts. In their eagerness to commence their arguments, students sometimes fail to state the applicable rule of law first. Remember, the *R* in either format stands for *Rule of law*. Defining the rule of law *before* an analysis of the facts is essential in order to allow the grader to follow your reasoning.

Third, it is important to treat *each side of an issue with equal detail*. If a hypothetical describes how an elderly man was killed when he ventured upon the land of a huge power company to obtain a better view of a nuclear reactor, your sympathies might understandably fall on the side of the old man. The grader will nevertheless expect you to see and make every plausible argument for the other side. Don't permit your personal viewpoint to affect your answer! A good lawyer never does! When discussing an issue, always state the arguments for each side.

Finally, remember to **state your opinion or conclusion** on each issue. Keep in mind, however, that your opinion or conclusion is probably the **least** important part of an exam answer. Why? Because your professor knows that no attorney can tell his or her client exactly how a judge or jury will decide a particular issue. By definition, an issue is a legal dispute that can go either way. An attorney, therefore, can offer the client only his or her best opinion about the likelihood of victory or defeat on an issue. Because the decision on any issue lies with the judge or jury, no attorney can ever be absolutely certain of the resolution.

Discuss All Possible Issues

As we've noted, a student should draw **some** type of conclusion or opinion for each issue raised. Whatever your conclusion on a particular issue, it is essential to anticipate and discuss **all of the issues** that would arise if the question were actually tried in court.

Let's assume that a personal jurisdiction hypothetical involves the full range of issues pertaining to the minimum contacts test. If the plaintiff fails to show purposeful contacts, the defendant will prevail. Nevertheless, even if you feel strongly that the defendant should prevail, you **must** go on to discuss all of the other potential issues as well (relatedness, general jurisdiction, the potential presumption of reasonableness, etc.). If you were to terminate your answer after a discussion of the purposeful-contacts element only, you would receive an inferior grade.

Why should you have to discuss every possible issue if you are relatively certain that the outcome of a particular issue would be dispositive of the entire case? Because at the commencement of litigation, neither party can be **absolutely positive** about which issues he or she will prevail upon at trial. We can state with confidence that every attorney with some degree of experience has won issues he or she thought he or she would lose, and has lost issues on which victory seemed assured. Because one can never be absolutely certain how a factual issue will be resolved by the fact finder, a good attorney (and exam writer) will consider **all** possible issues.

To understand the importance of discussing all of the potential issues, you should reflect on what you will do in the actual practice of law. If you represent the defendant, for example, it is your job to raise every possible defense. If there are five potential defenses, and your pleadings rely on only three of them (because you're sure you will win on all three), and the plaintiff is somehow successful on all three issues, your client may well sue you for malpractice. Your client's contention would be that you should be liable because if you had only raised the two additional issues, you might have prevailed on at least one of them, and therefore liability would have been avoided. It is an attorney's duty to raise *all* legitimate issues. A similar philosophy should be followed when taking essay exams.

What exactly do you say when you've resolved the initial issue in favor of the defendant, and discussion of any additional issues would seem to be moot? You should begin the discussion of the next issue with something like, "Assuming, however, the plaintiff prevailed on the foregoing issue, the next issue would be . . . . " The grader will understand and appreciate what you have done.

The corollary to the importance of raising all potential issues is that you should avoid discussion of obvious nonissues. Raising nonissues is detrimental in three ways: First, you waste precious time; second, you usually receive absolutely no points for discussing an issue that the grader deems extraneous; and third, it suggests to the grader that you lack the ability to distinguish the significant from the irrelevant. The best guideline for avoiding the discussion of a nonissue is to ask yourself, "Would I, as an attorney, feel comfortable bringing this issue to the attention of a judge or one of the lawyers working with me or against me in a case?"

Delineate the Transition from One Issue to the Next

It's a good idea to make it easy for the grader to see the issues you've found. One way to accomplish this is to cover only one issue per paragraph. Another way is to underline each issue statement. Provided that time permits, we recommend that you use both techniques. The essay answers in this book contain numerous illustrations of these suggestions.

One frequent student error is to write two separate paragraphs in which all of the arguments for one side are made in the initial paragraph, and all of the rebuttal arguments by the other side are made in the next paragraph. This organization is *a very bad idea*. It obliges the grader to reconstruct the exam answer in his or her mind several times to determine whether all possible issues have been discussed by both sides. It will also cause you to state the same rule of law more than once. A better-organized answer presents a given argument by one side and follows that immediately in the same paragraph with the other side's rebuttal to that argument.

Understanding the "Call" of a Question

The statement *at the end* of an essay question or of the fact pattern in a multiple-choice question is sometimes referred to as the "call" of the question. It usually asks you to do something specific such as "discuss," "discuss the rights of the parties," "list X's rights," "advise X," "give the best grounds on which to find the statute unconstitutional," "state what D can be convicted of," "recommend how the estate should be distributed," and so forth. The call of the question should be read carefully because it tells you exactly what you're expected to do. If a question asks, "what are X's rights against Y?" or "what is X liable to Y for?" you don't have to spend a lot of time on Y's rights against Z. You will usually receive absolutely no credit for discussing issues or facts that are not required by the call. On the other hand, if the call of an essay question is simply "discuss" or "discuss the rights of the parties," then *all* foreseeable issues must be covered by your answer.

Students are often led astray by an essay question's call. For example, if you are asked for "X's rights against Y" or to "advise X," you may think you may limit yourself to X's viewpoint with respect to the issues. This is *not correct*! You cannot resolve one party's rights against another party without considering the issues that would arise (and the arguments the other side would assert) if litigation occurred. In short, although the call of the question may appear to focus on the rights of one of the parties to the litigation, a superior answer will cover all the issues and arguments that person might *encounter* (not just the arguments he or she would *make*) in attempting to pursue his or her rights against the other side.

The Importance of Analyzing the Question Carefully Before Writing

The overriding *time pressure* of an essay exam is probably a major reason why many students fail to analyze a question carefully before writing. Five minutes into the allocated time for a particular question, you may notice that the person next to you is writing furiously. This thought then flashes through your mind: "Oh my goodness, he's writing more than I am, and therefore he's bound to get a better grade." It can be stated *unequivocally* that there is no necessary correlation between the number of words on your exam paper and the grade you'll receive. Students who begin their answer after only five minutes of analysis have probably seen only the most obvious issues and missed many, if not most, of the subtle ones. They are also likely to be less well organized.

Opinions differ as to how much time you should spend analyzing and outlining a question before you actually write the answer. We believe that you should spend 15 minutes analyzing, organizing, and outlining a one-hour question before writing your answer. This will usually provide sufficient time to analyze and organize the question thoroughly *and* enough time to write a relatively complete answer. Remember that each word of the question must be scrutinized to determine if it (1) suggests an issue under the operative rules of law or (2) can be used in making an argument for the resolution of an issue. Because you can't receive points for an issue you don't spot, it is usually wise to read a question *twice* before starting your outline.

When to Make an Assumption

The instructions for a question may tell you to *assume* facts that are necessary to the answer. Even when these instructions are *not* given, you may be obliged to make certain assumptions about missing facts in order to write a thorough answer. Assumptions should be made only when you are told or when you, as the attorney for one of the parties described in the question, would be obliged to solicit additional information from your client. On the other hand, assumptions should *never be used to change or alter the question*. Don't ever write something like "if the facts in the question were . . . , instead of . . . , then . . . would result." If you do this, you are wasting time on facts that are extraneous to the problem before you. Professors want you to deal with *their* fact patterns, not your own.

Students sometimes try to "write around" information they think is missing. They assume that their professor has failed to include every piece of data necessary for a thorough answer. This is generally *wrong*. The professor may have omitted some facts deliberately to see if the student *can figure out what to do* under the circumstances, and sometimes the professor may have omitted them inadvertently.

The way to deal with the omission of essential information is to describe (1) what fact (or facts) appears to be missing and (2) why that information is important. For example, in a personal jurisdiction essay involving a contractual relationship between a forum resident and a nonresident of the forum, the question may not include any facts pertaining to the precontractual negotiations between the parties. If that is so, it would be worth mentioning that such facts would help illuminate whether the contract was one under which the nonresident defendant could foresee being haled into a court of the forum state. That would be the case if the negotiations demonstrated that the nonresident defendant was an "active" buyer seeking a product with specific design specifications.

Assumptions should be made in a manner that keeps the other issues open (i.e., they lead to a discussion of all other possible issues). Don't assume facts that would virtually dispose of the entire hypothetical in a few sentences. For example, suppose that A called B a "convicted felon" (a statement that is inherently defamatory—that is, a statement that tends to subject the plaintiff to hatred, contempt, or ridicule). If A's statement is true, he has a complete defense to B's action for defamation. If the facts don't tell whether A's statement was true or not, it would *not* be wise to write something like, "We'll assume that A's statement about B is accurate, and therefore B cannot successfully sue A for defamation." So facile an approach would rarely be appreciated by the grader. The proper way to handle this situation would be to state, "If we assume that A's statement about B is not correct, A cannot raise the defense of truth." You've communicated to the grader that you recognize the need to assume an essential fact and that you've assumed it in a way that enables you to proceed to discuss all other issues.

Case Names

A law student is ordinarily *not* expected to recall case names on an exam. The professor knows that you have read a large number of cases for each course and that you would have to be a memory expert to have all of the names at your fingertips. If you confront a fact pattern that seems similar to a case you have reviewed (but you cannot recall its name), just write something like, "One case we've read held that . . ." or "It has been held that . . . ." In this manner, you have informed the grader that you are relying on a case that contained a fact pattern similar to the question at issue.

The only exception to this rule is in the case of a landmark decision (e.g., *International Shoe Co. v. State of Washington*). Landmark opinions are usually those that change or alter established law. These cases are usually easy to identify, because you will probably have spent an entire class period discussing each of them. *Erie Railroad v. Tompkins* is an example of a civil procedure case that would fall into this category. In these special cases, you may be expected to recall the case by name, as well as the proposition of law it stands for. However, this represents a very limited exception to the general rule that counsels against wasting precious time trying to memorize and reproduce case names.

How to Handle Time Pressures

What do you do when there are five minutes left in the exam and you have only written two-thirds of your answer? One thing *not* to do is write something like "No time left!" or "Not enough time!" This gets you nothing but the satisfaction of knowing you have communicated your personal frustrations to the grader. Another thing *not* to do is write a brief list of ideas and topics you meant to cover but didn't have time to write about. Professors will rarely give credit for undeveloped ideas.

First of all, it is not necessarily a bad thing to be pressed for time. The person who finishes five minutes early has very possibly missed some important issues. The more proficient you become in knowing what is expected on an exam, the greater difficulty you may experience in staying within the time limits. Second, remember that (at least to some extent) you're graded against your classmates' answers and they're under exactly the same time pressure as you. In short, don't panic if you can't write the "perfect" answer in the allotted time. Nobody does!

The best hedge against time-management problems is to *review as many old exams as possible.* These exercises will give you a familiarity with the process of organizing and writing an exam answer, which, in turn, should result in an enhanced ability to stay within the time boundaries. If you nevertheless find that you have about 15 minutes of writing to do and 5 minutes to do it in, write a paragraph that summarizes the remaining issues or arguments you would discuss if time permitted. As long as you've indicated that you're aware of the remaining legal issues, you'll probably receive some credit for them. Your analytical and argumentative skills will already be apparent to the grader by virtue of the issues that you have previously discussed.

Formatting Your Answer

Make sure that the way you write or type your answer presents your analysis in the best possible light. In other words, if you write, do so legibly. If you type, remember to use many paragraphs instead of just creating a document with all of your ideas merged into a single lengthy block of print. Remember, your professor may have a hundred or more exams to grade. If your answer is difficult to read, you will rarely be given the benefit of the doubt. On the other hand, a paper that is easy to read creates a very positive mental impact upon the professor.

The Importance of Reviewing Prior Exams

As we've mentioned, it is *extremely important to review old exams*. The transition from blackletter law to essay exam can be a difficult experience if the process has not been practiced. Although this book provides a large number of essay and multiple-choice questions, *don't stop here*! Most law schools have recent tests online or on file in the library, by course. If they are available only in the library, we strongly suggest that you make a copy of every old exam you can obtain (especially those given by your professors) at the beginning of each semester. The demand for these documents usually increases dramatically as "finals time" draws closer.

You should look at the exams for each course *throughout the semester*. Review them as you complete each chapter in your casebook. Sometimes the order of exam questions follows the sequence of the materials in your casebook. Thus, the first question on a law school test may involve the initial three chapters of the casebook; the second question may pertain to the fourth and fifth chapters; and so forth. In any event, *don't wait* until the semester is nearly over to begin reviewing old exams.

Keep in mind that no one is born with the ability to analyze questions and write superior answers to law school exams. Like any other skill, it is developed and perfected only through application. If you take the time to analyze numerous examinations from prior years, this evolutionary process will work smoothly. Don't just *think about* the answers to past exam questions; take the time to *write the answers down*. It's also wise to look back at an answer a day or two after you've written it. You will invariably see (1) ways to improve your organizational skills and (2) arguments you missed.

As you practice spotting issues on past exams, you will see how rules of law become the sources of issues on finals. As we've already noted, you have to *understand* how rules of law translate into issues in order to achieve superior grades on your exams. Reviewing exams from prior years should also reveal that certain issues tend to be lumped together in the same question. For instance, where a fact pattern involves a false statement made by one person about another, three potential theories of liability are often present—defamation, invasion of privacy (false, public light), and intentional infliction of severe emotional distress. You will need to see if any or all of these legal remedies apply to the facts.

Finally, one of the best means of evaluating if you understand a subject (or a particular area within a subject) is to attempt to create a hypothetical exam for that subject. Your exam should cover as many issues as possible. If you can write an issue-packed exam, you probably know that subject well. If you can't, then you probably haven't yet acquired an adequate understanding of how the principles of law in that subject can spawn issues.

As Always, a Caveat

The suggestions and advice offered in this book represent the product of many years of experience in legal education. We are confident that the techniques and concepts described in these pages will help you prepare for, and succeed at, your exams. Nevertheless, particular professors sometimes have a preference for exam-writing techniques that are not stressed in this book. Some instructors expect at least a slight reference to the *prima facie* elements of all pertinent legal theories (even though one or more of those principles are *not* placed into issue). Other professors want their students to emphasize public policy considerations in the arguments they make on a particular issue. Because this book is intended for nationwide consumption, these individualized preferences have *not* been stressed. The best way to find out whether your professor has a penchant for a particular writing approach is to ask him or her to provide you with a model answer to a previous exam. If a model answer is not available, speak to second- or third-year students who received a superior grade in that professor's class.

One final point. Although the rules of law stated in the answers to the questions in this book have been drawn from commonly used sources (casebooks, hornbooks, etc.), it is still conceivable that they may be slightly at odds with those taught by your professor. In the area of civil procedure, there are differences from jurisdiction to jurisdiction, and your professor will probably advise you as to how you should handle such differences. In instances in which a conflict exists between our formulation of a legal principle and the one taught by your professor, *follow the latter*! Because your grades are determined by your professors, their views should always supersede the views contained in this book.

Essay Questions

Question 1

APOW owns and operates a nuclear power plant. For one hour on each of three successive days, the plant emitted heavy radiation over the surrounding area, which has a population of 10,000. Several individuals injured by the radiation emitted on the third day brought a class action for "damages" in an appropriate federal district court against APOW on behalf of all those injured on one or more of the three days. After describing the relevant facts, the complaint alleged only that APOW was responsible for "wrongful conduct." Jurisdiction was based properly and exclusively on diversity of citizenship.

1. APOW moved to dismiss the complaint for failure to state a claim upon which relief could be granted. The motion was denied.

2. APOW then opposed plaintiffs' motion to certify the class, arguing that there was no common issue and that plaintiffs' claims were not typical of the class. Certification was granted.

3. During discovery, plaintiffs requested that APOW produce a memorandum concerning possible legal liability for nuclear power accidents, prepared by APOW's legal staff prior to the accident, but following minor accidents at another company's nuclear power plant. APOW objected. The state in which the action was brought had abolished its own work product doctrine a year earlier. The court held that the memorandum could be discovered.

Were the court's rulings correct? Discuss.

Question 2

Owner was the driver and Rider a passenger in Owner's expensive auto when it collided on a State X highway with a pickup truck driven by Trucker, a citizen of adjoining State Y. Both vehicles were damaged. Owner, Rider, and Trucker were injured.

Owner, a citizen of State X, sued Trucker in a U.S. district court in State X, claiming $80,000 in property damage to his auto. In his answer, Trucker denied negligence and asserted contributory negligence as a defense. After a nonjury trial, the court expressly found that Trucker was not negligent. Judgment was entered for Trucker and that judgment is now final.

Subsequently, Rider commenced a $400,000 personal injury suit against Owner in an appropriate State X court. State X has adopted the Federal Rules of Civil Procedure. Prior to trial, Owner timely moved that the suit be dismissed on the ground that Trucker was an indispensable party and had not been made a defendant. After a hearing, the court denied Owner's motion.

Before trial, Trucker timely petitioned to intervene as a plaintiff, and the court granted the petition over Owner's objection.

Trucker's complaint in intervention sought $200,000 for personal injury and property damage against Owner, who counterclaimed for $150,000 in personal injury damages. Rider was permitted to assert a $400,000 crossclaim against Trucker, over Trucker's objection.

None of the claims asserted is barred by a statute of limitations.

1. In the State X court action, did the court correctly rule that
   a. Trucker was not an indispensable party?
   b. Trucker could intervene?
   c. Rider could crossclaim against Trucker?

Discuss.

2. In the State X court action, what effect, if any, should the federal district court action have on
   a. Rider's claim against Owner?
   b. Rider's crossclaim against Trucker?
   c. Trucker's claim against Owner?
   d. Owner's counterclaim against Trucker?

Discuss.

Question 3

Seler, a citizen of State S, and Byer, a citizen of State B, met in State B and signed a written contract by which Seler agreed to sell Whiteacre, located in State W, to Byer. The contract provided that the purchase price of Whiteacre was $85,000. Seler returned to State S and sent Byer a deed conveying good title to Whiteacre.

Byer did not send Seler any money but brought an action against Seler for reformation of the contract to correct an alleged error in the contract price. Byer alleged that the agreed price was $37,500, and that the $85,000 figure in the contract was a typographical error. The action was brought in a federal district court in State B. Subject matter jurisdiction was based on diversity. Personal jurisdiction over Seler was based on service of process under State B's long-arm statute.

A. Seler moved to dismiss the action, alleging lack of personal and subject matter jurisdiction. The motion was denied.

B. Seler then filed an answer asserting that the written contract accurately stated the agreed price. In addition, he counterclaimed for the $85,000 purchase price set forth in the contract and demanded a jury trial. Byer answered the counterclaim and moved to strike the demand for jury trial. The motion was denied.

C. Seler then served Byer with interrogatories demanding responses to the following questions: "(1) Have you had Whiteacre appraised? (2) If so, state by whom, state the appraised value or values, and attach copies of all written reports received from all appraisers." Over Byer's timely objections to the interrogatories, the court ordered disclosure only of the identity of appraisers and the property's appraised values.

D. At trial, Byer testified that the agreed price was $37,500 and that the $85,000 figure in the written contract was a typographical error. An appraiser testified on behalf of Byer that the value of Whiteacre when the contract was signed was, at most, $42,200. Byer rested his case. Seler testified that the agreed price was $85,000, and judgment was entered accordingly. Byer promptly moved for "judgment as a matter of law" under FRCP 50. The court granted the motion. No other motions were made during or after trial.

1. Did the court rule correctly on the motion to dismiss? Discuss.
2. Did the court rule correctly on the motion to strike the demand for a jury trial? Discuss.

3. Did the court rule correctly on the objection to the interrogatories? Discuss.

4. Was the evidence admitted at trial such that the court was correct in granting the motion for judgment? Discuss.

5. What procedural argument or arguments should Seler have made in opposition to the motion for judgment? Discuss.

Question 4

Daw had just spent five days of vacation in State X and was on his way home to State A when his car collided with a vehicle driven by Paul. The collision occurred in State Y, ten miles beyond the State X border.

Paul, a citizen of State X, filed an action against Daw in a State X state court. Paul alleged that he had suffered $700 in property damage when his car was struck by Daw's car. Daw was served at his home in State A and moved to quash service of process on the ground that the court lacked personal jurisdiction over him. The motion was denied.

Daw then filed an answer that denied negligence on his part and alleged contributory negligence.

Paul served interrogatories on Daw that requested the substance of a conversation that Daw had with his wife and his attorney's investigator soon after the accident. When Daw refused to answer those interrogatories, Paul moved to compel answers, and the court granted the motion. A $700 default judgment was entered against Daw when he refused to comply with the discovery order. State X follows the Federal Rules of Civil Procedure with regard to discovery sanctions. Daw did not appeal the judgment, which then became final.

Paul filed a complaint against Daw in the U.S. district court in State X for $78,000 for personal injuries arising out of the accident. In his answer, Daw denied negligence and alleged contributory negligence. He also counter-claimed for damages for personal injuries resulting from the accident.

Both Paul and Daw moved for summary judgment based on claim preclusion (*res judicata*) and issue preclusion (collateral estoppel).

1. Was the State X court correct in denying Daw's motion to quash? Discuss.

2. Was the State X court correct in granting a default judgment against Daw? Discuss.

3. How should the U.S. district court rule on
   a. Paul's motion for summary judgment on his complaint and on Daw's counterclaim? Discuss.
   b. Daw's motion for summary judgment on Paul's complaint? Discuss.

Question 5

Two years ago, Worker was injured by a defectively constructed machine while he was working in an industrial plant in State A. The machine was manufactured by Macco, a State B corporation. While Worker was being treated for his injuries in Hospital in State A, Doctor, Worker's physician, prescribed medicine to which Worker was allergic. Worker's condition worsened gradually after that, but it was not clear whether his decline was due to the medicine or his injuries.

Worker sued Hospital in a state court in State A for negligence. Hospital's defenses were that (1) it was not responsible for the acts of Doctor since she was an independent contractor, (2) Doctor had not been negligent, and (3) Worker's present condition was caused by his injury, not the medicine. The trial court, sitting without a jury, found that Doctor had not acted negligently and that Doctor was not an agent of Hospital. The court made no finding on the cause of Worker's worsened condition. Judgment was entered for Hospital. No appeal was taken.

One month ago, Worker died and Worker's widow, Paula, who had lived in State A for five years, returned to her original home in State C. As executrix of her husband's estate duly qualified in State C, she has now filed suit in a state court in State C against Macco for the wrongful death of her husband. She has also filed suit against Doctor in a state court in State A for the damages she sustained as a result of the death of her husband. None of these suits is barred by a statute of limitations.

Macco sells its machinery in 40 states and maintains an office in State C. During the past ten years, Macco has sold its products in State C. Its annual sales volume in that state is between $400,000 and $500,000. The machine that injured Worker was originally sold to a corporation in State A, which sold it to Worker's employer.

A statute in State C provides: "The courts of this state may exercise jurisdiction over a person and property to the full extent permitted by the Constitution of the United States."

1. Assuming appropriate objection by Macco, may State C exercise jurisdiction over Macco in Paula's suit as executrix? Discuss.

2. What effect, if any, does Worker's suit in State A have on

    a. Paula's action in State C against Macco? Discuss.

    b. Paula's action in State A against Doctor? Discuss.

Question 6

Paul, a citizen of State X, brought suit against Dave, a citizen of State Y, in the U.S. district court in State Y for property damage caused to Paul's car when Dave's car ran into it in State Y. Jurisdiction was based on diversity of citizenship. The action was filed two weeks before the expiration of the period of State Y's one-year statute of limitations for negligent torts.

One month later, Paul filed an amended complaint that added a claim for personal injury arising out of the car accident. Dave moved to dismiss the personal injury claim. Because State Y had no rule allowing an amendment to relate back to the time of the original pleading under any circumstances, the district court granted Dave's motion, holding that the personal injury claim was barred by the State Y statute of limitations.

Dave next filed a third-party complaint impleading Insco, which he alleged was his auto insurer. Dave claimed Insco owed him the duty to defend against Paul's suit and to reimburse him for any loss. Insco, a State Y corporation, moved to dismiss the third-party complaint on the following grounds: (a) the third-party complaint was not authorized under the Federal Rules of Civil Procedure, (b) the district court lacked subject matter jurisdiction over that claim, and (c) the insurance policy had been fraudulently obtained. The district court dismissed Dave's third-party complaint.

At trial, over objection, the district court admitted the testimony of Dave's witness, Wit. Wit had not been listed by Dave in the pretrial order prepared pursuant to the Federal Rules of Civil Procedure. Though Dave could not demonstrate a valid reason why he had not included Wit in the pretrial order, the district court was of the view that no prejudice had resulted to Paul since he had been aware of Wit's existence.

Did the district court err in

1. granting Dave's motion to dismiss the personal injury claim? Discuss.
2. dismissing Dave's third-party complaint impleading Insco? Discuss.
3. admitting the testimony of Wit? Discuss.

Question 7

On March 15, 1987, Pat brought suit against Truco, a corporation, as sole defendant, in the U.S. district court in State Red. The State Red statute of limitations for personal injury claims caused by negligence is two years.

The complaint alleged (1) that Pat "resided" in State Red at the time of the events complained of and had become a "resident" of State White on March 1, 1987; (2) that Truco was a citizen of State Red; and (3) that on March 20, 1986, in State Red, Dan, a citizen of State Red and an employee of defendant Truco, negligently drove a motor vehicle, striking Pat and causing various personal injuries. The complaint sought a damage judgment against Truco for $100,000. Truco moved to dismiss the complaint on the following grounds: (1) lack of subject matter jurisdiction, and (2) failure of the complaint to join Dan as a defendant.

After its motions were denied, Truco's answer denied all of the allegations of Pat's complaint except that its citizenship is in State Red and that Dan was negligent.

At the pretrial conference, Pat and Truco stipulated that (1) plaintiff's actual damages were $85,000, and (2) Truco would be liable to Pat if Dan was an employee of Truco.

At trial on February 1, 1990, undisputed testimony admitted into evidence established that Pat was a citizen of State White at the time the complaint was filed, and that on March 20, 1986, when the accident occurred in State Red, Dan was driving a car owned by Truco with defendant's permission, but was *not* employed by Truco.

After each party rested, (1) Truco moved for a judgment as a matter of law, based on the stipulation and evidence introduced at trial; and (2) Pat moved for (a) permission to amend her complaint to insert a claim based upon a statute of State Red imposing liability upon the owner of a motor vehicle for the negligence of a driver operating the vehicle with the owner's permission, and (b) a judgment as a matter of law in her favor against Truco on the complaint as amended, for $85,000.

How should the court have decided

1. Truco's initial two motions to dismiss?
2. Truco's motion for a judgment as a matter of law?
3. Pat's post-trial motions?

Discuss.

Question 8

Albert is a touring professional golfer domiciled in State Red. Par Golf Clubs is incorporated and has its central administrative office in State Red, but its major manufacturing facility is located in State Green. Par pays Albert $25,000 per year for Albert's endorsement of a set of golf clubs that it manufactures in State Red and sells through independent retailers in every state. Albert uses these clubs in the tournaments in which he plays throughout the United States. Whenever he is interviewed, he specifically endorses the clubs.

Harold lives in State White. He is a weekend golfer. While at a golf tournament in State Red, he heard Albert's endorsement of the Par Golf Clubs and purchased a set from a golf shop in State Red.

While in State White, Harold was using one of the clubs for the first time. As a result of a metallurgical defect, the head of the club flew off the shaft and seriously injured Frances and Robert, both of whom are residents of State Green and were on a golfing holiday with Harold in State White.

Frances sued Par and Albert in a state court in State White. Par was sued as the manufacturer and Albert as the endorser of a defective product. Frances's complaint was based on theories of negligence and strict liability in tort. Two copies of the summons and complaint were personally delivered to Albert, who was "served personally and also on behalf of Par." At the time, Albert was physically present and playing in a tournament in State White. A copy of the complaint and summons was also personally delivered to the president of Par while he was on vacation in Hawaii. State White statutes authorize such service in actions for injuries received within the state.

1. Assuming all appropriate objections are properly made, may State White take jurisdiction over Albert and Par? Discuss.

2. Was Par validly served? Discuss.

3. Assuming Albert and Par desire to remove Frances's case to the U.S. district court in State Red, what arguments should Frances make in opposition? Discuss.

4. Assuming a final judgment on the merits is obtained in *Frances v. Albert and Par Golf Clubs, Inc.*, in a subsequent action by Robert in State Green, what use may Robert make of the judgment? What use may Par and Albert make of the judgment? Discuss.

Question 9

Pete, a citizen of State X, saw an advertisement in a newspaper published in adjoining State Y, but distributed also in State X. It described a new chemical process just developed by Devco, a State Z corporation, which has its principal place of business in State Z. The advertisement claimed the new process would revolutionize the industrial dye industry and urged readers to purchase stock in Devco. Pete wrote Devco requesting more information about the new process. Devco sent Pete promotional brochures that directed persons interested in buying Devco stock to consult Bull, a stockbroker.

Bull is a State X citizen, but his brokerage office is in State Y. Most of Bull's business has been selling Devco stock, for which Devco has paid him a commission. Devco did no business in either State X or State Y. Pete purchased 20,000 shares of Devco stock through Bull. Pete is the only Devco shareholder who is domiciled in State X. Shortly after Pete purchased his stock, it was found that the new chemical process developed by Devco had no commercial value. As a result, the value of Pete's Devco stock declined.

Pete sued Devco in the U.S. district court in State X, alleging jurisdiction based on diversity of citizenship. The complaint purported to state a claim for relief based solely on common law fraud and contained a demand for a jury trial.

Devco then moved to dismiss the complaint on the ground that the court lacked personal jurisdiction over it. Under State X law, a court has jurisdiction over a foreign corporation only if it is doing business in the state. The motion was denied, the court holding that it had jurisdiction to the full extent permitted by Fourteenth Amendment due process.

Devco moved to have Bull joined as a party-defendant. The motion was granted. Bull then moved for dismissal of the action against him on the ground that the district court in State X lacked subject matter jurisdiction. The motion was granted.

Devco answered the complaint and moved to strike Pete's demand for jury trial on the ground that factual issues in the case involved very complex scientific matters beyond the intellectual capabilities of the average juror, and therefore it had no adequate remedy at law. The district court struck Pete's jury trial demand and set the case for a bench trial.

1. Did the district court in State X have personal jurisdiction over Devco? Discuss.

2. Did the district court in State X have subject matter jurisdiction over the action against Bull? Discuss.

3. Assuming the district court in State X had subject matter jurisdiction over the claim against Bull, was the court correct in ordering Bull joined as a party-defendant? Discuss.

4. Did the district court err in striking Pete's demand for a jury trial? Discuss.

Question 10

Valco is a corporation incorporated in State B. Its principal office and sole manufacturing plant is in State A. It manufactures pressure valves for compressed air tanks. It purchases the "collars" affixed to the pressure valves, which are used to attach the valve to the air tank, from Mity, a State A corporation

The Valco pressure valve on a piece of machinery owned by Peter and Quincy and used by them in State C exploded. Peter and Quincy were seriously injured. At all times, Peter was a citizen of State C. At the time of the explosion, Quincy was a citizen of State A, but after the accident he moved to State B, where he is now domiciled.

Peter and Quincy wish to assert claims against Valco and Mity on the theory that the valve exploded because of a defective collar. Valco has informed Peter and Quincy that it will claim that a written notice recalling the valves had been sent to them and to all other users of this model valve, and that Peter and Quincy ignored the notice.

1. If Peter, as sole plaintiff, institutes an action against Valco, as sole defendant, in the U.S. district court in State C, may Valco object to the failure by Peter to join Mity as a defendant? May Valco bring Mity into the case as a defendant, and, if so, how? Discuss.

2. If Peter and Quincy institute an action against Valco and Mity in the U.S. district court in State C for $100,000 damages each, what issues may be raised as to joinder of parties plaintiff, joinder of parties defendant, joinder of causes of action, jurisdiction over the defendants, and jurisdiction over the subject matter? How should the trial court rule on each issue? Discuss.

3. If an action by Peter, as sole plaintiff, against Valco and Mity is commenced and tried in the U.S. district court in State A, should the trial court apply State A law, State C law, or federal law on the issues of (a) whether plaintiff must plead freedom from contributory fault, and (b) who has the burden of persuasion on the issue of contributory fault? Discuss.

Question 11

Don Pickles was a teenage comedian. In early September, Merv Griffey, a talent agent, took Don under his wing, and in two months made Don a star. In early December, Merv told Don that he had booked him to give a performance at the Palladium in California on New Year's Eve. Don immediately advised Merv that he had a verbal agreement with Ms. Bigbucks, a prominent New York attorney, to play at the latter's New Year's Eve party (where Don had previously performed). Merv advised Don to "cancel out" Bigbucks since "verbal contracts are unenforceable," which Don immediately did via telegram. Don and Merv both lived in Chicago, Illinois.

Two weeks later, when in Massachusetts en route to New Jersey to visit his girlfriend, Don stopped at a roadside restaurant. As he exited his car, he was served with a summons and complaint in an action filed by Bigbucks against Don and the Palladium Corporation in the U.S. district court for Massachusetts. The complaint alleged that Don was liable for breach of contract and that the Palladium Corporation was liable in the amount of $75,000 for inducing breach of the Don-Bigbucks agreement. Bigbucks asked for an injunction precluding Don from playing at the Palladium because her remedy at law was inadequate. Bigbucks premised this assertion on the grounds that Bigbucks had already invited many of her major clients to the party and would "lose face" if Don played somewhere else. The Palladium is located in California, owned by Palladium Corporation, a New York corporation (where its board of directors meets monthly). Palladium Corporation was served by delivering a copy of the summons and complaint to the president's personal secretary at its corporate offices in New York.

Don answered by denying all but the jurisdictional allegations of Bigbucks's complaint (i.e., he admitted that he was an Illinois citizen). Don also filed a third-party complaint against Merv for misadvising him as to his legal obligations to Bigbucks. Palladium Corporation filed an answer denying Bigbucks's allegations and a third-party complaint against Merv, claiming that Merv never advised them of an outstanding contract for Don's services. Palladium Corporation also filed a motion to transfer pursuant to 28 U.S.C. §§1404 and 1406, asking that the matter be transferred to the appropriate U.S. district court in California, but this motion was denied.

Before Merv was served with Don's third-party complaint, Don called him and complained about being "in the middle of a federal case." Don advised Merv that unless the latter "got him out of this mess, he was going to find another agent." Don also advised Merv to "come see him right away" in

Boston, Massachusetts. Immediately after Merv arrived at the airport, Don asked Merv if the Palladium show was going to be canceled. When Merv said "No," Don motioned to a process server who handed Merv the third-party complaint and summons. The Palladium Corporation served Merv by mailing a certified letter containing a copy of the summons and complaint to his office in Chicago. Merv's secretary signed for it and later gave the documents to him. This type of service was permissible under Massachusetts law. Merv responded to the third-party complaints by making the appropriate motions to dismiss them. When these motions were denied, he filed an answer denying liability to both Don and the Palladium Corporation.

The trial judge determined that she would hear the request for injunctive relief first (as was permissible under Massachusetts law) since this was the "lynchpin" issue. At trial, Don raised the defense of minority against Bigbucks's action, even though he had not stated it as an affirmative defense in this answer. The court, upon objection by Bigbucks, held that this defense was at variance with the pleading and could not now be raised. The court also held that Bigbucks was entitled to the relief she sought from Don. The jury decided that (1) Bigbucks was entitled to recover on her claim against the Palladium Corporation, and (2) Don and the Palladium Corporation were entitled to prevail on their third-party claims against Merv.

Discuss the issues that could be raised on appeal.

Question 12

Ped is a citizen of State A. Driver is a citizen of State D. Health is a corporation incorporated in State H. Its sole place of business is a hospital and corporate headquarters in State A. Ped was injured when struck by a motor vehicle operated by Driver in State A and hospitalized in the Health hospital. His injuries were allegedly aggravated as a result of Health's negligence.

Ped sued Driver and Health in a State A court, claiming damages in the sum of $100,000 and alleging that he was uncertain which defendant was responsible for which portion of his damages.

Upon Health's timely petition, the case was removed to the U.S. district court in State A. Thereafter, Ped moved to have the case remanded to the state court. Ped's motion was granted.

After remand, Health demurred on the grounds of improper joinder of parties. The demurrer was overruled.

Both Health and Driver filed answers denying liability and damages. Ped then filed a timely request for admissions asking that each defendant admit liability, reserving for trial only the issue of damages. Both defendants filed timely objections on the grounds that the requests called for legal conclusions. The objections were sustained.

Following a jury trial, a verdict was returned in favor of Ped and against both defendants in the sum of $43,652.89. Ped moved for a new trial on the issue of damages and, in the alternative, on all issues. He supported his motion by the affidavits of five jurors who stated that: (1) immediately after entering the jury room, the jurors took a ballot on the issue of whether Ped should recover and the vote was 12 to 0 in favor of Ped and against both defendants; (2) each juror then wrote down his or her idea of the amount of the recovery; the figures were totaled, divided by 12, and the result was $43,652.89; and (3) all jurors then agreed that their verdict would be $43,652.89. Based upon defendants' objections, the court refused to consider the affidavits and denied Ped's motion for a new trial.

Discuss the correctness of the court's rulings, setting forth the arguments that might reasonably be made in support of and in opposition to each of the following:

1. Ped's motion to remand
2. Health's demurrer
3. Ped's request for admissions
4. Ped's motion for a new trial

Question 13

Abel, an African American citizen of State Red, attempted to rent an apartment in a building in State Red owned by Cozy Nook, Inc., a State Red corporation. Abel's offer to rent was refused, and the apartment was rented to Dod for a term of two years.

Abel then obtained housing in State White, and sued Cozy Nook in a State White court of general jurisdiction, alleging a racially motivated denial of housing in violation of a federal statute. The complaint prayed for money damages and a mandatory injunction that would require Cozy Nook to give Abel possession of the apartment he had offered to rent or a similar apartment in the same building. Cozy Nook maintained a bank account in State White at Bank, but had no other business dealings in that state. Abel attached this account after notice and a hearing attended by Cozy Nook's president.

The federal statute authorized actions to be brought in "appropriate state or local courts of general jurisdiction," as well as federal court. The statute has been construed by the U.S. Supreme Court to require trial by jury in federal court suits. State White law does not provide for a jury trial in such cases.

Cozy Nook filed a motion to dismiss for failure to join a required party (Dod), lack of personal jurisdiction, and forum non conveniens. In addition, Cozy Nook made a timely demand for jury trial if the action was not dismissed.

How should the court rule on each ground set forth in the motion to dismiss and on the demand for jury trial?

Discuss.

Question 14

Tinselware, Inc., an Arizona corporation, sells widgets only in Phoenix, Arizona. Maureen, an employee of Tinselware, initiated telephone negotiations with Don, hoping he would purchase widgets for resale in California. Don, domiciled in San Francisco, responded to Maureen's telephone call by driving to Phoenix.

While in Phoenix, Don bought 75,000 widgets at $1 each. After returning to California, he discovered that the widgets did not function properly. He filed a breach of contract action against Tinselware in the U.S. district court in San Francisco.

Summons and complaint were hand-delivered to Maureen in Arizona, on behalf of Tinselware, Inc. Don then mailed a copy of the summons and complaint to the president of Tinselware—assume that this is a permissible means of service of process under California law.

Tinselware successfully moved to have the action dismissed because of (1) lack of subject matter and personal jurisdiction, and (2) lack of proper service. If Tinselware's motions had been denied, it would have attempted to have the action transferred to the U.S. district court in Nevada so that each party could travel an approximately equal distance to attend trial. Don then filed a new complaint against Maureen in the U.S. district court in San Francisco. However, the applicable statute of limitations had run after dismissal of the first suit and prior to refiling the second suit, so his action was dismissed.

1. Was the court's dismissal of the original action on each of the grounds stated correct?

2. Could the court have transferred the action to a federal district court in Nevada?

3. Was the dismissal of Don's action against Maureen correct?

Question 15

Defendant Delightful Skies, Inc. ("D") is a discount airline. D's Flight 007, carrying passengers and cargo from Boston to Philadelphia, skidded off the runway during takeoff, causing minor injuries to all the passengers. There were 40 passengers aboard from various states. Pete was one of the passengers. Pete is domiciled in Arizona, but owns several apartment houses in Los Angeles (which is in the Central District of California).

Pete files a diversity class action against D in U.S. District Court for the Central District of California. Pete seeks an $80,000 recovery for his minor personal injuries and to recover for injuries suffered by each of the other passengers. There is some evidence that the engine on the plane, manufactured by Boing, Inc., may have malfunctioned during takeoff, causing the accident. Boing is a Delaware corporation with its principal place of business in Massachusetts.

D is incorporated in Massachusetts, where its corporate headquarters are located. However, the majority of its flights originate and land on the West Coast, and D's main booking terminal and reservation center is in Arizona. D would prefer to defend in Massachusetts, where the crash occurred and where it believes juries are less liberal.

In response to P's complaint, D filed motions to dismiss the complaint for lack of subject matter jurisdiction and improper venue, to dismiss the class allegations, and to transfer the case to the appropriate federal district court in Massachusetts. D also filed a motion to implead Boing.

Discuss the likely outcome of D's motions and its impleader action.

Question 16

Photo Celebrities, Inc. ("P") is a Florida corporation with its principal place of business in Florida. Its primary business is the sale of candid celebrity photographs to purveyors of celebrity news. Many of the photographed celebrities live and work in Southern California. P has a Los Angeles office, employs Los Angeles-based photographers, has a registered agent for service of process in California, and pays fees to the California Franchise Tax Board. Dish the Dirt Inc. ("D") is an Ohio corporation with its principal place of business in Ohio. D operates a popular website called chit-chat.net (12 million unique U.S. visitors and 70 million U.S. page views per month). The website covers celebrities in the entertainment industry and features photo galleries, videos, and short articles. Visitors to the site may post comments on articles, vote in polls, subscribe to an e-mail newsletter, and submit news tips and photos of celebrities. The website posts third-party advertisements for jobs, hotels, and vacations in California and features a "Ticket Center," which is a link to the website of a third-party vendor that sells tickets to nationwide events, some of which are in California. In addition, D has agreements with several California businesses. A California firm designed Gossip's website and performs site maintenance. A California Internet advertising agency solicits buyers and places advertisements on chit-chat.net. A California wireless provider designed and hosts a version of chit-chat.net accessible to mobile phone users. Finally, D has entered a "link-sharing" agreement with a California-based national news site, according to which each site agrees to promote the other's top stories. D has no offices, real property, or staff in California, is not licensed to do business in California, and pays no California taxes.

In 2008, a photographer working for P shot 35 pictures of a celebrity couple — Froggie, a popular hip-hop singer who performs with the Black Eyed Beans, and Josh Who, an actor with credits in several poorly received movies — while the couple was bathing, sunning, and jet skiing in the Bahamas. P registered its copyright in the photos and posted the photos on its website. D then reposted the photos on chit-chat.net without first receiving permission from P.

P sued D in the U.S. district court for the Central District of California, alleging that D infringed P's copyright in the photos. P sought an injunction barring D from further dissemination of the photos, as well as actual and statutory damages. D has now filed a timely Rule 12(b)(2) motion to dismiss for lack of personal jurisdiction.

Describe and evaluate the arguments that each side is likely to make in support of or in opposition to this motion. You may assume that California has a due process style long-arm statute. Address both general and specific jurisdiction. Explain how you think the court should rule on D's motion.

Question 17

Smith, a citizen of State X, was an employee of Zonco, a State X corporation. A truck owned by Zonco, while driven by Smith, struck Patricia, a citizen of State Y. Patricia was injured and sued Zonco for $150,000 in the U.S. district court in State X, alleging that Zonco and Smith were negligent. She did not sue Smith.

Zonco made a motion to dismiss the complaint for failure to join Smith. The motion was overruled. Thereafter, Zonco answered, denying the negligence of either Zonco or Smith, and further denying that Patricia was injured.

Patricia then served Zonco with a notice to produce a written statement made and signed by a coworker of Smith who was riding with Smith at the time of the accident. The statement had been obtained by an adjuster for Zonco's insurance carrier shortly after the accident. Zonco refused to produce the statement, and the court sustained that refusal.

Patricia took the deposition of Smith at which Smith testified under oath that (1) Patricia was crossing the intersection in the pedestrian crosswalk with the green light, and (2) the truck driven by Smith ran into Patricia because the brakes failed. Patricia filed the deposition with a motion for summary judgment on the issue of liability, reserving for the jury only the question of damages. The motion was denied.

The action was tried before a jury. At the conclusion of the evidence, Zonco moved for a judgment as a matter of law. There was uncontradicted testimony introduced at trial that Smith was employed by Zonco and that Patricia had suffered a severe, painful injury as a consequence of the accident, and that her special damages for medical and hospital bills and loss of earnings were $80,000. The jury returned a verdict in the sum of $85,000. Zonco moved for a judgment notwithstanding the verdict. This motion was denied. Patricia moved for a new trial solely on the issue of damages. The trial judge ordered that the motion should be granted, unless Zonco consented to an increase in the judgment to $95,000.

Discuss the arguments that might reasonably have been made to the trial court in support of, and in opposition to, the court's rulings on

1. Zonco's motion to dismiss for failure to join Smith;
2. Patricia's notice to produce;
3. Patricia's motion for summary judgment;
4. Zonco's motion for judgment notwithstanding the verdict; and
5. Patricia's motion for a new trial.

Question 18

Plato decided to build a temple to reason in State X. He hired Derrida to provide blueprints for the project. All was going well until the foundation of the temple unexpectedly deconstructed in a morass of literary confusion. Plato was seriously injured in the chaos that ensued, and he has sued Derrida in a State X federal district court, properly invoking that court's diversity jurisdiction. Plato filed his claim, which is well recognized under the laws of State X, within the applicable State X statute of limitations, but did not serve Derrida until after the statute of limitations had run. Assume that a newly enacted federal statute provides as follows: "The filing of the complaint in a United States District Court shall operate to toll any applicable statute of limitations as to the claims asserted." 28 U.S.C. § A. State X law provides that the statute of limitations is tolled only by proper service of process on the defendant. Derrida has filed a motion to dismiss, arguing that Plato's claim was inherently meaningless and, more to the point, barred by the statute of limitations.

1. How would you analyze the statute-of-limitations question presented in Derrida's motion?

2. Suppose that instead of being part of a federal statute, the above tolling provision was embodied in an amended version of Rule 3 of the Federal Rules of Civil Procedure. How then would you analyze the statute-of-limitations question presented in Derrida's motion?

3. Finally, suppose that the quoted tolling provision was not embodied in a statute or a formal rule, but reflected the substance of federal judge-made doctrine applied in federal question and diversity cases. How then would you analyze the statute-of-limitations question presented in Derrida's motion?

Question 19

Salco is a corporation, incorporated and having its principal place of business in State A. Its sole business is the sale of products by mail order. It advertises its products in national magazines. None of these magazines is published in State B. Salco employs no agents or salespeople in State B.

Poe, a citizen of State B, commenced a class action in a competent State B court against Salco for fraud and misrepresentation in the sale of certain hi-tech alarm clocks to him and other citizens of State B. He alleged that 300 such clocks were sold to citizens of State B, and that he and each such person was damaged in the sum of $250. He asked for actual damages in the amount of $75,000, and punitive damages in the sum of $25 million. In accordance with State B law, process was served on Salco by sending a copy of the complaint and summons by registered mail, return receipt requested, to the president of Salco at the company's principal place of business in State A.

Salco filed a petition for removal from the State B court to the U.S. district court in State B. After removal, Salco filed a motion to dismiss pursuant to FRCP 12(b)(2) and (5). The motion was denied. Poe then filed a motion to remand to the State B court on the ground that the complaint did not state a claim within the jurisdiction of the U.S. district court. The motion was denied. Salco then moved for a more definite statement. This motion was also denied. The action then proceeded to trial. Judgment on the merits was rendered in favor of Salco.

After the judgment was final, Jones, a citizen of State B, filed an action in a State B court against Salco, based on the same claims of fraud and misrepresentation in the sale to him of one of the 300 alarm clocks. Salco filed a motion to dismiss upon the ground that the judgment in *Poe v. Salco* was a bar to the action by Jones. The motion was granted.

1. Was the U.S. district court correct in its rulings on
   a. Salco's the FRCP 12(b) motion to dismiss?
   b. Poe's motion to remand?
   c. Salco's motion for a more definite statement?
2. Was the State B court correct in its ruling on the motion to dismiss in *Jones v. Salco*?

Question 20

Paula, a citizen of the State of Calvada, purchased a box of breakfast cereal produced by Krispy at a grocery store in Calvada. As part of a promotional campaign by Krispy, there was a certificate in the box that stated that by sending "the certificate and $1 to Glassco, A Street, Central City, State of Black, USA," the sender would receive by return mail six cocktail glasses. Paula sent in the certificate and $1 and thereafter received the glasses. While she was washing them for the first time, one shattered in her hand, cutting the tendons and permanently injuring her.

Paula sued Glassco for $100,000 in a Calvada state court, basing jurisdiction on a Calvada statute giving its courts jurisdiction over "any person who commits a tortious act in this state with respect to any cause of action arising out of such act." The statute further provided that in such cases, process could be served on a foreign corporation by mailing a copy of the summons and complaint by registered mail, return receipt requested, to the corporation at its "place of business outside of the state." Glassco was incorporated in and had its principal place of business in State White.

Copies of the summons and complaint were mailed by registered mail, return receipt requested, addressed to "Glassco, A Street, Central City, State of Black, USA" and were returned with the notation "not accepted by addressee."

After the statutory time for appearance had expired, the default of Glassco was entered and the case heard as a default matter. Other than medical testimony regarding the extent and nature of her injuries, the only evidence received was Paula's testimony concerning the manner in which she obtained the glasses and the fact that while she was carefully washing one glass it shattered in her hand. Judgment was in Paula's favor for $25,000.

1. Is the Calvada verdict a valid judgment? Discuss.

2. Assuming that it is a valid judgment, may Glassco nevertheless have it set aside, and, if so, on what grounds? Discuss.

3. Assuming that the judgment is set aside and a new trial is held, is Paula likely to prevail if the only evidence offered by her is the same as that presented at the hearing at which the default judgment was rendered? Discuss.

Question 21

Peter is a citizen of State Red. Stanford James is a citizen of State White. On August 20, 2006, in State White, Peter was injured when the car he was driving collided with a car owned and driven by Stanford James. The applicable statute of limitations in both States Red and White is two years and is tolled by the filing of the complaint.

On August 16, 2008, Peter filed suit in the U.S. district court for State Red to recover for personal injuries he received in the collision. The complaint set forth the correct date and place of the collision, but erroneously named the defendant as James Stanford. Peter sought $80,000 in damages.

On August 30, 2008, while Stanford James was in State Red at the invitation of Peter to discuss the settlement of Peter's claim, he was personally served with the summons and complaint. Thereafter the following occurred:

Stanford James filed a timely Rule 12(b) motion to dismiss the action, or, in the alternative, to transfer the action to the U.S. district court in State White. Both motions were denied.

Two weeks after Sanford James filed his Rule 12(b) motion, Peter moved to amend his complaint to name Stanford James as defendant in place of James Stanford. The motion was granted.

Stanford James then filed an answer that, among other matters, alleged that Peter's claim was barred by the statute of limitations. Stanford James then moved for judgment on the pleadings on that ground. The motion was granted.

Assuming all appropriate grounds were urged in support of and in opposition to each of the motions mentioned, was the trial court correct in its rulings on

1. Stanford James's Rule 12(b) motion? Discuss.
2. Stanford James's motion to transfer? Discuss.
3. Peter's motion to amend the complaint? Discuss.
4. Stanford James's motion for judgment on the pleadings? Discuss.

Question 22

While visiting Austin, Texas, Paul was arrested outside Silley's Department Store, an exclusive men's clothing store. As he was departing, Mary Poppins, the cashier at Silley's, shouted "Stop, thief!" Bill Joe Bobb, a police officer who responded to Mary's shout, tackled Paul and applied a chokehold, allegedly causing Paul serious, permanent injuries.

Both Poppins and Bobb are citizens of Texas. Bobb lives in Austin. Paul is a citizen of Oklahoma. Bobb owns a 5 percent limited partnership interest in an eight-unit apartment house in Oklahoma. The limited partnership was formed in Texas and is operated by a general partner who is domiciled in Texas. As a limited partner, Bobb has no say in how limited partnership assets are operated. Silley's does a mail order business from its department store, and 14 percent of its mail order sales are to persons in Oklahoma (this represents 3 percent of Silley's total business). Silley's is a Texas corporation with its principal place of business in Texas.

1. Paul sued Bobb and Silley's in the U.S. district court in Oklahoma. He claimed that the defendants falsely imprisoned him and were each liable to him for $85,000. Silley's and Bobb do **not** desire to stand trial in Oklahoma. Describe their procedural alternatives. Assume the Texas and Oklahoma long-arm statutes give their courts all requisites of personal jurisdiction consistent with due process.

Assume Paul did not commence an action in Oklahoma, but filed his suit in a U.S. district court sitting in Texas. In this suit, Paul sued Bobb under a federal civil rights statute and for the state-law tort of assault and battery. He also sued Mary and Silley's as defendants, claiming that each was liable for the state-law tort of false arrest..

2. Can Paul join all of these parties in a single action? (Assume personal jurisdiction is satisfied.)

3. Would the U.S. district court in Nebraska have subject matter jurisdiction over Paul's claim?

Question 23

Pam, a patient injured in a nursing home fire, brought a suit for $77,000 against the home's operators, D Inc., in U.S. district court in State X, where the nursing home in which P resides is located. Jurisdiction was properly based on diversity of citizenship because even though P resides in State X, her domicile is actually in State Y. Under the law of State X, the failure of a nursing home to install smoke detectors in each patient's room is considered negligence *per se.* P alleged D's failure to install the device; D's answer denied all allegations in the complaint.

P promptly moved for summary judgment as to liability, attaching her own sworn affidavit stating that no smoke detector had been installed in her room. D's attorney responded with a memorandum asserting, "My client stands by its Answer in this case." The court denied the motion.

P then initiated discovery. She first served an interrogatory on D asking whether it had installed a smoke detector in P's room. The appropriate corporate official responded, "No."

P also requested D to produce for inspection its fire investigator's report, hoping that the investigator's early investigation of the since-demolished home showed no smoke detectors present. D refused to comply with the discovery request. P moved to compel production, and the court ordered D to produce the report for inspection and also held D in contempt of court for refusing the discovery request.

At trial, M, D's maintenance director, testified that smoke detectors had been installed in P's room; P's motion to disallow M's testimony as inconsistent with the interrogatory answer was denied.

Was the district court correct in its ruling

1. on P's motion for summary judgment as to liability?
2. on P's motion to compel production of the fire investigator's report?
3. holding D in contempt for refusing P's discovery request?
4. on P's motion to disallow M's testimony concerning the installation of a smoke detector in P's room?

Discuss.

Question 24

Borrow, a resident of State A, obtained a $12,000 car loan from Finco. Finco is incorporated and has its principal place of business in State A. When Borrow began making installment payments against the loan, she was dismayed to learn that her required monthly payments were in an amount greater than she had expected.

Borrow brought suit against Finco in a state court in State A, asserting a claim under the federal Truth-in-Lending Act ("TLA"). TLA specifically requires lenders to disclose to a borrower in a consumer loan transaction the amount of the monthly loan payment. TLA further provides that a borrower whose rights under TLA have been violated may bring an action against the lender in a U.S. district court, or in any other court of competent jurisdiction.

Finco filed its answer denying liability and asserting a counterclaim against Borrow under state law for recovery of the full amount owed on the loan. Finco then timely removed the suit to the U.S. district court for the district of State A. In the district court, Borrow moved to remand the action. The motion was denied.

Shortly thereafter Borrow moved to amend her complaint to (1) add an additional defendant, Dealer, the company that had sold her the car, (2) allege that Dealer violated State A's Consumer Protection Law ("CPL") by providing her erroneous information about the terms of her loan, and (3) allege that Dealer's CPL violation had resulted in $20,000 in damages. Dealer is incorporated in State A and conducts all of its business there. The district court denied the motion to amend on the ground that the court lacked subject matter jurisdiction over Borrow's claim against Dealer.

Borrow next moved for partial summary judgment that, if granted, would preclude Finco from denying that its lending agreement violated TLA. In support of this motion, Borrow offered uncontradicted evidence that in previous lawsuits brought by other borrowers in federal court, final judgments had been entered against Finco on holdings that, under circumstances identical with those in the present lawsuit, Finco's failure to make the required loan payment disclosure violated TLA. Borrow's motion was denied.

Were the district court's rulings correct as to

1. Borrow's motion to remand?
2. Borrow's motion to amend her complaint?
3. Borrow's motion for partial summary judgment?

Discuss.

Question 25

On March 1 of last year, Paul, a citizen of State X, was involved in a three-car accident in State Y with Dave and Al, both of whom are State Y citizens. Wilma, Paul's wife, was a passenger in his car. Immediately after the accident, Wilma obtained signed statements from two witnesses. Later, Paul employed Len, a lawyer, to study the statements and advise him. Len made some handwritten notes on the statements and placed them in his files.

On February 15 of this year, Paul filed a complaint against Dave in the U.S. district court for State Y. All allegations of the complaint and the prayer for relief are set forth below:

1. Plaintiff is a citizen of State X. Defendant is a citizen of State Y. The amount in controversy, exclusive of interest and costs, exceeds $75,000.

2. On March 1 of last year, Defendant negligently operated his automobile and collided with Plaintiff's automobile.

3. As a result, Plaintiff suffered personal injuries, pain of body and mind, and incurred medical expenses in the sum of $25,000.

Wherefore, Plaintiff prays for a judgment against Defendant of $250,000.

Dave timely answered Paul's complaint as follows:

Defendant neither admits nor denies the allegations of Plaintiff's complaint, but demands strict proof of each and every allegation.

Paul did not amend his complaint, but moved for judgment on the pleadings. Dave countered with his own motion for judgment on the pleadings. The district court denied both motions.

On May 1 of this year, Paul successfully moved to amend his complaint, adding Al as an additional defendant. After being properly served with a copy of the amended complaint, Al moved to dismiss on the ground that the applicable one-year statute of limitations for personal injury actions had expired at the time the amendment was filed and before he had notice of Paul's action. A statute of State Y provides:

If an action is filed within the limitations period provided by law, a new defendant added after the running of that period shall not be entitled to dismissal on the ground that the period has run, if the claim against the new defendant arises out of the same occurrence as the original claim.

In the belief that this statute was controlling, the district court denied Al's motion.

Thereafter, Al served an interrogatory on Paul asking whether Paul took "the statements of any witnesses to the accident" and requesting the submission of "copies of any such statements." Paul asserted that the interrogatory was "objectionable on grounds of work product" and refused to provide any answer or produce any documents. Al moved for an order compelling (1) an answer to the interrogatory, and (2) the production of the requested documents. The motion was granted.

Did the court rule correctly on

1. the motions for judgment on the pleadings?
2. Al's motion to dismiss?
3. Al's motion to compel an answer to his interrogatory and the production of documents?

Discuss.

Question 26

Danielle was flying her small airplane through the dark of night from her home in State X to a resort in State Y. Before she could reach her destination, she made a forced landing on a highway in State Z and hit a truck driven by Price, a resident of State Y. The truck was demolished, and Price sustained personal injuries resulting in medical expenses in excess of $75,000. Although a State Z statute requires the use of headlights after sunset, the truck's headlights were not on at the time of the accident, and Danielle did not see the truck.

Price sued Danielle in the U.S. district court of State Z, basing jurisdiction on diversity of citizenship. The complaint stated in relevant part, "Defendant negligently failed to operate her plane in a safe manner including, specifically, failure to use carburetor heat, causing her engine to fail and causing her to crash into Plaintiff."

Danielle filed an answer denying negligence on her part. Neither the complaint nor the answer made any allegations of contributory negligence or the lack thereof.

Prior to trial, Danielle filed a timely motion requesting that the owner of the truck, Trucko, be made a party on the ground that Trucko is indispensable to the full and final resolution of the dispute. Trucko is incorporated in State X. The court denied the motion on the grounds that Trucko was not a required party.

Price moved for an examination of Danielle by a physician to determine whether Danielle's eyesight, hearing, and physical dexterity were adequate for piloting an airplane. Over Danielle's opposition, the motion was granted.

At a pretrial conference, the court entered an order stating that the case would be tried on the issue of Danielle's negligence. The issue of contributory negligence was not discussed.

At the trial, Danielle introduced evidence without objection, showing that the engine failed without any known cause, that this presented a sudden emergency, and that Danielle could not see Price's truck because its headlights were off.

Over Price's timely objections, the court instructed the jury that it could consider the issue of possible contributory negligence on the part of Price.

Was the court correct in

1. denying Danielle's motion to make Trucko a party and allowing the case to go forward without the presence of Trucko?
2. granting Price's motion for a physical examination of Danielle?
3. allowing the jury to consider the issue of contributory negligence?

Discuss.

Question 27

In 1985, the town of Paz entered into a waste management contract with Daz, Inc., by which Paz agreed to build a wastewater treatment plant and to make the plant available to Daz for the treatment of wastewater. Under the contract, Daz agreed to pay the operating costs of the facility for the first ten years and thereafter to pay a "reasonable" user charge for the continuing use of the facility. In 1995, the Environmental Protection Agency ("EPA") informed Paz that the Clean Water Act ("CWA"), a federal statute, required Paz to implement a user charge system whereby each user of the plant must pay a proportionate share of the cost of operating and maintaining the entire wastewater treatment system based upon that user's contribution to the total waste flow. The EPA also advised Paz that the user charge system currently applied to Daz was inconsistent with the user charge system required by the CWA. In general, the CWA creates a federal regulatory scheme designed to promote clean water for the benefit of the public. The provisions of the CWA are enforceable by the EPA. The statute includes no private enforcement mechanism.

Paz filed a lawsuit against Daz in a U.S. district court seeking to force Daz to comply with the EPA/CWA mandated user charge system. Paz alleged that the lawsuit came within the court's federal question jurisdiction. The essence of Paz's claim is that the waste management contract between Paz and Daz requires Daz to pay any user charges mandated by state or federal law. Since the CWA mandated the imposition of specific type of user charge, Daz was contractually obligated to pay that charge. Daz has filed a motion to dismiss under FRCP 12(b)(1). How should the court rule? Explain.

Question 28

Abe is a commercial real estate developer. He entered into a contract with Bob under which Bob agreed to construct a strip mall on property owned by Abe. As part of the contract, Carl was named as a surety—that is, an insurer—for Bob's performance under the contract. After the commencement of the construction, a dispute arose between Abe and Bob in which Abe claimed that Bob was in default under the contract. Bob claimed that Donna, Abe's agent, was preventing Bob from completing the project. Abe and Carl are citizens of California. Bob and Donna are citizens of Arizona. Abe has sued Bob in a U.S. district court claiming breach of contract. He seeks damages of over $100,000. In answering the following questions, be certain to address the applicable FRCP and any pertinent jurisdictional statutes.

1. May Bob implead Carl? Explain.

2. Assuming for purposes of this subpart that Bob is allowed to implead Carl, may Carl file a claim against Abe related to the construction project? Explain.

3. Assuming for purposes of this subpart that Bob is allowed to implead Carl, may Carl file a claim against Abe unrelated to the construction project? Explain.

4. Assuming for purposes of this subpart that Bob is allowed to implead Carl, may Abe file a claim against Carl related to the construction project? Explain.

5. If Bob does not attempt to implead Carl, may Carl intervene? Explain.

6. May Bob file a counterclaim against Abe, joining Donna as a defendant on that counterclaim, asserting that Abe and Donna have undermined Bob's ability to complete the construction project? Explain (as to both Abe and Donna).

7. Assuming that Bob does not file a counterclaim against Abe and Donna, may Donna intervene, claiming that Bob's performance under the contract amounts to tortuous interference with Donna's ability to perform as Abe's agent on the construction project? Explain. (Assume that Donna has stated a claim on which relief can be granted.)

8. Assuming for purposes of this subpart that Donna is allowed to intervene as a plaintiff, may Abe file a claim against Donna related to the underlying dispute between Abe and Bob? Explain.

Question 29

Delmore, a citizen of California, entered into a contract with the city of Industry, California, to perform repair work on Industrial Blvd., the city's main thoroughfare. The contract required Delmore to provide a payment bond to ensure that he would pay all subcontractors and suppliers for the project. Pursuant to this requirement, Delmore obtained a payment bond from Surety, Inc., a New York corporation. Thereafter, Delmore subcontracted with Patricia, also a citizen of California, for certain labor, material, supplies, and services for the Industrial Blvd. project. Patricia performed her obligations under the subcontract. Pursuant to the subcontract, Delmore owes Patricia $100,000. However, he refuses to pay her based on a preexisting debt owed to him by Patricia. Patricia has filed two suits. The first was filed in a California state court against Delmore claiming breach of contract and seeking $100,000 in damages. The second was filed in a U.S. district court sitting in California against Surety seeking to enforce the payment bond in that same amount. In the federal action, Surety has filed a motion to dismiss under FRCP 12(b)(7), claiming that Delmore is a person who should be joined in the federal proceeding and without whom the federal court cannot proceed. How should the federal district court rule on Surety's motion?

Question 30

A and B entered into a long-term delivery contract under which B was obligated to deliver certain goods to A on July 1 of each year from 2001 until 2011. For the first two years of the agreement (2001-2002), B performed as required, but in 2003, B failed to make the required delivery until mid-December of that year. A sued B in a State X court claiming breach of contract and seeking damages for the failure to make the 2003 delivery in a timely fashion. B defended on the ground that there was an intervening act of God (a 100-year flood) and that the contract was procured by A through fraud. B also claimed that the contract allowed him to make the delivery either on July 1 or within four months of that date. All issues were fully litigated. The court found that there had been no 100-year flood, that there was no fraud, and that the contract permitted B to ship the goods within four months of the July 1 date. Judgment was entered for A, the court finding that B failed to make the shipment within four months of July 1, 2003. In 2004, B again failed to meet the July 1 delivery date, but did make a delivery on August 30 of that year. A again sued B in a State X court seeking damages for breach of contract.

1. Is A bound by the finding in the first proceeding that the contract allowed B to make the delivery within four months of July 1?

2. If B raises a defense of claim preclusion, how should the court rule? Does it matter whether the breach at issue in the first proceeding was considered material?

3. Since the court in the first proceeding made several findings, is B bound by the finding of no fraud? Explain.

4. Suppose in the first case that the court found for B despite the fact that B had not shipped within four months of July 1, concluding both that there was a 100-year flood and that the contract was procured through fraud. Would A be precluded from bringing the second suit?

5. Suppose that while making the August 30, 2004, delivery, B's driver, D, negligently damaged A's loading dock. A files a negligence suit against D. Judgment, however, is for D. If A now attempts to sue B for damages to the loading dock, may B rely on the prior judgment in favor of D as bar to that suit?

6. Same facts as part 5, except that the judgment in the *A v. D* proceeding was against D and in favor of A. Would B be bound by that judgment?

Question 31

Phyllis ("P"), a resident of State X, was injured when the water heater in her home exploded. She had just recently purchased the water heater at a local appliance store in State X. The water heater was manufactured by Dumdum Radiator, Inc., a State Y corporation ("D"). The pressure valve on the water heater was manufactured in State Z by Twisty Valves, Inc., a State Z corporation ("TV"). TV shipped the valve to D in State Y where it was fabricated onto the water heater. TV has sold an average of 15,000 such valves to D each year for the past four years. D water heaters are sold throughout the country, with steady sales in State X through various retail outlets.

P sued D in a U.S. district court sitting in State X on a theory of products liability. She seeks $80,000 in damages. D then brought TV into the lawsuit seeking indemnity from TV and claiming that a defective TV valve caused the explosion. TV has no agent in State X; nor does TV do any business within that state. P's claims against D have not settled. Nor has she filed a claim against TV.

TV was served in State Z at its headquarters. Macduff, a professional process server, handed a copy of the summons and D's third-party complaint to a receptionist seated in TV's main lobby. According Macduff, he told the receptionist, whose name was Hecate, that he was handing her legal process to be delivered to TV's chief executive officer. Also according to Macduff, he asked Hecate if she was authorized to accept process on behalf of the corporation and she replied that she was. According to Hecate, however, Macduff simply walked in, tossed some papers at her and said, "Take these to your leader," and walked out. Hecate denies that she was authorized to accept service of process, having been hired only recently. She did deliver the papers to the chief executive officer who received them that day. Both Macduff and Hecate have signed affidavits attesting to their respective versions of the event.

TV has filed a timely motion to dismiss D's third-party complaint pursuant to FRCP 12(b)(2) and 12(b)(5).

1. Assuming that under the facts presented, the State X long-arm statute would *not* allow the exercise of personal jurisdiction over TV, might D rely on FRCP 4(k)(2) as an alternative method of establishing jurisdiction over TV? Explain.

2. Assuming that under the facts presented, the State X long-arm statute would allow the exercise of personal jurisdiction over TV, would the standards of due process be satisfied by that exercise? Explain.

3. How should the U.S. district court rule on TV's FRCP 12(b)(5) motion? (In answering this question you may assume that the State X law pertaining to service of process is identical to federal law.)

Question 32

Delmore ("D"), a citizen of State X, placed his 1964 Ford Galaxie for sale on eWay, an online auction through which private parties buy and sell goods and services worldwide. Sellers on eWay are able to limit the geographic region in which their product is sold. D's eWay listing described the car as a "64 Ford Galaxie 500 XL in cherry condition, fully restored, rust-free chrome, recently rebuilt engine and ready to drive." The listing was placed at auction throughout the world, the buyer to pay for and arrange delivery from State X.

Pierre ("P"), a citizen of State Y, saw the ad while browsing on his computer from his home. P bid $34,106 for the Galaxie and was notified through eWay that he was the winning bidder. P and D communicated via e-mail to arrange for the pickup of the vehicle in State X. P ultimately hired a transport company and the Galaxie arrived in State Y a month after the sale. Upon delivery, P discovered that the car was not a 500 XL as advertised, and noted a variety of other problems, including a motor that would not turn over, rusted chrome, and extensive dents on the body of the vehicle. P contacted D in an attempt to rescind the purchase, but those efforts failed.

P sued D in the U.S. district court in State Y. He has raised several state-law claims sounding in breach of contract and fraud, all of which are premised on the "falsehoods" in D's eWay posting. State Y has a due process style jurisdictional statute and its service of process statute provides, among other things, that service may be effected on an out-of-state resident via certified mail so long as the out-of-state resident signs the accompanying return receipt.

On the day after the suit was filed, P's attorney mailed D a Request for Waiver of Service in full compliance with FRCP 4(d). The Request was sent via certified mail. D received the mailing in a timely fashion and signed the return receipt, but he did not return the Waiver of Service form included in the mailing. On advice of State X counsel, D did not make an appearance. Three months after filing the complaint, P's lawyer filed a motion for a default judgment for the amount of the purchase price. The motion was granted. P has now filed an enforcement action in a State X state court.

1. Was service of process on D effective?
2. Assuming effective service of process, did the U.S. district court sitting in State Y have personal jurisdiction over D?
3. In what court may or must D raise his challenges to service of process and personal jurisdiction?

Question 33

Beginning in 1970 and up through 1990, Big Chemicals, Inc. ("BC"), a New York corporation with its principal place of business in New Mexico, used Happy Acres, a deserted 10-acre parcel of land in California's Mojave Desert, as a disposal site for its chemical wastes. The chemicals were stored in sealed metal drums and buried beneath the surface of the land. BC's all-purpose insurer, ProTectU ("PTU"), is a New York corporation with its principal place of business in California.

Today Happy Acres is a large housing tract known as Happy Acres Estates ("the Estates"). The Estates were developed by Good Homes ("GH"), a New Mexico partnership with all partners residing in New Mexico.

Lately, residents of the Estates have been experiencing a series of health problems, including severe rashes and flu-like symptoms. They have also noticed "chemical odors" emanating from their tap water. The source of these toxins and odors is quite likely seepage from the Happy Acres dump site.

A public report issued by the Environmental Protection Agency ("EPA"), a federal administrative agency, disclosed that a recent inspection of Happy Acres revealed evidence of dangerous chemical residues. The residues are of the type disposed of by BC. BC, however, denies responsibility, claiming that leakage from the sealed drums was all but impossible.

The Federal Toxic Waste Cleanup Act ("FTWCA") imposes a "cleanup duty" on any person or business that has disposed of toxic pollutants in a manner that endangers public health, regardless of when the disposal occurred. The FTWCA does not provide a private right of action; rather, the cleanup duty is enforceable only by the EPA. The EPA has yet to take any action against BC.

Alice and Bernice, both lifelong Californians, are residents of the Estates, each living in different sections of the community. Alice has experienced rashes and flu-like symptoms. As a consequence of her illness, she has been unable to work for the past year. She has suffered over $100,000 in medical bills and lost wages. Bernice can no longer drink the water from her tap due to the overwhelming chemical odors. To remedy the situation, she installed a state-of-the-art water filtration system that cost her $2,500. Both Alice and Bernice believe that leakage from the BC disposal site is at the root of their problems.

Alice and Bernice have joined together as plaintiffs suing BC in a U.S. district court sitting in California. They have each asserted claims for negligence and negligence *per se*, the latter being based on BC's alleged violation of the FTWCA "clean-up duty." BC has filed a motion to dismiss pursuant to FRCP 12(b)(1). BC has also filed an alternative motion to join PTU as a third-party defendant on the theory that PTU must pay BC for any losses incurred by BC in this litigation. After receiving the above motions, Alice and Bernice filed and amended complaint in order to assert claims against GH premised on the theory that when GH undertook to construct the Estates it knew or should have known the extent of the pollution.

1. How should the U.S. district court rule on BC's motion to dismiss?

2. Should the district court allow BC to join PTU as a third-party defendant?

3. May GH be joined as a co-defendant with BC in the amended complaint?

Question 34

Paula sued her former employer, DBA, Inc., in a federal district court claiming violations of Title VII of the Civil Rights Act of 1964 ("Title VII"), a federal statute that prohibits various forms of discrimination in the workplace. Paula claimed that she was fired because of her sex, a protected category under Title VII, and in retaliation for having filed charges against her employer with the Equal Employment Opportunity Commission ("EEOC"). The EEOC is a federal agency charged with enforcing Title VII. In terms of remedies, Paula seeks back pay and benefits, future pay and benefits (collectively totaling $13 million), punitive damages, and attorneys fees. At the time she was fired, Paula's annual salary and benefits package exceeded $500,000. By way of contrast, DBA's most recent quarterly profits were over $700 million. In addition, DBA claims that the most Paula could possibly recover in compensatory damages would be $1.2 million.

In the context of an allegedly unlawful termination of employment based on sex, Title VII requires the plaintiff to prove that she was terminated from her employment and that sex was "a" motivating factor — not necessarily "the" motivating factor — in her employer's decision to fire her. In the context of a claim for unlawful retaliation, Title VII requires the plaintiff to show that she engaged in activity protected by Title VII (e.g., filing charges with the EEOC), that an adverse employment action occurred, and that there was a causal connection between the protected activity and the adverse employment action.

In her complaint, Paula alleged as follows:

1. Defendant is a Delaware corporation engaged in the international sales of securities.

2. Plaintiff was employed by DBA in its New York office from August 23, 1999 until October 23, 2001, when she was fired by her supervisor.

3. Plaintiff was hired by DBA as a senior salesperson in its U.S.-based Asia-Pacific Sales Desk ("the Desk"). At that time, the manager of the Desk was Karl, who informed Paula, who was already an experienced securities salesperson, that she would be considered to fill his position when he returned to his position at DBA's London office.

4. On January 29, 2001, Karl wrote a performance evaluation of Paula's work and indicated that during the year 2000 she had either fully met or exceeded all performance objectives. She received the highest possible rating for "teamwork."

5. Paula was awarded a substantial bonus for her work in 2000, the second highest in the history of the Desk.

6. Karl relocated to DBA's London office at the end of January 2001.

7. On information and belief, Paula was not considered for Karl's replacement. Instead, DBA hired Frederick to assume Karl's responsibilities.

8. During Frederick's tenure as manager, Paula was the only female senior salesperson working the Desk.

9. From the outset, Frederick treated Paula differently than he treated her male counterparts.

10. Among other things, Frederick ridiculed and belittled Paula in front of coworkers, asking her if "anybody liked her"; excluded her from work-related outings with male coworkers and clients; made sexist remarks in her presence, such as stating that he had "yellow fever," meaning he liked Asian women; instructed Paula not to go to the gym during lunch as it would set a bad precedent, yet placed no such restrictions on male coworkers; and isolated Paula from other senior salespersons (all male) by seating her apart from them.

11. On information and belief, Frederick took no similar actions with regard to any male salesperson.

12. Frederick's discriminatory treatment of Paula was part of the "male" culture at DBA.

13. During this same period of time, male-written peer reviews of Paula instructed her to "smile more" and be "softer," reflecting the view that she did not comport with the DBA stereotype of women as passive and accommodating toward men.

14. Paula complained about the above unfair treatment to the Managing Director of International Equity Sales, the Managing Director of Global Asian Sales, the Executive Director of Human Resources and the Associate Director of Human Resources.

15. On information and belief, the defendant took no action to discipline Frederick, despite the fact that the Executive Director of Human Resources agreed that Frederick was "a problem."

16. In July 2001, shortly after Paula had complained to the individuals described in paragraph 14, Frederick retaliated against her by criticizing her in that month's performance review and describing her as insubordinate, unsupportive, and abrasive. Although Paula asked Frederick to provide specific examples, he did not do so.

17. On August 16, 2001, Paula filed a charge of discrimination against DBA with the Equal Employment Opportunities Commission ("EEOC"), describing Frederick's discriminatory treatment of her.

18. On information and belief, Frederick was made aware of the EEOC charges on August 21, 2001.

19. On October 9, 2001, Paula received a letter signed by Frederick stating that her employment with DBA was terminated as of October 23, 2001.

20. DBA, through its agent, Frederick, terminated plaintiff's employment because of her sex and in retaliation for her having filed charges with the EEOC.

DBA has filed a Rule 12(b)(6) motion to dismiss both of Paula's claims. How should the district court to rule on this motion?

Question 35

Using the same facts as the previous question, assume for purposes of the following questions that the motion to dismiss was denied. Paula's attorney has now properly served DBA with a request that DBA "produce all electronically stored information concerning any communications by or between five specified DBA employees from August 1999 to December 2001 concerning Plaintiff." The "specified" group includes Frederick, Frederick's supervisor, a DBA human relations officer who had been assigned to handle issues concerning Paula, and two of Paula's coworkers at the Desk. E-mail was an important means of communication at DBA during the relevant time period. Each salesperson on the Desk received approximately 200 e-mails each day.

1. Does this request to produce satisfy the standards of FRCP 26(b)(1) and 34(a)(1)(A)?

2. What should DBA do if some of the e-mails involve discussions between Frederick and a DBA in-house counsel regarding Paula's EEOC charges?

In response to the above request, DBA produced 100 pages of e-mails, all of which were retrieved from readily accessible online sources. DBA did not, however, search its backup system. Under that system, which is required by the Securities and Exchange Commission, "deleted" e-mails are preserved each month to backup tapes. These tapes are kept for three years and then destroyed. Restoration of an undestroyed tape takes approximately five days. A total of 77 backup tapes held by DBA potentially included e-mails that fall within the request to produce. DBA estimates that the cost of doing such a search would be $300,000. Paula has filed a motion to compel DBA to search all 77 backup tapes for purposes of responding to her discovery request.

3. Which sections (or subsections) of the federal rules are relevant to resolving this question? How should the district court rule on this motion?

4. What should DBA do if some of the e-mail exchanges between Frederick and in-house counsel (noted above) were inadvertently included in the 100 pages of e-mails provided to Paula? Which federal rule or rules are pertinent to answering this question? What must Paula do in response to any action taken by DBA?

Suppose that in response to Paula's motion to compel, the district court ordered DBA to produce, at its own expense, e-mails responsive to the request to produce from any five backup tapes selected by Paula and to prepare an affidavit detailing the results of its search, as well as the time and money spent.

5. Why, in terms of federal discovery principles, would the district court make such an order?

DBA has now complied with the district court's order regarding the five backup tapes. The results of that compliance are as follows: The search of the five selected backup tapes reveals 800 pages of e-mails responsive to the request to produce. The total cost of the restoration and search (including attorney and paralegal time) was $20,000. IBS estimates the cost of restoring and searching the remaining 72 tapes to be $275,000; of that figure, $100,000 is attributable to attorney and paralegal time. DBA now requests either that no further restoration be required or that the cost of any further restoration and search be shifted to Paula. In response, Paula cites 68 e-mails produced in the sample restoration and search as "highly relevant" to her claims. Some of those e-mails reflect facts that refute assertions made by DBA in defense of the EEOC charges, some involve discussions of how to best phrase complaints about Paula, some attest to the positive quality of Paula's performance (including one from Frederick), and others reveal the hostility between Frederick and Paula. In addition, the restoration revealed that Frederick had deleted e-mails from online sources after the EEOC charges were filed and after DBA attorneys had advised him to save all materials pertaining to Paula. Accordingly, Paula has asked the court to order the restoration and search of the remaining 72 backup tapes and that DBA bear the entire cost.

6. How would you advise the court to rule on these matters?

Essay
Answers

Answer to Question 1

Did the court properly deny APOW's motion to dismiss?

Yes. A motion to dismiss for failure to state claim can be premised on either the procedural or the substantive sufficiency of the complaint. As to the former, the question is whether the complaint satisfies the "short and plain statement" requirement of FRCP 8(a)(2) in that it provides the opposing party sufficient notice of the claim asserted against it. APOW ("D") might contend that the facts described in the complaint (that emissions from the plant had injured people) are not sufficient to put it on notice of the nature of the action against it because the plaintiffs failed to specify the precise type of claim asserted. However, plaintiffs would argue that the allegations were sufficient to satisfy the liberal standards of notice pleading and that D should be able to recognize a variety of legal theories (strict liability, nuisance, negligence, and trespass) that could be inferred from those allegations. The Supreme Court has described the proper standard as one of "plausibility," and the facts alleged here would appear to satisfy that standard as they outline obviously plausible claims (as noted above). Therefore, D was on proper notice of the claims against it, which is all that the rule requires. The substantive sufficiency of a complaint pertains to the question of whether the claim asserted is one that is legally recognized. The claims described above are well recognized at law; hence there is no sound argument that the complaint is substantively insufficient. The motion to dismiss was, therefore, properly denied.

Was the grant of certification proper?

For a class action of this type to be maintained, (1) there must be common questions of law or fact, and (2) the representative's claim must be typical of the class represented. D probably argued that since the plaintiffs were injured on the third day of the emissions, their claims are not representative of persons harmed on the first and second days. Also, each plaintiff may have been injured to a different extent and possibly in a different manner (if different types of emissions were involved). If so, there would be no common factual issues. However, if it is likely that the emissions were all from the same source (e.g., a malfunctioning valve), certification was probably proper. The types of claims for all three days would be identical and the question of D's liability would be common to the entire class. In such instance, the representative's claims would be typical of the class (at least until it can be established that each day's emissions were from a different source).

Was the memorandum discoverable?

The discoverability of the memo depends initially on the FRCP. If it would be discoverable under the FRCP, no conflict with state law would exist (since the state has no work product doctrine). If it would *not* be discoverable under the FRCP, the federal court would be required to determine if application of the federal rule would be consistent with the standards of the Rules Enabling Act (REA).

Under FRCP 26(b)(3), a party may discover documents prepared in anticipation of litigation or for trial by another party or her counsel only upon showing a substantial need for the items and that they (or their "substantial equivalent") cannot otherwise be obtained without undue hardship. Plaintiffs probably contended that the memo involved was not within this privilege because it was not prepared in anticipation of litigation (i.e., there is no indication that anyone was threatening suit against D over minor accidents at *another* company's plant). The rule, however, has not been so narrowly construed. D could successfully argue that (1) the memo was created to assist D in responding to claims which would inevitably be made when similar "incidents" occurred at a D plant; (2) there was no reason why plaintiffs could not recreate the memo by doing their own research; and (3) to the extent that the memo contained the lawyer's impressions or conclusions, it would not be subject to discovery under any circumstances. Since D's position is consistent with the standards of FRCP 26(b)(3), the memo would *not* be discoverable under the FRCP.

Assuming the memo was *not* discoverable under the FRCP, plaintiffs might have contended that, under the *Erie doctrine*, where state substantive law conflicts with the FRCP, state law controls. The FRCP are not, however, limited by the *Erie* doctrine. D, therefore, would have argued that *Hanna v. Plumer* held that a valid federal rule trumps state law to the contary. The measure of that validity is provided by the REA, under which a federal rule must be rationally classifiable as procedural and may not abridge, enlarge, or modify a substantive right. Rule 26(b)(3) is rationally classifiable as procedural since it regulates the manner in which information is exchanged between parties to a federal lawsuit. Next, although state law creates a "right" to discovery of this material, that right arises only in the context of litigation and therefore cannot be properly characterized as substantive. In other words, this state rule does not regulate primary human activity. As a consequence, FRCP 26(b)(3) does not abridge, enlarge, or modify a state substantive right.

Plaintiffs could contend that by abolishing the work product doctrine the state legislature evinced a strong desire to permit discovery of any relevant unprivileged information. Plaintiffs would further contend that FRCP 26(b)(3) conflicts with this "substantive" state policy. Therefore, the memo should be discoverable. However, no Supreme Court decision has ever held that a state substantive policy can override or invalidate a formal federal rule of civil procedure.

Answer to Question 2

Was Trucker ("T") a party who ought to be joined in the State X action?
Under FRCP 19(a)(1), a person must be joined if it is feasible to do so and if "(A) in that person's absence, the court cannot accord complete relief among existing parties; or (B) that person claims an interest relating to the subject of the action and is so situated that disposing of the action in the person's absence may: (i) as a practical matter impair or impede the person's ability to protect the interest; or (ii) leave an existing party subject to a substantial risk of incurring double, multiple, or otherwise inconsistent obligations because of the interest." We can assume feasibility since nothing in the facts suggests to the contrary. As to whether T ought to be joined, complete relief can be given to the existing parties in his absence—that is, Rider ("R") can obtain a judgment for the full amount of his injuries from Owner ("O"). Also, T's interests are not likely to be prejudiced if he is not joined since nothing in the *R v. O* proceeding would seem to impair T's interests in any legal or practical way.

O might contend, however, that since he and T were joint tortfeasors, he could be liable for the entire judgment if T were not joined (whereas if T were joined, and they were deemed to be joint tortfeasors, O would have a right of contribution against T). Thus, the failure to join T exposes O to excessive liability. However, an absent party's status as a joint torfeasor is never, standing alone, a sufficient basis on which to require joinder of that party under Rule 19(a). *Temple v. Synthes Corp., Ltd.* (1990).

Was the State X court correct in granting T's motion to intervene?
Under FRCP 24(a), a party has a right to intervene when the disposition of an action may, as a practical matter, impair his interests and these interests are **not** likely to be adequately represented by the existing parties. T would probably **not** come within this standard because his interests would not appear to be affected by the *R v. O* litigation. Since R's conduct with respect to the accident was different from T's, whether R won or lost would have no effect on a possible subsequent lawsuit by T against O.

However, under FRCP 24(b), one may be permitted to intervene where there is a common question of law or fact between (1) the existing action, and (2) the claim or defense sought to be asserted by the intervenor. A trial court arguably could determine that R and T share a common claim with respect to the transaction (i.e., that O operated his vehicle in a negligent manner). Thus, the trial court's decision to permit T to intervene was probably correct.

Was the State X court correct in permitting R to crossclaim against T?
Under FRCP 13(g), a party may assert a crossclaim against a co-party if his action arises out of the occurrence that is the subject of the original action. Since both R and T are co-party plaintiffs and since R's claim against T arises out of the collision between O and T, it appears that the court was correct in permitting R to cross-claim against T. Some courts, however, have interpreted Rule 13(g) as permitting crossclaims between co-plaintiffs only when those co-plaintiffs have been joined as co-parties to a counterclaim filed by a defendant. Under this approach, R would not be entitled to crossclaim against T.

What is the effect of the federal action on R's action against O?
Since R was not a party to the federal action, R is not be bound by the judgment in that action. Hence, O could not assert either claim or issue preclusion against R. R might, however, be able to preclude O from asserting, as a defense, that the accident was caused by T's negligence. This would be an example of nonmutual, offensive issue preclusion, which is recognized by federal courts. R is, however, unlikely to use this argument since R would also like to show that T was negligent. As a consequence, the effect of the federal action on R's suit against O is likely to be nil.

What is the effect of the federal action on R's crossclaim against T?
Under *res judicata* principles of claim preclusion, where there has been a prior, final judgment between the parties or their privities with respect to the cause of action being asserted in a subsequent lawsuit, the latter action is barred. However, O and R do not appear to be in privity with each other. O was not R's legal representative (sometimes called "procedural privity"), nor was there any type of legal relationship between O and R (sometimes called "substantive privity"). Thus, the prior federal lawsuit would have no effect upon R's crossclaim against T since R, as a nonparty and as someone who was not in privity with a party, cannot be bound by that judgment consistent with principles of due process. In addition, a theory of "virtual representation," —that is, that O virtually represented R since O and R shared an interest in establishing T's negligence—would not be of any avail since the Supreme Court has found this doctrine to be inconsistent with the due process clause. *Taylor v. Sturgell*, 553 U.S. 880 (2008).

What is the effect of the federal action upon T's claim against O in the federal district court?
Under FRCP 13(a), a party must assert a counterclaim that she has against the opposing party if it (1) arises out of the occurrence that is the basis of

the latter's claim against the former, and (2) there is no need for the presence of third parties over whom the court cannot acquire jurisdiction. If this is not done, the claim is barred. Since (1) T's claim for personal injury damages arose out of the collision between O and T (which was the basis for the former's state court action against the latter), and (2) R's presence was not necessary to T's claim against O, T's claim against O will be treated as having been a compulsory counterclaim in the previous lawsuit and will be barred.

What is the effect of the federal action upon O's counterclaim against T? The State X court must apply the law of preclusion that would be applied by the court that first entered judgment, that is, the federal court sitting in State X. Since a federal court exercising diversity jurisdiction will borrow the preclusion law of the state in which it sits, the State X law of preclusion will apply. *Semtek Int'l Inc. v. Lockheed Martin Corp.*, 531 U.S. 497 (2001). Whether claim preclusion bars O's counterclaim depends, therefore, on how State X defines "claim" for purposes of that doctrine. If State X follows the majority "same-transaction" rule, O's counterclaim for personal injuries will be barred since it arises out of the same transaction as O's prior claim for property damage. On the other hand, if State X follows the "primary rights" definition of claim, O's claim for property damage in the first suit is not the same as his claim for personal injuries in the second suit. In short, under the majority approach, O's claim will be barred; under a minority approach, it will not.

Answer to Question 3

The motion to dismiss based on subject matter jurisdiction:

The only plausible basis for subject matter jurisdiction under these facts is diversity of citizenship. To satisfy this standard, the parties must be of diverse citizenship (no plaintiff and no defendant may be citizens of the same state) and the amount in controversy must exceed $75,000. The first part of the diversity requirement is satisfied since Seler ("S") and Byer ("B") are citizens of different states. The amount in controversy requirement, however, is not satisfied. S would argue that the amount in controversy alleged by B is only $47,500—that is, the amount of the alleged error in the contract. This argument is correct since the disputed amount between the parties is precisely this amount. However, B might contend that in an action for equitable relief most courts will measure the amount in controversy by the greater of the amount either the plaintiff stands to gain or the defendant stands to lose. While this legal position is well taken, here the amount the plaintiff stands to gain and the defendant stands to lose is identical for both parties, namely, $47,500. Regardless of who prevails, one party will gain and the other party will lose $47,500. Hence the amount in controversy is not satisfied under these facts.

The motion to dismiss based on personal jurisdiction:

For a court to take personal jurisdiction over an out-of-state defendant: (1) there must be a long-arm statute that permits it to do so (since the facts are silent, we'll assume that State B's long-arm statute gave its courts the authority to exercise personal jurisdiction to the extent permitted by due process), and (2) the defendant must have sufficient minimum contacts with the forum so as not to offend traditional notions of fair play and substantial justice. This latter standard requires a showing of (1) purposeful availment by the out-of-state resident (or activity purposefully directed toward the forum), (2) a relationship between the purposeful contacts and the claim, and (3) reasonableness. B would contend that since the contract was signed in State B, S has sufficient minimum contacts with that jurisdiction. In support of that position, B would argue that S's contacts with the forum state were purposeful and that the claim arose out of those contacts. S would argue in response that an isolated appearance in one state for the purpose of concluding a business transaction pertaining to property in another state is *not* constitutionally adequate to create personal jurisdiction. S is likely correct. To satisfy the minimum contacts test, S's contacts would have to be of a quantity and quality that would make the exercise of jurisdiction reasonable. In the absence of some showing of a continuing relationship between S and State B with respect to this particular transaction, that standard would not be satisfied. Thus, the district court erred in denying S's motion to dismiss for lack of personal jurisdiction.

S's demand for a jury trial:

Pursuant to FRCP 38(a) and the Seventh Amendment, each party is entitled to a jury trial with respect to legal issues. While reformation has traditionally been recognized as an equitable (rather than legal) claim, S could have contended that the reformation question is inextricably associated with the legal issue of whether B breached the contract by refusing to pay S $85,000 for Whiteacre. Since *Beacon Theatres, Inc. v. Westover*, 359 U.S. 500 (1959), held that legal claims must be tried prior to equitable ones, S's demand for a jury trial should *not* have been denied.

Disclosure of the appraisers' identities and the appraisals:

Pursuant to FRCP 34, documents and other tangible things must be obtained by a request to produce. Since S demanded the appraisal reports within the context of interrogatories, B was arguably not required to comply. On the other hand, given the liberality of the federal rules, S's interrogatories could be treated as requests for production, thus requiring B's compliance. Indeed, interrogatories and requests for production are often served together. The court's ruling, although perhaps technically correct, is suspect under the liberal standards of the federal rules.

B probably objected to the other information requested on the ground that it was irrelevant (appraisal reports would not necessarily indicate the price the parties agreed to) and, possibly, that it represented B's work product.

The first objection probably would *not* be successful because a party may ordinarily obtain disclosure of any information that is reasonably calculated to lead to the discovery of admissible evidence. FRCP 26(b)(1). If the appraisals were made *prior to* the commencement of the action, they would tend to show the fair market value of Whiteacre, and therefore the probable purchase price agreed upon by the parties.

If B's appraisals showed that the land was worth $85,000, it is unlikely that S would have sold it to him for $37,500. Conversely, if the land was worth $37,500, it would tend to corroborate that a mistake had been made (i.e., B probably would not have agreed to pay $85,000 for Whiteacre). If the appraisals were made *after* the litigation had commenced, they would still be discoverable (to the extent they did not contain advice or suggestions to B's attorney) because S would have the right to know the nature of the evidence that B intended to present, so that he might counter it.

The second objection will *not* be successful with respect to any expert B expects to call at trial. Under FRCP 26(a)(2), an expert who may be called to testify must prepare a report containing (1) the expert's opinions and the basis for them, (2) the data considered by the expert, (3) any exhibits the expert will use, (4) the expert's qualifications, (5) the compensation she is receiving, and (6) a list of other cases in which she has testified within the prior four years. Thus, while B would not have to hand over work product documents, B would have to provide the information requested by S concerning the identity of testifying witnesses and their opinions within 90 days of the trial, or the court would have to exclude B from using this evidence at trial. FRCP 37(c)(1).

However, B's second objection probably will succeed with respect to any appraisers B has retained in anticipation of litigation, but who will not testify in the action. The federal rules allow discovery of such experts only upon a showing of *exceptional circumstances.* FRCP 26(b)(4)(B). Since S could retain its own appraisers, the court should not have allowed S to discover the opinions of these experts.

Thus, the court ruled correctly with respect to B's objections concerning the opinion of witnesses B expected to use at trial, but was in error to the extent the order encompassed nontestifying experts.

Evidence submitted with respect to the motion for judgment:
A jury's determination of a factual issue may not be disturbed, unless there was an insufficient evidentiary basis for it. B probably contended that the preponderance of the evidence favored him since he had introduced expert testimony that the land was worth only $42,200. Nevertheless, based upon the demeanor of the witnesses, the jury could have believed S while disbelieving the testimony of B and his appraiser. Additionally, the jury might have believed that even though Whiteacre was worth only $42,200, B may have exercised poor business judgment and entered into the transaction anyway. Thus, the court was probably *not* correct in granting B's motion for judgment.

Procedural arguments:
Pursuant to FRCP 50(b), a party seeking a motion for judgment after the entry of judgment—that is, seeking to reverse a previously entered judgment—*must* have made a motion for a judgment as a matter of law at the

close of the evidence or prior to submission to the jury. The post-judgment motion is essentially a renewal of the earlier motion. Since the facts do not indicate that B made a motion for judgment at the close of the evidence or prior to submission to the jury, S should have contended that B's post-judgment motion was not properly before the court.

Answer to Question 4

Motion to quash:

The State X court was *not* correct in denying Daw's motion to quash. For a court to exercise personal jurisdiction over an out-of-state defendant, the latter must have sufficient minimum contacts with the forum so as not to offend traditional notions of fair play and substantial justice. There seems to be little question that Daw ("D") did *not* have sufficient minimum contacts with State X since (1) the accident did not occur in that state, (2) D owns no property there, and (3) D visited the jurisdiction only for a short period of time.

The fact that D filed an answer after the motion to quash was denied is irrelevant and does not constitute a waiver of his personal jurisdiction argument in a majority of jurisdictions. Once a trial court denies a motion to quash, finding that personal jurisdiction has been established, in most states the defendant is free to defend on the merits without waiving the right to challenge the trial court's ruling on appeal. In some states, however, the defendant is required to file a writ of mandate against the trial court in order to challenge that court's denial of the motion to quash. In such jurisdictions, then, D would have waived any further objection to the trial court's jurisdiction.

Default judgment against D:

Whether the State X court was correct in granting a default judgment depends upon the resolution of two issues: (1) whether D properly refused to answer the interrogatory, and (2) if he should have answered, whether a default judgment was an excessive sanction.

Was D's conversation with the investigator and his wife privileged?

D probably contended that the conversation was not admissible because "confidential" communications to one's spouse and to one's attorney are ordinarily privileged. P probably asserted that (1) the statement to D's wife was not confidential since it was made in front of the investigator, (2) the statement to the investigator was not confidential because it was made in front of D's wife, and (3) the investigator was not D's attorney. However, D should have been able to successfully argue in rebuttal that both conversations were "confidential" since (1) the statements were made in front of persons whom D reasonably believed would retain his statements in confidence, and (2) the attorney-client privilege ordinarily extends to "essential" personnel of the attorney, such as the investigator.

Assuming the statement was not privileged, is summary judgment an appropriate sanction?

Under FRCP 37(b)(2)(A), if a party refuses to obey a court order after being directed to do so, the court may make such order as is "just" (including the right to render a default judgment against the disobedient party). However, it could be contended by D that the order was not just in this instance since the failure by D to respond to this inquiry didn't materially hinder the ability of P to present his case. Also, even if D had advised his wife and the investigator that he was at fault, he might have been incorrect (not being an attorney, he would not be capable of making this determination, even if he believed he could). Thus, regardless of how damaging D's statements might appear, they would not necessarily be dispositive of the case. On the other hand, the relatively small size of the judgment and the fact that a factual admission by D (e.g., "I ran a stop sign") may have eliminated the need for further litigation, the court might have been within its discretion in imposing this modest sanction. Ultimately it would seem that the court should have taken at least the interim step of ordering an in camera inspection of the contested statements to determine their likely utility.

How should the district court rule?

P's summary judgment:

P's summary judgment motion may have been premised on the doctrine of *res judicata*. That doctrine bars the assertion of a claim that has previously gone to judgment—claim preclusion—and of issues that have been previously litigated and decided—issue preclusion. Under the principles of intersystem preclusion and the Full Faith and Credit statute, the federal court will be required to apply the law of preclusion that would be followed by a state court sitting in State X.

Claim preclusion applies only when a prior claim has been asserted. Therefore, P has no argument based on claim preclusion since D raised no claims in the prior lawsuit. Summary judgment on this basis therefore would be inappropriate.

On the other hand, most state courts follow the federal model with respect to counterclaims and require that a defendant assert all counterclaims that he may have against a plaintiff when those counterclaims are transactionally related to the plaintiff's claims against him. If a defendant fails to assert a transactionally related counterclaim in the initial proceeding, he will be barred from later asserting that claim in any other proceeding, the counterclaim being deemed compulsory in the first proceeding. If State X follows this majority rule, D will be barred in this second proceeding from asserting any claim against P arising out of the accident that was the subject of the first proceeding. The federal court in the second proceeding will honor that state rule under the compulsion of the *Erie doctrine* since allowing D to proceed with his counterclaim under such circumstances would be outcome determinative at the forum shopping stage, the federal forum being available to adjudicate D's claim while the state forum would not. Thus, if State X has a "transactional" compulsory counterclaim rule, summary judgment in favor of P on D's counterclaim would be appropriate.

P might also rely on issue preclusion as a basis for summary judgment on his own claim against D, specifically on the issue of D's negligence. Again, the federal court would be required to apply the law of State X. Under universally accepted principles of issue preclusion, the issue must have been actually litigated in the prior proceeding. However, the issue of D's negligence was never "actually litigated" (i.e., P was granted a default judgment in the context of sanctions). Therefore, issue preclusion would not be available under these circumstances. Thus, P's summary judgment motion relying on issue preclusion should be denied.

D's summary judgment on P's complaint:

D's motion for summary judgment would seek to apply the doctrine of claim preclusion against P. Again, under the standards of intersystem preclusion, the federal court will follow the law of State X in determining whether the doctrine applies. Under the majority rule, the doctrine of claim preclusion requires a plaintiff to file all transactionally related claims he has against the D in a single proceeding. Once the initial proceeding goes to final judgment, all rights of action arising out of the transaction that was the subject of that proceeding are subject to preclusion. If P prevails in the first proceeding, any unasserted rights of action are "merged" into the judgment. If P loses in that proceeding, any unasserted rights of action are "barred." In this case, since P's personal injury claims arise out of the same set of facts (i.e., the same transaction) as P's property damage claims, and since the property damage proceeding has gone to final judgment, P would now be precluded from asserting those personal injury claims in any other proceeding against D. Accordingly, D would be entitled to summary judgment.

On the other hand, if State X is a minority jurisdiction that follows the "primary rights" definition of a claim, summary judgment would be inappropriate. Under the primary rights approach, a claim is defined by the interest the claim is designed to protect. Interests in property and interests involving personal injuries are deemed separate primary rights. In essence, a party is allowed to split her cause of action, filing separate lawsuits to vindicate different primary rights. Under this theory, P would be allowed to file a second proceeding to vindicate his primary right to be free from personal injury.

Answer to Question 5

May State C assert personal jurisdiction over Macco ("M")?
We'll assume that (1) the lawsuit was properly filed and served, and (2) the State C court is competent to hear this matter.

A State C court may exercise "specific" personal jurisdiction over M only if the standards of the minimum contacts test are satisfied. Paula ("P"), therefore, would have the burden of establishing that M purposely availed itself of the opportunity of doing business in State C and that P's cause of action arose out of those purposeful contacts. If P satisfies these elements, the assertion of jurisdiction would be presumptively reasonable, and M would have the heavy burden of rebutting that presumption. Alternatively, P could attempt to demonstrate that State C could exercise "general" jurisdiction over M on the theory that M's contacts with the state are so continuous and systematic that M should be subjected to personal jurisdiction even over claims unrelated to those contacts. The standards for general jurisdiction are quite high and require a relationship with the state that is tantamount to being at home in that state.

It would be difficult for P to satisfy either of these tests. As to specific jurisdiction, while M clearly has purposeful contacts with State C—an office in the state and up to $500,000 in annual business over a ten-year period—none of those contacts appears to be related to P's wrongful death claim, which arose in State A. P, therefore, could not satisfy the second element of the test. As to general jurisdiction, M's contacts are not sufficient to establish the type of relationship with the state that would satisfy the applicable standards. Unless M's contacts with State C represent essentially the sum total of M's business, or at the very least, a very substantial portion thereof, the assertion of general jurisdiction over it would be quite unlikely.

Effect of Worker ("W")'s prior lawsuit on P's action against M:
Since the initial proceeding was in a State A court, the Full Faith and Credit Clause will require the State C court to apply the principles of preclusion that would be applied by a State A court. This intersystem preclusion principle will have little importance in the immediate case, however, since under universally accepted principles of preclusion, the prior judgment will have no effect on P's action against M.

Under *res judicata* principles, where there has been a final, valid judgment on the merits between the parties (or their privies) with respect to a claim that is being asserted in a subsequent lawsuit, the latter action is barred under the doctrine of claim preclusion. Similarly, issues that have been litigated, decided, and were essential to a prior proceeding against the same parties (or their privities) will be precluded from relitigation under the doctrine of issue preclusion. Neither doctrine is satisfied here. As to claim preclusion, two elements are lacking. First, this suit does not involve the same parties. Although P, as executrix, will be treated as having been in privity with W, M was not a party to the prior proceeding nor in privity with any party to that proceeding. Second, the claims asserted in these suits are not the same claims. The first suit involves the negligence of Doctor ("D") and the responsibility of Hospital ("H") for that negligence; the second suit involves the liability of M for the accident.

As to issue preclusion, the only issues litigated, decided, and essential in the first proceeding pertained to the negligence of D and the liability of H for the actions of D. Neither issue is relevant to the second proceeding. Hence, issue preclusion would not apply.

Effect of W's prior lawsuit upon P's action against Doctor:
D might be able to assert issue preclusion against P. While P was not a party to that proceeding, as explained above, as the executrix of W's estate, she will be treated as being in privity with W in the first proceeding. Hence, she is bound by that proceeding. The question is whether D, a nonparty who is not in privity with a party, can benefit from that proceeding. The concept of mutuality prohibits assertion of issue preclusion by a person who would not be bound by the first proceeding. D clearly falls into that latter category. Hence, if State A adheres to the principle of mutuality, a State C court, under the principles of intersystem preclusion described above, would not permit D to assert issue preclusion against P. On the other hand, most jurisdictions have now abandoned the mutuality requirement for defensive assertions of issue preclusion. If State A falls into that category, then State C will be required to allow D to assert issue preclusion against P even though D is not himself bound by the prior judgment.

Assuming State A has abandoned the mutuality requirement, under the doctrine of issue preclusion, where a particular issue has been actually litigated in a prior action, a court may preclude it from being relitigated where that issue was essential to the outcome of the earlier case. D could contend that the issue of his D's negligence was actually litigated, decided, and essential to the previous judgment.

P could argue that the findings by the State A court were "alternative" findings, either of which standing alone would support the judgment. As such, neither finding should be treated as "essential" to the prior judgment. Courts have adopted three approaches to such alternative findings. First, some courts hold that unless both findings are appealed and then affirmed on appeal, neither finding will be treated as essential. Under this approach, since there was no appeal of the State A proceeding, neither finding would be binding on P in a subsequent lawsuit. Next, some courts have held that so long as the issue was thoroughly and carefully addressed in the initial proceeding, it will be treated as binding in all subsequent proceedings. Under this approach, P would be bound by the finding that D was not negligent if that question was thoroughly and carefully addressed in the prior proceeding. Finally, a few courts follow the principle that both alternative findings are binding regardless of care with which either finding was made. Under this approach, P would be bound by the finding that D was not negligent. Hence, the result here will depend on the rule adopted by State A, which, under principles of intersystem preclusion, must now be applied by State C.

Answer to Question 6

Did the court err in granting Dave ("D")'s motion to dismiss?

FRCP 15(c) allows relation back with respect to an amendment that adds a claim to a pleading under two circumstances. First, an "amendment to a pleading relates back to the date of the original pleading when . . . the law that provides the applicable statute of limitations allows relation back." FRCP 15(c)(1)(A). Since the accident occurred in State Y, State Y law would provide the statute of limitations. Furthermore, since State Y has no rule allowing an amendment to relate back "under any circumstances," subsection (c)(1)(A) would not permit relation back. Next, under subsection (c)(1)(B), an amendment relates back if the claim asserted in the amended pleading "arose out of the conduct, transaction, or occurrence set out—or attempted to be set out—in the original pleading." This standard would appear to be satisfied since P's amended pleading raises a claim that arises out of the same accident that was the subject of his initial pleading. Hence, under the language of FRCP 15(c)(1)(B), Paul ("P") would be entitled to have his amendment relate back to the date of the original filing.

Nonetheless, the U.S. district court's ruling denying relation back may have been correct. The essential question is whether application of FRCP 15(c)(1)(B) to these facts would be proper in light of the standards of the Rules Enabling Act ("REA"). To resolve that question, three subsidiary questions must be answered: (1) Is the federal rule broad enough to control, and, if so, is there a direct collision between it and the state law? (2) Assuming a conflict, is the federal rule rationally classifiable as procedural? (3) Assuming affirmative answers to the first two questions, would application of the federal rule abridge, enlarge, or modify a substantive right?

On the first question, FRCP 15(c)(1)(B) would appear to be broad enough to control since it addresses the specific circumstances under which relation back would be allowed. In addition, since the federal rule allows relation back (and, in fact, seems to require it) and state law does not, there would seem to be a conflict between the federal rule and state law. However, this conflict can be avoided. FRCP 15(a)(1)(B) permits a plaintiff to amend a pleading as of right if done within 20 days of the date on which the original pleading was filed. Otherwise, in the absence of consent by the adverse party, the pleading may be amended only by leave of court that shall be freely given "when justice so requires." The amendment here was filed one month after the initial pleading and it would not appear that D consented to it. Hence, the district court could avoid any conflict with state law by simply concluding that justice would not be served by allowing P to file this amendment. In essence, it would not be just to allow a plaintiff in federal court to enjoy the benefits of relation back when a plaintiff in state court would not reap those fruits. Since there is no conflict, the district court's ruling would be correct.

Assuming there is a conflict, the two elements of the REA must be satisfied if relation back is to be allowed—that is, the procedural and substantive components of the statute must be applied. As to the first, FRCP 15 is rationally classifiable as procedural since it adopts a method through which to amend pleadings and provides standards for determining the effect of those pleadings. Hence, this low threshold test is easily satisfied here.

Next, assuming a conflict and assuming that the rule is rationally classifiable as procedural, we must determine whether application of the rule would abridge, enlarge, or modify a substantive right. D has a very strong argument that allowing relation back when the effect of doing so will be to revive a claim that otherwise would be barred by the state statute of limitations does abridge his right to be free from liability on claim that is no longer enforceable under state law. Similarly, D could argue effectively that the application of relation back enlarges P's right to assert that claim by essentially resurrecting the moribund state-created cause of action.

In short, D's motion to dismiss the personal injury claim was correctly decided, either because the district court avoided the conflict with state law by refusing leave to file the amended pleading or because application of FRCP 15(c)(1)(B) under these circumstances would abridge, enlarge, or modify the underlying substantive rights asserted by P.

Did the court err in dismissing D's third-party complaint?
Insco ("I") has asserted three independent grounds for its contention that the district court should dismiss the third-party complaint against it.

(a) Lack of authorization under the FRCP: This assertion should not have prevailed since FRCP 14 specifically authorizes third-party claims premised on a claim of indemnity.

(b) Lack of competency: Since D and I are both citizens of State Y, I's argument was probably that the U.S. district court was not competent to hear the impleader because diversity subject matter jurisdiction requires that no plaintiff and no defendant be citizens of the same state. However, impleader by a defendant falls within the court's supplemental jurisdiction. Thus, dismissing D's complaint on this basis would have been erroneous.

(c) Lack of substantive claim: I's argument appears to be that D, in fact, has no right of recovery against it since the policy in question was fraudulently obtained. However, FRCP 14(a) permits an impleader claim whenever the impleaded party "may" be liable to the third-party plaintiff (i.e., the impleading party). Since whether the policy was wrongfully obtained appears to be a factual issue (to be decided at trial), dismissal of D's third-party complaint was therefore improper.

Admission of Wit's testimony:

Pretrial orders pursuant to FRCP 16(e) ordinarily describe matters that the parties have agreed on with respect to the conduct of the trial. Such matters can be modified at trial only to prevent "manifest injustice." Even though P might have been aware of Wit, he would have no reason to prepare to cross-examine him as a consequence of D's failure to list Wit in the pretrial order. Since (1) there is no indication that D had just discovered Wit, and (2) there was the possibility that Wit's testimony could tip the evidence in favor of D, the district court probably erred in permitting Wit to testify.

Answer to Question 7

Truco ("T")'s Motions to Dismiss

(a) Lack of subject matter jurisdiction: Where subject matter jurisdiction is based on diversity, the complaint must allege that no plaintiff and no defendant are citizens of the same state. T's contention that the complaint should be dismissed because of a lack of subject matter jurisdiction was probably based upon the fact that Pat ("P") has asserted only that she was a "resident" of State White. Thus, P could have resided in State White and yet have been a citizen of State Red. Yet, the word "resident" is often used synonymously with "domicile" or "citizenship." And under standards of notice pleading, P's allegations of residence probably would suffice as far as pleading goes. If there were any doubt as to whether P was, in fact, a citizen of State White, the district court would have a duty to require P to provide more specific proof as to her state of citizenship. Since the evidence later established that P was a citizen of State White at the time of filing, we can assume that the district court met its duty in this regard.

The fact that P was a citizen of State Red at the time the action arose is irrelevant because subject matter jurisdiction is determined at the time the complaint is filed. Since P had apparently made a bona fide relocation to State White before the action was commenced, diversity existed.

In summary, T's lack of subject matter jurisdiction defense was quite likely properly rejected.

(b) Failure to join Dan ("D"): Under FRCP 19(a)(1), a person must be joined if it is feasible to do so and if "(A) in that person's absence, the court cannot accord complete relief among existing parties; or (B) that person claims an interest relating to the subject of the action and is so situated that disposing of the action in the person's absence may: (i) as a practical matter impede or impair the person's ability to protect the interest; or (ii) leave an existing party subject to a substantial risk of incurring double, multiple, or otherwise inconsistent obligations because of the interest." The Supreme Court has made it clear, however, that an absent party's status as a joint tortfeasor is not sufficient, standing alone, to satisfy the requirements of FRCP 19(a). *Temple v. Synthes Corp., Ltd.,* 498 U.S. 5 (1990). In any event, P can clearly get complete relief from T in D's absence. Moreover, disposition of the action will not impair or impede any discernible interest of D; nor will it leave P or T subject to a substantial risk of incurring multiple liability. At most, if P prevails, T will be required to file a separate proceeding against D to enforce any joint liability between them and D will have ample opportunity to defend his rights against T in that proceeding.

T's motion for a judgment as a matter of law:

T would next contend that since it and P had stipulated in a pretrial order that "T would be liable to P if D was an employee of T," and since it was proved that D was not employed by T, a judgment as a matter of law was appropriate. P could make two arguments in rebuttal. First, P and T agreed only that T would be liable if D were T's employee, not that there could be no other grounds on which T's liability to P could be established. Thus, liability could be predicated on the State Red statute, which enforces liability on the owner of the vehicle who gave the driver causing the accident permission to use his car.

Second, a pretrial order may be modified to "prevent manifest injustice." FRCP 16(e). It would arguably be unjust to permit T to avoid liability simply because P had inadvertently alleged an incorrect basis for recovery—especially since T was in a superior position to know that D was not its employee. However, T could respond that (1) a reasonable construction of the language in question would lead T to have assumed that liability could be premised only upon a finding that D was T's employee, and (2) there is no "manifest injustice" in holding P to a pretrial order into which she had voluntarily entered, especially when the stipulation in question probably induced T to refrain from contesting the admission of evidence that tended to show that D was driving the car with T's permission (since it would have been extraneous to T's potential liability). Under these circumstances, the stipulation, as interpreted by T, probably should be enforced.

P's motion to amend her complaint:

Assuming the stipulation was not deemed dispositive, P would argue (as mentioned above) that where an issue is actually "tried," the pleadings are deemed to conform to such evidence. FRCP 15(b)(2). However, T could contend that the question of whether D drove the vehicle involved in the collision with T's permission was not "tried" since T had no reason to contest the introduction of this evidence because it was irrelevant to whether D was T's employee. Where evidence is objected to as being at variance with the pleadings, a court may nevertheless allow the pleadings to be amended at trial where "doing so will aid in presenting the merits" and the objecting party fails to establish prejudice. FRCP 15(b)(1). P alternatively could contend that justice is served by permitting the amendment since T knew (or should have known) from the commencement of the action that liability based on D driving with T's permission was a possible basis of recovery by P. However, T probably could successfully contend in rebuttal that an injustice would result by permitting such a post-trial amendment because, in light of the pretrial stipulation, it had no reason to rebut P's evidence bearing upon whether T permitted D to drive the vehicle that injured P.

Answer to Question 8

Does State White have personal jurisdiction over Albert ("A")?

A traditional basis for personal jurisdiction has been service of process upon the defendant when he was physically present in the forum. *Pennoyer v. Neff*, 95 U.S. 714 (1877). The Supreme Court reaffirmed that principle in *Burnham v. Superior Court*, 495 U.S. 604 (1990), where it held that the mere presence of a nonresident in the forum state is sufficient for the forum state to assert personal jurisdiction over him as long as service is made on the person while he is in the forum state. A's lack of other contacts with State White are irrelevant, so long as he was served in State White. Thus, State White may assert personal jurisdiction over A.

Does State White have personal jurisdiction over Par ("P")?

Since the question does not identify a State White tailored long-arm statute, we'll assume that the State White legislature has enacted a long-arm statute that gives its courts the full range of personal jurisdiction permitted by due process. Thus, there are no statutory interpretation issues.

To establish personal jurisdiction over P, Frances ("F") will have to satisfy the minimum contacts test by showing that P had purposeful contacts with State White and that F's claim arises out of those contacts. If F makes such a showing, then the burden will shift to P to demonstrate that the exercise of jurisdiction would nonetheless be unreasonable. As to purposeful availment, F might rely on the stream of commerce ("SOC") theory, arguing that P's clubs are distributed into the SOC, thereby subjecting P to jurisdiction in those states that may be included within that stream. Under this approach, the reach of purposeful availment is extended from the state of manufacture to the state of retail sale. The difficulty in applying SOC here is that the club that caused the injury was purchased by a consumer in State Red. As a consequence, the SOC ended in State Red. Although Harold ("H") did bring the club into State White where the accident occurred, his actions are not attributable to P. Moreover, while F could argue that other clubs manufactured by P do wind up being sold at retail in State White, thus establishing purposeful availment of the State White market, those clubs were not the cause of her injuries. In short, F will not be able to show her claim arises out of any purposeful activity directed toward State White by P. The standards of minimum contacts not being satisfied, the court may not exercise jurisdiction over P.

Was P validly served?

First, it is unlikely that state law would permit service on A to constitute service on P. Although A is under contract to P, nothing in the facts indicates that he is authorized to accept service on behalf of P and that he could be reasonably presumed to have such authority. Cf. FRCP 4(h) (serving a corporation, partnership, or association). Moreover, service of process, even if in conformity with the applicable state law, must comport with due process (i.e., give such notice as is reasonably calculated under the circumstances to apprise the defendant of the action). P might contend that service of process for it on A, a non-officer, is not constitutionally adequate. However, since P's president was also personally served, F should prevail on this issue.

Removal to the U.S. district court in State Red:

First, a case may be removed only to the federal district court embracing the geographic location of the state court. Hence, a case cannot be removed from a State White court to a federal court sitting in State Red. In theory, A and P could remove the case to a State White federal court and then seek to have it transferred to a State Red federal court pursuant to 28 U.S.C. §1404(a). The problem, however, is that there is no basis on which this case could be removed from state to federal court.

Removal is proper only if the case could have originally been filed in federal court. This means that the case would have to satisfy a federal court's subject matter jurisdiction. Since no federal question is presented by these facts, the only plausible basis for jurisdiction is diversity. Thus, F could initially contend that diversity does not exist since she and P are citizens of State Green. This assertion is premised on the argument that a corporation is a citizen of its state of incorporation and of the state in which it has its principal place of business. Since P's major manufacturing facility is in State Green, under a "place of activity" or "muscle" approach to determining "principal place of business," P would be a citizen of that state, thus destroying diversity.

The defendants would successfully argue in rebuttal, however, that the exclusive test for determining a corporation's principal place of business is now the "nerve center" test. *Hertz Corp. v. Friend*, 130 S.Ct. 1181 (2010). Under that approach, a corporation's headquarters will be treated as the entity's principal place of business in all but the most unusual circumstances, e.g., where an internet company has no geographic headquarters. Here, P's central administrative offices in State Red would easily qualify that state as being P's principal place of business.

Assuming that P is a citizen of State Red only, removal would be permitted so long as both defendants joined in the petition for removal and so long as neither defendant was a citizen of the forum state. The facts suggest that A and P joined in the petition for removal and neither of them is a citizen of State White. The next issue is whether the defendants' motion to transfer under §1404(a) should be granted.

Section 1404(a) allows a federal court to transfer a case in the interests of justice to another federal court where it could have been brought. Since both A and P are citizens of State Red, both would be subject to personal jurisdiction there. Moreover, if the case was properly removed to State white federal court, verve would be automatically proper in that court. *See* 28 U.S.C. §1390(e). Thus, the case could have been filed in a State Red district court. The question, therefore, is whether the transfer from State White to State Red would be in the interests of justice. Given that the accident took place in State White and that much of the evidence would be in State White and given that State Red has no direct interest in this accident, it is quite unlikely that the State White federal court would grant the motion to transfer, especially considering the preference for plaintiff's choice of forum.

What use may Robert ("R"), P, and A make of the judgment?
(a) Assuming that F was successful, may R assert issue preclusion against P and A? Under the issue preclusion aspect of *res judicata* doctrine, where an issue that was essential to the outcome of a case was actually litigated and decided in a prior lawsuit, and essential to the judgment in that case, relitigation of that issue by the defendant in a subsequent case between the same parties is precluded. Since F prevailed in the first lawsuit, it is fair to infer that the defectiveness of the golf club was litigated and decided in that proceeding. Moreover, in order for F to prevail, the resolution of that issue was essential. The question is whether R, a nonparty and nonprivity to the prior proceeding, can use the resolution of this issue to establish an element of his claims against A and P—so-called offensive issue preclusion. The answer to this question depends on whether State White (assuming that the case remained in State White) has abandoned the doctrine of mutuality in the context of offensive uses of issue preclusion. (Note that under principles of intersystem preclusion, the State Green court would be compelled to follow the law that the State White court would apply to this issue.) That doctrine provides that only parties bound by a judgment can benefit from it. If State White has not abandoned this doctrine as to offensive uses of issue preclusion, then R, who is not bound by the State White

proceeding, may not assert issue preclusion against A and P. Moreover, even if State White has abandoned mutuality in this context, the circumstances under which a person in R's position can use the doctrine are limited. If, for example, R could have joined in the prior litigation, a court is unlikely to allow him to assert issue preclusion in a subsequent proceeding because he has adopted an "inefficient" wait-and-see posture. In addition, if there is any unfairness to the defendants, issue preclusion will not be allowed. Thus, a determination of whether R may assert issue preclusion depends on the law of State White and on an examination of why R did not join in the earlier proceeding.

(b) Assuming that P and A were successful, could they assert collateral estoppel against R? Robert was not a party to the previous proceeding, nor was he in privity with a party. Hence neither claim nor issue preclusion may be asserted against him in a subsequent proceeding.

Answer to Question 9

Did the U.S. district court in State X have personal jurisdiction over Devco ("D")?

In order for the U.S. district court to assert personal jurisdiction over D, both the standards of the state long-arm statute and the requirements of Fourteenth Amendment due process must be satisfied.

The state long-arm statute provides that jurisdiction may be asserted over a foreign corporation "only if" that corporation is "doing business" in the state. Hence, this statute provides the exclusive means provided by State X for asserting personal jurisdiction over a foreign corporation. The question, therefore, is whether D is "doing business" in State X within the meaning of this long-arm statute, as construed by the courts of State X. The facts state that D did "no business in State X." If this statement is dispositive, then Pete ("P") is out of luck. Indeed, D's only contacts with State X are the advertisement that was placed in a State Y newspaper and that also circulated in State X, and, arguably, the mailing of the stock certificate to Pete in State X. Unless the courts of State X would treat these contacts as "doing business," there would appear to be no statutory basis through which to assert jurisdiction over D in State X. The U.S. district court is, of course, bound by state law under these circumstances and cannot exercise personal jurisdiction over D in the absence of a state long-arm provision that would allow it to do so. This is true even if the standards of due process would be satisfied. Note, however, that some state courts construe their specific act statutes to extend jurisdiction to the full extent of due process. If State X is such a state, then the term "doing business" could be construed quite broadly to include the solicitation of business through a newspaper advertisement. If that is the case, then the statute might well be satisfied. Thus, whether the state long-arm statute is satisfied depends on how liberally the courts of State X have construed and applied that statute. Those constructions are binding on the U.S. district court.

Assuming that the state long-arm does allow for the assertion of personal jurisdiction over D, it must be determined whether the exercise of that jurisdiction would comport with the minimum contacts test embodied in the Fourteenth Amendment's due process clause. To satisfy this test, P must show that D engaged in purposeful activities directed toward State X and that P's claim arises out of those contacts. If this standard is satisfied, the reasonableness of the exercise of personal jurisdiction will be presumed; however, D can then attempt to meet the heavy burden of rebutting that presumption by demonstrating that the exercise of jurisdiction would nonetheless be unreasonable.

Arguably, D has at least two purposeful contacts with State X: the newspaper advertisement circulated in State X and the delivery of the stock certificates to P in State X. As to the former, assuming D knew of the circulation in State X, this contact might well qualify as a purposeful contact, especially if the advertising had run over a lengthy period of time. In essence, D was soliciting business from potential clients in State X, a classic purposeful contact. On the other hand, the mailing of the stock certificate to P in State X, assuming that is what happened, might not qualify as a purposeful contact. If the certificate was mailed to P at his home address in State X, the contact might be seen as P's contact and not D's. As such, it represents a classic "unilateral" contact by the plaintiff that cannot be counted in the minimum contacts analysis. See *Hanson v. Denckla*, 357 U.S. 235 (1958). On the other hand, P could argue that the mailing was part of the overall solicitation of stock purchases within the state—that is, D chose to promote its stock in the State X market, and both the advertisement and the mailing were, in essence, part of the same purposeful transaction, which would distinguish this case from *Hanson* where the non-resident defendant did nothing to promote its business in the forum state.

The next question is whether these purposeful contacts with State X—the newspaper advertisement and the mailing—are sufficiently related to Pete's claim to satisfy the standards of due process—that is, does his claim arise out of D's purposeful contacts with State X? The resolution of that question depends on how strictly a court applies the "arises out of" principle. If that principle can be satisfied by a loose "but for" test—that is, but for the advertisement P would not have purchased the stock, and but for that purchase he would not have been damaged—then the test would seem to be satisfied. If, as some courts do, the court requires that the D contacts with the forum be substantively relevant to P's claim—that is, the contacts constitute an element of the claim—then the test would be satisfied only if the content of the advertisement were part of the fraud, which is certainly a possibility.

Assuming that the foregoing elements of the minimum contacts test have been satisfied, then D will have an opportunity to rebut the presumption that the exercise jurisdiction under these facts is reasonable. However, the burden here is a "heavy" one and is not likely to be met. D would have to demonstrate either that State X has no interest in this case—unlikely given that P is from State X—or that the burden on D of litigating in State X will be particularly onerous and prejudicial—the facts suggest no basis for such an argument.

In short, if the U.S. district court finds that both the state long-arm statute and the standards of due process are satisfied, it may exercise jurisdiction over D. As to the former, the resolution depends on how broadly the courts of State X have construed their long-arm statute. As to the latter, it depends on a combination of the sufficiency of the limited purposeful contacts and the relationship between those contacts and P's claim.

Did the U.S. district court in State X have subject matter jurisdiction over the action against Bull ("B")?

For a U.S. district court to be competent based upon diversity, (1) no plaintiff and no defendant may be a citizen of the same state; and (2) the amount in controversy must exceed $75,000, exclusive of interest and costs. It is assumed that the latter requirement is satisfied. The former criterion, however, would not be met if B is joined as a party-defendant. Individuals are considered citizens of the state in which they are domiciled (i.e., presently live and intend to remain). Although B works in State Y, for diversity purposes he is a citizen of State X. Thus, the U.S. district court would not have subject matter jurisdiction over the claim against B. Nor would the court have supplemental jurisdiction over this claim. Although any claim P would have against B would be part of the same constitutional case as P's claim against D, hence satisfying the standards of 28 U.S.C. §1367(a), since this is a diversity case, the limitations imposed by §1367(b) would apply. That section precludes the exercise of supplemental jurisdiction in diversity cases when doing so would violate the above principle of complete diversity and when the claim is one by a plaintiff, here P, against a party joined pursuant to FRCP 19, here B.

Assuming the U.S. district court had subject matter jurisdiction over P's claim against B, was it correct in ordering the latter to be joined as a party-defendant?

D's motion to bring B into the case would have been made pursuant to FRCP 19. Under FRCP 19(a)(1), a person must be joined if it is feasible to do so and if "(A) in that person's absence, the court cannot accord complete relief among existing parties; or (B) that person claims an interest relating to the subject of the action and is so situated that disposing of the action in the person's absence may: (i) as a practical matter impede or impair the person's ability to protect the interest; or (ii) leave an existing party subject to a substantial risk of incurring double, multiple, or otherwise inconsistent obligations because of the interest." It would not appear that B's joinder would satisfy any of these standards. Certainly, P can get complete relief without B's presence and there is nothing in the facts to suggest that

D would be seeking any type of relief from B. Moreover, there is nothing in the facts to indicate that any interest of B would be impaired by the *P v. D* proceedings or that D would somehow be subjected to multiple liability. Hence, the standards of FRCP 19(a) having not been satisfied, joinder was improper. Moreover, as noted in the previous answer, the district court would not have subject matter jurisdiction over any claim by P against B; therefore, even if subsection (a) had been satisfied, under FRCP 19(b), B's joinder would not have been feasible. In that case, the district court could have proceeded without B since his absence would not prejudice him or the parties to the suit.

Did the district court err in striking P's demand for a jury trial?

Where a "common law" claim is brought in a federal district court, either party normally has a right to a jury trial, whether state law permits a jury trial or not. FRCP 38. A "common law" claim is one that courts of law recognized prior to the adoption of the Seventh Amendment in 1791. However, there appears to be a division of authority as to whether a case can be so exceedingly complex that the Fifth Amendment right to due process can be deemed to override the Seventh Amendment right to a jury trial. Some federal courts have suggested that, in rare instances, a denial of a jury trial is appropriate. Others, however, have refused to recognize a "complex case" exception to the Seventh Amendment.

In any event, this case does not appear to constitute a situation where denying the normal right to a jury trial would be appropriate since lay-persons should be able to determine if (1) the statements contained in the advertisement and promotional brochures were incorrect; and (2) D knew, or should have known, that those statements were (a) false, or (b) made without adequate knowledge as to their truth or falsity. Since P has asserted only common law fraud (rather than a federal securities violation) and such actions were recognized at "common law," the court erred in striking P's demand for a jury trial.

Answer to Question 10

Valvo ("V")'s objection to Peter ("P")'s failure to join Mity ("M") as a defendant:

Under FRCP 19(a)(1), a person must be joined if it is feasible to do so and if "(A) in that person's absence, the court cannot accord complete relief among existing parties; or (B) that person claims an interest relating to the subject of the action and is so situated that disposing of the action in the person's absence may: (i) as a practical matter impede or impair the person's ability to protect the interest; or (ii) leave an existing party subject to a substantial risk of incurring double, multiple, or otherwise inconsistent obligations because of the interest." If any of these factors is satisfied, the nonparty should be made a party if she is subject to service of process and the court will not be deprived of subject matter jurisdiction if the party is joined.

In this instance, none of the above elements is satisfied. P can obtain complete relief (i.e., a judgment for the full amount of his injuries) against V. M's interest in the subject matter of the action will not be impaired (i.e., any judgment against V will not have a preclusive effect upon M since this preclusion cannot be asserted against a nonparty who is not in privity with party).

V will not be exposed to double multiple liability since (1) it would retain the right to pursue an indemnity action against M if P were successful against it; and (2) in any event, a tortfeasor cannot complain about a plaintiff's decision to abstain from suing all possible joint tortfeasors. Thus, any objection by V that P must be joined would be incorrect.

May V bring M into the case as a defendant?

V could bring M into the case as a third-party defendant (assuming personal jurisdiction over the latter was satisfied) by means of a third-party complaint (sometimes called "impleader"). FRCP 14(a). This procedural device is appropriate where the third-party defendant (the impleaded party) may be liable to the third-party plaintiff (the impleading party) for all or part of the plaintiff's judgment against the latter. Subject matter jurisdiction would not be a problem even though V and M are each citizens of State A since impleader actions filed by defendants fall within the court's supplemental jurisdiction.

Joinder of parties (P and Q v. V and M):

Parties may be joined, as either plaintiffs or defendants, if (1) the claim asserted (or defended against) by them, jointly, severally, or in the alternative, arises out of the same transaction or occurrence or series of transactions or occurrences; and (2) there is a common question of law or fact. FRCP 20(a). These requisites appear to be satisfied in this instance since both claims arise from the same occurrence (the explosion) and there are common questions of fact (i.e., whether the valve "collar" was defectively or negligently made, whether the plaintiffs were advised of a possible malfunction). Thus, joinder of parties (subject to competency and personal jurisdiction questions discussed below) would be appropriate.

Joinder of causes of action (P and Q v. V and M):

A party asserting a claim to relief may ordinarily join all the causes of action she has against a particular defendant. FRCP 18(a). Since the plaintiffs probably would be asserting negligence, products liability, and breach of the implied warranty of merchantability against V and M, joinder of claims is appropriate.

Personal jurisdiction over the defendants:

Since this appears to be a diversity action, the U.S. district court would use (i.e., "borrow") the long-arm statute of State C, the forum in which it is located. FRCP 4(k)(1)(A). Since the facts do not state otherwise, it is assumed that the State C long-arm statute affords its courts the full range of personal jurisdiction permitted by the due process clause (and thereby avoids any possible statutory interpretation problems). The assertion of personal jurisdiction over the defendants would still have to satisfy due process (i.e., the defendants must have such minimum contacts with the forum so as not to offend traditional notions of fair play and substantial justice). In determining if this standard is satisfied, the courts consider (1) the extent to which the defendant has purposefully availed itself of the benefits of the forum or purposefully directed activities toward that state; (2) whether the claims by the plaintiff arise out of the defendant's forum contacts; and (3) assuming the first two elements have been satisfied, whether the defendant has rebutted the presumption of reasonableness.

The facts are not sufficient to determine whether the standards of due process have been satisfied. Certainly if V shipped the machinery into State C as part of a sale to P and Q, then the standards of due process would be satisfied. Such a direct sale would have been purposefully directed toward the forum state, and the plaintiffs' claims arising out of the explosion would also be deemed to arise out of the contacts. Moreover, under such circumstances, it would be highly unlikely that V could rebut the presumption of reasonableness. As to M, if M sold the collar to V as part of a regular course of business, with the expectation that the collars would be used on valves to be sold in State C, under the stream of commerce test, the contacts of V with State C might be imputed to M. The current standards for this test are somewhat unclear. At a minimum, the plaintiffs would have to show that M either promoted its collars in State C or that there was a regular flow of those collars into the state. *J. McIntyre Machinery, Ltd. v. Nicastro*, 131 S.Ct. 2780 (2011). If the stream of commerce test is satisfied, M would have purposeful contacts State C. On the other hand, if the arrival of the machinery in State C was completely fortuitous—for example, P and Q purchased it from a third party in State X—then neither V nor M would be subject to personal jurisdiction in this State C proceeding. This is particularly true if the purchaser buys the product in one state and then brings it into another.

Subject matter jurisdiction over the parties:

For diversity subject matter jurisdiction to exist, (1) no defendant and no plaintiff may be citizens of the same state, and (2) the amount in controversy must exceed $75,000.

Since V and Q are citizens of State B (a corporation is a citizen of the states in which it is incorporated and has its principal place of business, and an individual is a citizen of his state of domicile at the time the action is commenced), a U.S. district court would *not* be competent to hear this matter.

Must P plead a lack of contributory negligence ("CN")?

U.S. district courts adhere to the FRCP whenever a valid federal rule is sufficiently broad to control the question presented. Under FRCP 8(c), CN must be set forth as an affirmative defense. Thus, P would not be required to plead that he was not contributorily negligent. Rather, the defense, if relevant, would have to be pled by the defendant.

Does P have the burden of persuasion on the issue of CN?

In a diversity case, where a matter is not dealt with directly in the FRCP and pertains to a substantive aspect of the case (the burden of proof on an issue would arguably constitute a substantive issue since it goes to establishing a claim or defense), state law will ordinarily be followed. Whether the federal judge will apply the law of State A (where the action has been commenced) or State C (where the cause of action allegedly arose) depends upon State A law. If State A applies its own law, the law of State A controls. However, if a State A court would, under its conflict of law rules, apply the law of State C, the federal judge must also apply the law of State C.

Answer to Question 11

Bigbucks ("BB") v. Palladium Corporation ("PC"):

(a) Subject matter jurisdiction: PC (or any party or the court itself) could successfully contend on appeal that diversity subject matter jurisdiction was lacking on either of two grounds: (1) PC and BB are citizens of New York, and (2) the amount in controversy is not "in excess" of $75,000. While BB could contend that PC waived these defects by filing an answer that failed to question the district court's subject matter jurisdiction, a lack of subject matter jurisdiction cannot be waived and can be raised at any time, FRCP 12(h)(3), including while on appeal. Thus, the court of appeals should dismiss the appeal and remand with instructions to the district court to dismiss the case for want of subject matter jurisdiction.

(b) Personal jurisdiction, service, and venue: Whatever objections PC may have to personal jurisdiction, service of process or venue were waived when PC filed an answer without raising these defects. Thus, although PC may have had a tenable personal jurisdiction argument, that argument is no longer available on appeal. As to service of process, even if the claim had not been waived, there is a plausible argument that the secretary to the president of a corporation falls within the meaning of FRCP 4(h)(1)(B)'s requirement that service on a corporation be made by delivering a copy of the summons and complaint to an "officer, managing or general agent, or to any other agent authorized by appointment or by law to receive service of process." As to venue, again assuming no waiver, it is unlikely that venue was proper in Massachusetts since all the defendants do not reside there (28 U.S.C. §1391(b)(1)) and since no events giving rise to the claim occurred there (§1391(b)(2)). Additionally, the fallback provision of §1391(b)(3) is not available since there are other states in which substantial events giving rise to the controversy occurred, including Illinois (the discussions between Don and Merv), New York (where the telegram was sent and the contracted breached), and possibly California (where the Pallidium concert was to take place and where negotiations between Merv and PC may have taken place). Importantly, subsection (b)(2) is designed to establish proper venue in a range of locations; in other words, the underlying assumption of that subsection is that there may be more than one place where substantial events giving rise to the claim occur.

(c) Motion to transfer venue: Any party may make a motion to transfer an action in U.S. district court to a different U.S. district court, provided the case could have been commenced in the latter court. In other words, both venue and personal jurisdiction must have been available in the potential

transferee forum at the time the original suit was filed. As to venue, venue is proper in a diversity action in a judicial district in which (1) any defendant resides, if all defendants reside in the same state; (2) a substantial part of the events or omissions on which the claim is based occurred or a substantial part of the property is located; or (3) if there is no jurisdiction where the suit may otherwise be brought, any defendant is subject to personal jurisdiction with respect to the claims asserted. 28 U.S.C. §1391(b). California would provide a proper venue if substantial events giving rise to the plaintiff's claim occurred in a judicial district in that state. It is possible that the negotiations between Merv and PC took place partly in California, where the Palladium is located. If that is the case, then the district in which the Palladium is located would have been a proper venue. Venue would not be proper in California under subsection (b)(3) since there are other districts where venue may have been proper, namely, Illinois and New York under subsection (b)(2). See discussion in the preceding subsection of this answer. However, in addition to establishing venue, the party seeking a transfer must also establish that personal jurisdiction over all defendants would have been available in the transferee state at the time the action was commenced. It is not clear that Don would have been subject to personal jurisdiction in California at that time since the facts do not indicate any contacts he may have had with California other than his plans to perform there on a future date. If personal jurisdiction were lacking, transfer to California would be inappropriate unless all the parties consented to the transfer. Assuming that California would be a proper transferee state—that is, both venue and personal jurisdiction would have been satisfied—it remains within the discretion of the district court to transfer or not in the interests of justice. In this case, the district court may have abused its discretion because Massachusetts has no connections with this case but California at least has some. The ultimate conclusion on this issue, however, would depend on a balancing of the interests of the parties, the witnesses, and the judicial system. Additional facts would be required to make that judgment.

BB v. Don Pickles ("D"):
(a) Personal jurisdiction: BB could successfully contend that she obtained personal jurisdiction over D since the latter was served within Massachusetts. In this specific regard, the U.S. Supreme Court has held that service in the forum state establishes personal jurisdiction over a defendant voluntarily in the state no matter how brief the defendant's presence in the state. *Burnham v. Superior Court,* 495 U.S. 604 (1990).

(b) Venue and waiver: Even if D prevailed on the issue of personal jurisdiction discussed immediately above and could have successfully objected to venue (see discussion of venue under *BB v. PC*), these objections were waived by his failure to raise them in his initial response to BB's complaint. FRCP 12(h)(1).

D v. Merv ("M"):

(a) The Federal Rules: Since BB was not seeking monetary damages from D, D's action against M was presumably for the lost income that D would have earned from appearing at the Palladium. This is not a proper claim for impleader since D does not allege that M may or will be liable to him for any liability D has to BB, the plaintiff. Hence, FRCP 14 is not available. Moreover, since D has not filed a counterclaim against BB, FRCP 13(h) (joinder of additional party to a counterclaim) is also not available. In fact, there are no federal rules that would allow D to file this claim, although he plausibly could have filed a motion to dismiss for failure to join a necessary party under FRCP 19. But the facts do not indicate the filing of any such motion. The claim against M, therefore, should be dismissed.

(b) Subject matter jurisdiction: Assuming there was a federal rule that allowed D to file his claim against M, the court would have supplemental jurisdiction over the claims since they arise from the same transaction as the plaintiff's primary claim. 28 U.S.C. §1367(a). Moreover, although this is a diversity suit, nothing in §1367(b) would preclude this claim by a defendant. The fact that D and M are citizens of the same state would be irrelevant.

(c) Service of process: Next, M could have argued that service of process should be quashed because he was "lured" into the jurisdiction (i.e., he entered Massachusetts in response to D's telephone call and D had a process server waiting at the airport). While D could argue that the thought of serving D at the airport occurred *after* the telephone conversation and there was nothing dishonest about his statements (i.e., D intended to seek another agent if BB's action against him was not dismissed), the court probably should have ruled in favor of M on this issue.

(d) Personal jurisdiction: M could argue that his temporary physical presence did not establish sufficient minimum contacts with the forum state for it to assert personal jurisdiction over him. D could counter that since M was served in Massachusetts, the district court in that state could constitutionally assert personal jurisdiction over M (see discussion of jurisdiction under *BB v. D*). However, in *Burnham v. Superior Court*, 495 U.S. 604

(1990), at least five members of the Court suggested that principles of fairness might limit the scope of territorial jurisdiction, and given the possibility that M was lured into the jurisdiction, that principle may apply here.

PC v. M

(a) Subject matter jurisdiction: Since PC is a New York corporation with its principle place of business in New York (by virtue of the "nerve center" test as adopted by the Supreme Court in *Hertz Corp. v. Friend*, 130 S.Ct. 1181 (2010)) and M is a resident of Illinois, diversity subject matter jurisdiction exists over this claim. However, assuming that PC is asserting an indemnification-type claim against M, the third-party action would also fall within the court's supplemental jurisdiction.

(b) Service of process by PC on M: FRCP 4(e)(1) allows a party to use the service of process standards of the state where the district court is located. The facts state that Massachusetts allowed the type of service used here (certified mail). Because the case was filed in a district court sitting in Massachusetts, service of process was proper under the rule. M could raise a due process objection (i.e., permitting service by mail without any initial attempt at personal delivery of the summons and complaint is arguably *not* reasonably calculated to inform the defendant of the lawsuit). However, given that M received actual notice, this argument is not likely to succeed. Moreover, since the summons and complaint were sent by certified mail, requiring a signature by a responsible party, it seems that the service was reasonably calculated to apprise M of the pending litigation.

(c) Personal jurisdiction and venue: Because the claim asserted by PC against M arises out of the same transaction as the claim asserted by D against M, if personal jurisdiction over the *D v. M* claim is established, then, upon proper service of the third-party complaint, personal jurisdiction may be exercised over M with respect to that claim as well. See discussion of personal jurisdiction in "*D v. Merv*," above; and see the discussion of service by PC on M in the previous subsection. Assuming venue was proper between the original parties, venue is proper for the third-party claim.

(d) Determination of BB's right to an injunction: Under FRCP 38(a) and the Seventh Amendment, there is an absolute right to a jury trial with respect to legal claims in federal courts. In *Beacon Theaters, Inc. v. Westover*, 359 U.S. 500 (1959), the Supreme Court held that in a federal court, legal claims *must* be tried prior to equitable ones in order to preserve a party's right to a jury trial. Since BB's right to injunctive relief would be premised

upon the "legal" question of whether D was in breach of his contract with BB, the judge incorrectly determined the equitable issue first. Under the Supremacy Clause of the U.S. Constitution, any state rule that is inconsistent with the Supreme Court's interpretation of the Seventh Amendment as applied to federal court cases will be superseded. Thus, the fact that Massachusetts law permits resolution of equitable issues first is irrelevant.

D's defense of minority:

Amendments to pleadings are permissible at trial if the court determines that (1) doing so will "aid in presenting the merits," and (2) the objecting party fails to satisfy the court that the admission of such evidence will prejudice that party's defense on the merits. FRCP 15(b)(1). Although D could have contended that this standard is satisfied because BB could not have defended against this assertion in any event (i.e., either D is under the age of majority or he is not), the court could have decided that D's making this assertion near the end of the litigation was prejudicial to BB. If the prejudice could not be avoided, then the district court's decision was correct. However, if any prejudice to BB could have been mitigated (e.g., by imposing costs on D), the district should have allowed the amendment.

Answer to Question 12

Ped ("P")'s motion to remand:

Removal to a U.S. district court when no federal question is involved is proper where (1) no defendant is a citizen of the state(s) in which the action has been commenced, and (2) "diversity" subject matter jurisdiction requirements are satisfied.

P could have contended that removal to the U.S. district court was improper on two grounds: (1) Health ("H") is a citizen of State A (a corporation is a citizen of the states in which it is incorporated and has its principal place of business) because that is where H's business is conducted (and therefore one of the defendants is a citizen of the state in which the action was commenced), and (2) "diversity" is lacking because P and H are both citizens of State A (diversity requires that no plaintiff and no defendant be citizens of the same state). Thus, federal court subject matter jurisdiction does not exist and the remand was proper.

H's demurrer:

In some states, defendants can be joined only if their liability to the plaintiff arises out of the same "transaction or occurrence." Thus, H would contend that joinder of D and H was not proper since two distinct occurrences were involved: (1) the traffic accident involving P and D, and (2) the treatment that P subsequently received at H's hospital.

In determining if claims arise from the same "transaction or occurrences," state courts typically apply one of two standards: (1) whether the events that serve as the basis for each claim are "logically related," *or* (2) whether "common evidence" would be introduced in trials regarding each claim. Either test appears to be met in this instance.

The claims are "logically related" in that H's liability should be diminished to the extent it can be shown P's injuries in the traffic accident are distinguishable from those that he allegedly sustained at the hospital. Also, an initial tortfeasor is ordinarily liable for additional injuries caused to the plaintiff by medical personnel acting in a negligent manner, unless the latter's conduct can be characterized as "reckless" (in which case, the initial tortfeasor is *not* responsible for the subsequent enhancement of the plaintiff's injuries). Since a determination of each defendant's conduct is pertinent to deciding the extent of liability properly allocated between them, the claims are probably "logically related." The "common evidence" test would also be satisfied for the reasons described above (i.e., evidence as to P's initial injuries and the conduct of H's medical personnel would be pertinent in an action against either D or H for purposes of determining each party's precise liability to P).

Finally, it should be mentioned that a few jurisdictions follow the FRCP. Under the applicable rule, claims against multiple defendants can be joined as long as (1) they arose out of the same transaction or occurrence or series of transactions or occurences, and (2) share at least one common issue of law or fact. FRCP 20(a). Since this provision has been liberally construed, it probably would be concluded that (1) P's claims against both D and H "arose" from the same transaction or series of transactions (i.e., the traffic accident and the consequent hospitalization), and (2) there are common questions of fact (i.e., the extent to which each defendant's conduct caused injury to P and whether H's personnel performed their duties in a reckless or merely negligent manner).

Thus, joinder of claims was proper, and H's demurrer was properly denied.

P's request for admissions:

In many states, requests for an admission of a legal conclusion are *not* permissible. However, requests for admissions relating to facts or the application of law to facts (e.g., leaving a rake on a sidewalk is negligent) are ordinarily proper. In states that follow the FRCP, a party may request admissions "relating to facts, the application of law to fact, or opinions about either." FRCP 36(a)(1)(A). P's request is probably improper because it asks H and D to do more than admit facts or the application of law to facts; instead, P asks for an admission of liability. As such, it is requesting admission of a purely legal conclusion. Thus, the court properly sustained the objections to P's request for admissions.

P's motion for a new trial:

Misconduct by jurors is an established ground for granting a mistrial. Quotient verdicts (i.e., where the verdict is determined by dividing a particular sum by the number of jurors) are usually viewed as improper since the figure does not represent the collective decision of the jury as to the actual damages sustained by a plaintiff. The verdict is arguably subject to this defect because the amount of P's damages was determined by adding the differing opinions as to liability and dividing by the total number of jurors.

In rebuttal, however, P could have made two arguments. First, some jurisdictions (including the federal courts) do not permit evidence of jury deliberations (except to show the possible influence of external factors upon the jurors). If this were such a jurisdiction, the affidavits could not be considered in the determination of whether a new trial should be granted. Second, the use of a quotient verdict as a ***starting point*** for discussing the amount of a judgment that should be rendered is not improper. Since the jury agreed on the $43,652.89 amount after that figure was derived from the quotient method, P probably could successfully argue that the verdict was proper (despite the occurrences described in the affidavits).

Assuming evidence of jury deliberations is admissible, D might also have contended that the total lack of discussion on the substantive issues was improper because ***immediately*** after entering the jury room, a vote of liability was taken and returned against the defendants. However, P could have argued that since the jury members presumably understood the legal issues under consideration, their verdict of liability evidenced a determination by each juror that P had successfully satisfied the burden of proof on the prima facie elements of his action.

In summary, the court's refusal to order a new trial (on any aspect of the case) was probably correct.

Answer to Question 13

Was Dod ("D") a required party?

Assuming that State White follows a compulsory joinder rule similar to FRCP 19, a person should be joined if, in her absence, (1) complete relief cannot be accorded to the existing parties, (2) disposition of the case will impair her ability to protect an interest that she has in the action, or (3) disposition of the action without her could result in an existing party's being exposed to multiple liability.

Cozy Nook ("CN") could contend that D is person who should be joined because (1) he has an interest in the action (the apartment D now occupies could be jeopardized) since Abel ("A") seeks to lease the dwelling now rented by D; and (2) CN would be exposed to multiple liability since a verdict in favor of A might oblige CN to dispossess D, thereby exposing CN to an action by the latter for breach of the lease agreement (and to potential inconsistent obligations).

However, A could argue in rebuttal that D's interest would not necessarily be affected by A's action because (1) A has alternatively sought a similar apartment in the building; and (2) even if no similar apartment were available, A probably could be adequately compensated by monetary damages (the rental differential between the initial apartment and the one in which A is now living, as well as any moving expenses attendant upon the relocation). Nonetheless, the actual relief that A seeks could require dispossession of D and the potential for Cozy Nook to be subject to mutually exclusive obligations.

But even though D may be a required party, D's joinder would not likely be possible since D does not appear to have any contacts with State White. Given that D's joinder is not feasible and assuming that D ought to be joined, D could not be characterized as a party without whom the court cannot proceed because the court could avoid any potential prejudice to CN or D by shaping the relief. Thus, should P prevail, CN could be ordered to give P an alternate apartment and/or to pay P an appropriate compensatory award. Accordingly, the court should overrule CN's motion to dismiss on this basis.

Did the court lack personal jurisdiction over CN?

CN will contend that attachment of a single account within a jurisdiction that is unrelated to the plaintiff's action does not constitute an adequate basis for making it stand trial within State White. Although A could argue that by maintaining the account, CN is availing itself of the protection of

State White's banking laws, CN is likely to prevail on this question given the ruling in *Shaffer v. Heitner*, 433 U.S. 186 (1977) that exercises of *quasi in rem* jurisdiction over personal property must comport with the minimum contacts test. At a minimum, Abel would have to establish some relationship between his claim and the attached property. The facts here indicate no such connection.

Is State White an inconvenient forum?

In its discretion, a court may decline to exercise jurisdiction. Factors considered in making this determination are access to proof, ability to secure attendance of key witnesses, the forum's relationship to the matter, and the potential necessity of viewing the premises.

CN could contend that since (1) the action arose in State Red, (2) D is domiciled in State Red, and (3) CN is a State Red corporation, dismissal is proper. A could then reinstitute the action in State Red.

However, A could argue in rebuttal that (1) the presentation of evidence would not be significantly impaired by conducting the trial in State White (i.e., the matter will primarily involve the oral testimony of A and CN's representatives; the mere fact that D subsequently rented the apartment desired by A does not make D's testimony essential), and (2) State White has an interest in affording its citizens a convenient forum. Thus, dismissal is unlikely.

Is CN entitled to a jury trial?

In *Dice v. Akron, Canton & Youngstown Railroad Co.*, 343 U.S. 359 (1952), the Supreme Court held that a state procedural rule (which did not permit a jury trial with respect to the particular issue under scrutiny) is overridden where it conflicts with a federal statute that allowed a jury trial on the claim in question. The court reasoned that where a procedural aspect is embodied in a U.S. statute that creates a federal cause of action and is important to the successful assertion of that claim, it must be observed by a state court. The only difference between the *Dice* case and the present situation is that in the latter the right to a jury trial has been judicially (as opposed to legislatively) created. However, since an interpretation of federal law by the U.S. Supreme Court is binding upon a state court, CN's demand for a jury trial should be granted (regardless of any contrary local procedure).

Answer to Question 14

Was dismissal because of lack of subject matter jurisdiction correct?

Federal district courts are competent to hear diversity actions where no plaintiff and no defendant are citizens of the same state and the amount in controversy exceeds $75,000, exclusive of interest and costs. Since there is no question that Don ("D") and Tinselware ("T") are citizens of different states, whether the court's dismissal was proper will turn on whether D's damages were in excess of $75,000.

T could contend that since D expended exactly $75,000 to purchase the widgets, the "in excess of" $75,000 requirement was not satisfied. However, since D intended to resell the widgets, he is entitled to recover consequential damages, including lost profits; his damages therefore meet the monetary requirement for diversity. Thus, assuming there was no "legal certainty" that D's claim would not exceed $75,000, dismissal for failure to satisfy the amount in controversy would not have been correct.

Did the court lack personal jurisdiction over T?

U.S. district courts "borrow" the long-arm statute of the state in which they are located. FRCP 4(k)(1)(A). Since the facts do not describe the California long-arm statute, it is assumed that the courts of that state have been legislatively authorized state courts to assert personal jurisdiction to the full extent permitted by the due process clause, which is, in fact, the law of California. The statutory analysis, therefore, collapses into the due process analysis and personal jurisdiction may be exercised over T if due process is satisfied (i.e., if T had such minimum contacts with California as not to offend traditional notions of fair play and substantial justice). To satisfy this test, D must demonstrate that T had purposeful contacts with California and that D's cause of action arose out of those contacts. T could contend that since (1) it does no business in California, (2) the contract was made in Arizona, and (3) the items in question were delivered to D in Arizona, it would not be constitutionally permissible to require it to defend the action in California. In essence, T would argue that it has no purposeful contacts with California.

In response, D will argue that Maureen ("M"), an employee of T, initiated this business transaction by placing a call on behalf of T to D in the state of California. Moreover, M's purpose was to promote resale of T's products in California and, as such, represents an effort by T to purposefully avail itself of the California market. A single contact with the forum state can be sufficient to establish personal jurisdiction over an out-of-state defendant so long as the claim arises out of that contact such that it is reasonably foreseeable for the defendant to expect to be haled into a court of the forum state. Here there is certainly a "but for" relationship between Maureen's phone call and the breach of contract action filed by D. However, given the paucity of contacts with the forum, a court might require a tighter substantive connection between the contacts and the claim. Hence, unless M made certain representations concerning the widgets that form a part of the breach of contract claim, a court might find the necessary relationship between the contacts and the claim inadequate for due process purposes.

In short, D has an argument that due process would be satisfied under these facts, but we would need more facts to fully assess the strength of that argument. In the absence of some additional facts showing a tighter connection between the contacts and the actual breach, the court's ruling was probably correct.

Was the court correct in dismissing the action because of lack of proper service?

Under the FRCP, service may be made upon a corporation by delivering a copy of the summons and complaint to an officer, a managing or general agent, or to any other agent authorized by appointment or law to receive service of process. FRCP 4(h)(1)(B). The burden is on the plaintiff to establish a proper inference of agency. M, as an employee of T, might well be authorized by T to accept service of process, and courts tend to be quite liberal in applying this principle. The fact that she is an employee with the authority to promote out-of-state business might support an inference of agency for service of process purposes. However, the facts here are insufficient to arrive at a definitive conclusion.

However, under FRCP 4(h)(1)(A) and 4(e)(1), a summons and complaint may be served on a corporation in accordance with the law of the state in which the U.S. district court is located.

Since California has a statute that permits service of process on a corporation by mailing, the issue is whether the application of this statute is constitutionally valid. Due process requires that a defendant be given such notice as is reasonably calculated under the circumstances to apprise him of the lawsuit.

While D might argue that service by mailing to the president of a corporation is proper, this assertion probably would fail. This is the correct result because pieces of mail sent to a corporation are rarely received directly by the individual addressee. Thus, there would be a significant possibility that the document could be received by an employee who is unhappy with management or might not understand the importance of legal papers. As a consequence, the summons and complaint could intentionally or inadvertently be discarded (without ever reaching the hands of the proper person). Thus, dismissal for improper service was probably correct.

Could the court have transferred the action to the U.S. district court in Nevada?

Under 28 U.S.C. §§1404(a) and 1406(a), a U.S. district court may transfer a case to any federal district court where the case could have filed originally. This requires that both personal jurisdiction and venue would have been satisfied in the transferee district at the time the action was commenced. As to personal jurisdiction, there are no facts indicating that T has any contacts with Nevada. Hence, under the given facts, there is no reason to believe that D could have commenced this action in Nevada against T. Venue is similarly problematical. Under the general federal venue statute, 28 U.S.C. §1391(b), venue is proper in a judicial district in which (1) any defendant resides, if all defendants reside in the same state; (2) a substantial part of the events or omissions on which the claim is based occurred or a substantial part of the property is located; or (3) if there is no other location where the suit may otherwise be brought, where any defendant is subject to personal jurisdiction with respect to the claims asserted. Nevada meets none of these criteria and subsection (b)(3) is unavailable since the case could have been filed in Arizona. On the other hand, if all both parties consented to jurisdiction and venue in Nevada, transfer would be proper under §1404(a) ("any district or division to which all parties have consented").

Was the dismissal of D's action against M correct?

D's action against M is not an amendment to an existing lawsuit (the initial case having already been dismissed). Hence, there is no basis on which to discuss relation back under FRCP 15(c). Moreover, in a diversity case, the federal court must apply the substantive law that a state court of the forum state would apply. Given that under the applicable law the state statute of limitations has run, a federal court would be required to enforce the statute of limitations and dismiss the case. To do otherwise would plainly violate the *Erie* doctrine and the refined outcome determinative test as defined by the Supreme Court in *Hanna v. Plumer*, 380 U.S. 460 (1965). Thus, dismissal of D's complaint against M was proper if the applicable statute of limitations had expired.

Answer to Question 15

Is the U.S. district court competent?

For diversity purposes, a corporation is deemed to be a citizen of the state in which it is incorporated and the state in which it has its principal place of business. Delightful Skies ("D") is incorporated in Massachusetts. Massachusetts is also D's principal place of business since its corporate headquarters are located there. *See Hertz Corp. v. Friend*, 130 S.Ct. 1181 (2010) (endorsing the "nerve center" test and explaining that corporate headquarters is the presumptive nerve center). Since P is a citizen of Arizona, diversity is satisfied.

There is, however, a problem with the amount in controversy alleged by P. In a class action based on diversity, the claim of the named plaintiff must exceed $75,000 unless, under the Class Action Fairness Act (CAFA), the aggregate claims of the class exceed $5 million. 28 U.S.C. §1332(d). The facts state that the $80,000 sought by P is meant to compensate him for his minor injuries *and* to compensate the injuries of the other passengers. This would seem to suggest that Pete's claim for his "minor" injuries does not itself satisfy the amount in controversy requirement and that the aggregate claims of the class would not meet the CAFA threshold. Hence, the face of the complaint suggests the absence of a good faith claim that would satisfy the jurisdictional minimums of §1332, including those aspects of §1332 premised on CAFA. The court, therefore, should either dismiss the case or require P to establish his good faith claim to an amount in excess of $75,000 or to an aggregate class-based claim that exceeds $5 million. As to the former, if P does satisfy the court that his personal claim exceeds $75,000, the court may exercise supplemental jurisdiction over claims by class members that do not meet the amount in controversy requirement. *Exxon Mobil Corp. v. Allapattah Services, Inc.*, 545 U.S. 546 (2005). As to the latter (i.e., the CAFA claim), if the aggregate claims of the class exceed $5 million, jurisdiction will be satisfied if any member of the class is diverse from the defendant (minimal diversity). P's diversity with D (discussed above) would satisfy this standard.

Is a class action maintainable?

For a class action to be maintainable, four requisites must be met: (1) the class is so numerous that joinder of all members is impracticable, (2) there are questions of law or fact common to the class, (3) the claims of the representative are typical of the class she seeks to represent, and (4) the representative is capable of fairly and adequately protecting the interests of the class. FRCP 23(a). Assuming these conditions are satisfied, P appears to be asserting an FRCP 23(b)(3) class action (i.e., common questions of law or fact predominate and a class action is superior to any other method of adjudication).

D could contend that (1) the class is not sufficiently numerous (only 40 persons); and (2) since each passenger's injuries are different, common questions of fact do not predominate.

While 40 is not a large number, joinder of these claims is probably impracticable since the plaintiffs are from various states, and therefore many members of the class could assert venue objections. Additionally, the objective of judicial economy is realized by combining 40 potential lawsuits into one action. Thus, a "numerosity" objection by D should be overcome.

Finally, while each plaintiff's injuries are different in type and extent, common questions of law or fact probably still predominate since the initial question of D's liability to the group for the accident is common to the entire class. Thus, a class action is probably appropriate.

Is venue proper?

A diversity action may be brought in a judicial district in which (1) any defendant resides, if all defendants reside in the same state; (2) a substantial part of the events or omissions on which the claim is based occurred or a substantial part of the property is located; or (3) if there is no location where the suit may otherwise be brought, any defendant is subject to personal jurisdiction with respect to the claims asserted. 28 U.S.C. §1391(b). This suit clearly could have been brought in Massachusetts under either subsection (b)(1) or (b)(2). D resides there, and the accident took place there. Therefore, subsection (b)(3)—the fallback provision—cannot be relied on to establish venue in the Central District of California. Nor will (b)(2) work since substantial events giving rise to the claim did not occur in the Central District of California. The only possibility is that D might be treated as a resident of California for purposes of subsection (b)(1). In this regard, §1391(c) provides that a corporation will be deemed a resident of any judicial district in which it would be subject to personal jurisdiction at the time the suit commenced. Hence, D will be treated as a resident of the Central District of California if its contacts with that district are sufficient to satisfy the minimum contacts test. The facts state that a majority of D's flights originate and land on the West Coast. The contacts are purposeful, but there are two problems here. First, the contacts are not necessarily with the Central District of California, and second and more importantly, there is no showing that the claim asserted by P arises out of the California contacts. Thus, unless D's contacts with California are so systematic and continuous so as to satisfy the standards of general jurisdiction, venue will not be proper under the residency prong of §1391(b)(1). This seems unlikely since the standards of general jurisdiction require a presence in the state that is the practical equivalent of citizenship or being "at home" in the forum. The facts here would not support such a claim. In short, it is unlikely that venue is proper in the Central District of California.

Should the action be transferred to Massachusetts?

On motion of any party, an action pending in a U.S. district court may be transferred to any other U.S. district court where the case could have originally been commenced, if the "convenience of the parties and witnesses" and "the interest of justice" so require. Since the accident occurred in Massachusetts (when the aircraft was taking off from Boston), the action could have been commenced in that state. (This, of course, assumes that the court has subject matter jurisdiction; if subject matter jurisdiction is lacking, the only option is to dismiss.) While a plaintiff's choice of forum is not easily disturbed, it is likely that all nonparty witnesses reside in Massachusetts and medical records pertaining to the victims are located in that jurisdiction (presumably, the victims were treated at the airport or taken to hospitals in the Boston area). In addition, as noted above, venue in the Central District appears to have been improperly laid. Therefore, under §1406(a), the district court has the option of dismissing (for improper venue) or transferring to Massachusetts.

Can Boing ("B") be impleaded by D?

A third-party claim (sometimes referred to as "impleader") is appropriate where the complainant has a indemnity-type claim against the third-party defendant (the party being impleaded). FRCP 14. B could contend that impleader is improper because (1) there is only "some" evidence of engine malfunction; (2) D and B are citizens of the same state (and thus, subject matter jurisdiction is lacking); (3) personal jurisdiction is lacking; and (4) venue is improper.

D would respond that (1) it is necessary only that the third-party claimant "may" have an indemnity-type claim against the third-party defendant (there need not be a strong likelihood that liability will actually be established at trial), (2) impleader actions satisfying the standards of FRCP 14(a) fall squarely within the court's supplemental jurisdiction under 28 U.S.C. §1367(a) and (b), (3) B is a citizen of Massachusetts and therefore subject to personal jurisdiction in that state (this of course assumes that the case has been transferred to Massachusetts), and (4) venue is established by the original parties to the case; hence if venue was proper as to the original parties, as it would be if transferred to Massachusetts, then the court will have supplemental venue over the impleader action against DC.

There is, however, one additional problem with D's impleader against B. If D is alleging that the accident was not its fault but the fault of B, then this is not a proper impleader. The only basis on which D may implead B is on allegations that if D is liable to P, B may or will be required to indemnify D, in whole or in part. Thus, the impleader is appropriate only if D is alleging that B, as a joint tortfeasor, is or may be liable for contribution and indemnity (or, less plausibly under these facts, as an insurer).

Answer to Question 16

Under FRCP 4(k)(1)(A), a federal court may exercise personal jurisdiction over a non-resident defendant to the same extent as a state court of the forum state. Since there is no applicable federal long arm statute and since neither FRCP 4(k)(1)(B) (the bulge rule) nor FRCP 4(k)(2) (a default provision for certain federal question cases) apply here, the court in this case may exercise jurisdiction over D if doing so is consistent with the California long-arm statute and with the minimum contacts standards imposed by the due process clause of the Fourteenth Amendment. Since California's long-arm statute permits the courts of California to exercise personal jurisdiction to the full extent of due process, the statutory analysis will collapse into the due process analysis. In addition, the federal court may exercise personal jurisdiction over D if any of the traditional bases have been satisfied.

Traditional Bases of Jurisdiction

The traditional bases of jurisdiction include physical presence, voluntary appearance, agent appointed for service of process within the state, and domicile. (Property found in the state is no longer an independent basis for the exercise of personal jurisdiction in the absence of satisfaction of minimum contacts standards.) Nothing in the facts supports the exercise of jurisdiction on any of these grounds. D, an Ohio corporation, is neither domiciled nor physically present in California. Neither do the facts suggest that D made a voluntary appearance in this proceeding or that D has appointed a California agent for receiving service of process.

Minimum Contacts/Due Process Standard

Under the minimum contacts test, a court may exercise personal jurisdiction over a non-resident defendant if that non-resident defendant has engaged in purposeful activity in or directed toward the forum state and those purposeful contacts are so substantial as to warrant the exercise of jurisdiction over that defendant over claims unrelated to the contacts (general jurisdiction) jurisdiction or, if not so substantial, the contacts are sufficiently related to the claim (specific jurisdiction) to create a presumption of reasonableness. The foregoing standards are satisfied, the defendant may rebut the presumption of reasonableness by presenting a compelling showing that the exercise of jurisdiction would be unreasonable or unfair.

Purposeful Contacts
D's Activities in CA

D has no office, real property, or staff in CA, is not licensed to do business in CA, and pays no CA taxes. Unlike the facts in *International Shoe Co. v. Washington*, 326 U.S. 310 (1945) where the non-resident defendant's enlisted in-state sales personnel to sell products in the forum state, D engages in no such direct activity in CA. D does have business relationships with a number of California companies, but those relationships are more effectively assessed as contractual relationships with forum residents (see below). The only other potential activity in CA is D's website, which is accessible in CA. Whether that website will constitute a sufficient contact with CA will be discussed under the effects test (see below). One aspect of the website, however, is worth mentioning here. The website hosts posts third-party advertisements, some of which promote connections to CA (jobs, hotels, vacations and tickets to events). These "activities" are, however, unilateral in the sense that they are not the activities of D, but the activities of a third-party and unlikely to be attributed to D as purposeful contacts, at least not without additional information.

D's Contractual Relationships with CA Residents

Whether a contractual relationship with a forum resident constitutes a purposeful contact with the forum state requires a realistic appraisal of the entire contractual relationship, including the negotiations leading up to the contract, the terms of the contract and the course of conduct under the contract. A classic example of this type of analysis is found in the *Burger King* case. *Burger King Corp. v. Rudzewcz*, 471 U.S. 462 (1985). In that case, an experienced MI businessman ("R") entered into a 20-year franchise agreement with Burger King, a FL corporation, under which R would operate a BK franchise in MI. After the franchise failed, BK sued R in a FL court. The Supreme Court examined the contractual relationship between the parties, including the active negotiations between the parties, the specific terms of the contract—a 20-year term, a $1 million commitment by R to BK, a FL choice of law provision—the fact that R knew that he was dealing with a FL business and that he was required to make payments in FL to that business. The Court found that the contractual relationship created a sufficiently purposeful affiliation with FL to put R on notice that he could be sued in FL for claims arising out of that contractual relationship.

D has four "agreements" with California businesses: a California firm designed and maintains D's website, a California Internet advertising agency solicits ads to be placed on the website, a California wireless provider hosts an D-related app for mobile users, and California news site has a "link-sharing" agreement with D. While none of these agreements mirror the detailed agreement in *Burger King*—for example, there is no evidence of a 20-year term or $1 million commitment in any of them—all of the contacts appear to be ongoing—that is, not one-shot sales—and they also appear to be of the type that would involve some degree of negotiation and active interaction. That would be particularly true of the design and maintenance of the website. Furthermore, this case is readily distinguishable from the "passive buyer" cases where non-resident buyers purchased a single, standard product from a forum seller. Quite likely then D's agreements with California business will be treated as purposeful contacts with the forum.

The Effects Test

A nonresident defendant whose activity outside the forum state causes a foreseeable effect in that state can be subjected to jurisdiction in that state for claims arising out the effect. The majority approach to the effects test requires that the non-resident defendant engage in some type of intentional, wrongful act outside the forum (some courts would say "intentional tort"), that is both aimed at the forum state and such that the non-resident defendant should know that the brunt of the harm would be felt in that state.

The argument here would be that D's posting of the photos on its website falls within the scope of the effects test. Preliminary to assessing that argument, it is useful to examine D's website under the *Zippo* sliding scale. Under *Zippo*, there are three types of websites: highly interactive commercial websites, completely non-interactive or passive websites, and those that fall somewhere in-between on the interactivity scale. Highly interactive websites, for example, amazon.com, are most likely to operate as purposeful contacts by the site operator with those forums in which that commercial interactivity occurs. Passive websites, for example, a non-interactive website that features photos from a family vacation, are unlikely to operate as a purposeful contact outside of the "home" state. Websites that fall in the mid-range can go either way and require a careful assessment of the interactivity to determine whether the interactivity constitutes a purposeful contact with the forum state.

[Note that *Zippo* is not a separate measure of purposeful contacts, but merely offers a perspective from which to apply the otherwise available tests of purposefulness, typically the contractual relations or effects tests.]

D's website appears to fall into *Zippo*'s middle category. It is certainly not an "amazon.com" style of commercial website. There is no indication that D itself actually sells any products on the site. On the other hand, the website is not completely passive since it allows visitors to "post comments on articles, vote in polls, subscribe to an e-mail newsletter, and submit news tips and photos of celebrities." To determine whether this moderately interactive website will support the exercise of personal jurisdiction over D, we turn to the effects test.

The first element of the effects test—intentional wrongful act—appears to be satisfied. The use of copyrighted material is certainly wrongful and D's reposting was just as certainly an intentional act. The second element—aimed at the forum—is somewhat more difficult to establish and one's conclusion will depend on the strictness with which the test is applied. In *Calder v. Jones* 465 U.S. 783 (1984), the Supreme Court found that the a defamatory article written in Florida was "aimed" at California for a combination of reasons: the author knew that the person about whom the article was written—the plaintiff—lived and worked in Southern California, the article was about the California-based activities of the plaintiff, the topic was of interest to the California readership (the entertainment industry), and California was the state of highest circulation for the newspaper in which the article appeared. By way of contrast P, a FL corporation, is not a resident of California, although much of its celebrity-based business is centered there (including a Los Angeles office and Los Angeles based photographers). In addition, the photos at issue were not a California-based topic other than in the sense that California is somewhat of a focal point for celebrity worship. The same difficulties attach to the brunt analysis. In *Calder*, the brunt of the harm would clearly be felt in California since that is where the plaintiff worked. Here P is a FL corporation and one could sensibly conclude that the loss of sales revenues caused by the copyright infringement will be felt in FL. Certainly, the case for the effects test is weaker here than in *Calder*.

One way to get around these difficulties is to focus on the likely size of D's California audience and the fact that D's website was built around the California-based entertainment industry. If the California share of the US visitors to D's site is proportional to the California population, one could certainly argue that the aim was California since that is site of D's largest market. Moreover, the advertising revenues generated by D seemed to be premised in part on third-party sales oriented toward California activities. In this sense, D's overall activities, as well as its reposting of the photos, are all aimed at California. As to "brunt," one could construe that word to require only that some harm be suffered in the state. This more open-ended approach to the effects test would be quite consistent with the approach endorsed in the Restatement (Second). Of course, the distinctions with *Calder* remain, but although many lower courts have treated *Calder* as stating the minimum standards of the effects test, that case can also be construed as doing no more than concluding that the facts before it were sufficient to satisfy the effects test.

In conclusion, the effects test is potentially satisfied but only if one takes a less-than-strict approach to that test.

General Jurisdiction

A court may exercise general jurisdiction over a non-resident defendant when that defendant's contacts with the forum are so substantial as to constitute the rough equivalent of domicile or being "at home" in the forum. D is not literally domiciled in California and its contacts with California — contracts, website, effects — are not sufficient to constitute being at home in the state.

The facts here do not come close to those in the *Perkins* case whether the defendant essentially operated its entire business, albeit temporarily, in the forum state. By contrast, D has no office and no employees in California and its principal place of business is in Ohio. Notably, *Perkins* is the only case in which the Court found that the standards of general jurisdiction were satisfied; moreover, in the recent *Goodyear* decision, the Court emphasized the relatively limited scope of the general jurisdiction principle.

Specific Jurisdiction

To satisfy the standards of specific jurisdiction, the plaintiff must show that defendant's purposeful contacts with the forum state relate the claim or claims asserted by the plaintiff. Essentially, there is a spectrum of possibilities from the loose "but-for" test to the much stricter "proximate-cause" or "substantive-relevance" standards. Between these ends of the relatedness spectrum is a middle ground variously described as "substantial connection," "lies in the wake," and "proximate cause with a but-for overlay." At a minimum, a contact must satisfy the but-for test in order to come within the scope of specific jurisdiction.

The but-for test would not seem to be satisfied by the Internet-advertising agreement, the wireless-provider agreement or the link-sharing agreement. It is possible to create some type of elongated but-for chain of causation, but not one that is likely to satisfy a court. On the other hand, the web-design-and-maintenance agreement ("web agreement") can be fairly described as the but-for cause of P's injury since "but for" the website the photos would not have been posted. The web agreement would not, however, be deemed the proximate cause of P's injuries; that honor would go to the act of posting the photos. Nor would the web agreement be relevant in any fashion to P's claim. One might plausibly argue, however, that the web agreement satisfies the middle-ground standards since it would be reasonably foreseeable that entering such an arrangement would lead to potential liability for items posted on the website.

The posting of the photos on a website accessible in the state—assuming the effects test is satisfied—would clearly satisfy the but-for test since but for the posting, no harm would occur. The posting can also be seen as the proximate cause of P's injuries and is certainly substantively relevant to P's copyright infringement claim. Hence, if the effects test has been satisfied, relatedness would be satisfied as well.

Reasonableness
Assuming that P has satisfied the standards of specific jurisdiction (purposeful contacts and relatedness), the burden would shift to D to rebut the heavy presumption that the exercise of jurisdiction would be reasonable. In determining whether a defendant has met this difficult burden, a court will examine five-factors or perspectives—the so-called Gestalt factors: the plaintiff's choice of forum, the defendant's burden, the forum state's interest, interstate harmony and efficiency, and relevant policy concerns. Nothing with respect to any of these factors would suggest that the exercise of jurisdiction would be unreasonable or unfair.

Recommendation
The court should deny the motion based on the satisfaction of the effects test—a somewhat flexible version of that test—and relatedness and the failure of D to rebut the presumption of reasonableness.

Answer to Question 17

Zonco ("Z")'s motion to dismiss for failure to join Smith:
A person who is subject to service of process and whose joinder will not deprive the court of subject matter jurisdiction must ordinarily be joined as a party to the action if "(A) in that person's absence, the court cannot accord complete relief among existing parties; or (B) that person claims an interest relating to the subject of the action and is so situated that disposing of the action in the person's absence may: (i) as a practical matter impede or impair the person's ability to protect the interest; or (ii) leave an existing party subject to a substantial risk of incurring double, multiple, or otherwise inconsistent obligations because of the interest." FRCP 19(a)(1)(A) and (B). First, complete relief can be afforded to Patricia ("P") since she could obtain a judgment against Z for the full amount of his injuries. Second, Smith ("S")'s interest in the action will not be impaired by his absence (in fact, his presence in the litigation could result in liability only to him). If, for example, a judgment is entered for P against Z, S will not be bound by that judgment since he was not a party to that proceeding and since, as an employee, he will not be treated as being in privity with his employer when a judgment is entered against the employer on a theory of respondeat superior.

Finally, the Supreme Court has held that the fact that an absent party is a potential joint tortfeasor is never, in itself, sufficient to require joinder under FRCP 19. *Temple v. Synthes Corp., Ltd.*, 498 U.S. 5 (1990).

Thus, the court correctly denied Z's motion to dismiss for failure to join S.

P's notice to produce:
A party may obtain discovery of documents prepared for litigation or trial (1) for another party, or (2) by or for that party's representative (including her insurer) only upon a showing that substantial need for such materials exists and they are otherwise unobtainable without undue hardship. FRCP 26(b)(3)(A).

Since the coworker's statement was made to Z's insurer, Z would likely contend that it is within the work product privilege. However, P could argue that there is a "substantial need" for the coworker's factual statement since it was given shortly after the accident and would therefore be the most reliable version of the incident. While Z could depose the coworker and obtain a non-contemporaneous version of the same information, the interview by the insurer would be superior both because of its proximity to the event and because it was taken in a non-adversarial context. As to the latter, since the coworker is employed by Z, she might be reluctant to make any statements that could adversely affect her employer in the litigation. Thus, despite the possibility of a deposition, the coworker's statements to Z's insurance adjuster (which were not made to an adversarial party) are arguably not otherwise available to P. While trial court may have been within its discretion in sustaining Z's refusal to produce the statement without at least an initial attempt by P to take the coworker's deposition, a strong case can be made that the material should have been discoverable.

P's summary judgment motion:
A summary judgment should be granted when there is no genuine dispute as to any material fact and the moving party is entitled to prevail as a matter of law. FRCP 56(c).

At trial, the burden of proof on the question of liability would be P's. Therefore, on summary judgment, P had the burden of producing sufficient evidence on which a rational trier of fact could find for P as to each element of the claimed liability. Thus, P would be required to introduce evidence (1) that S was driving the truck within the course of his employment by Z; and (2) that the cause of the accident was attributable to Z, either vicariously or directly. The deposition of S satisfies the second element by providing evidence that the cause of the accident was the malfunction of the brakes on the truck driven by S and owned by Z. If, in addition, the deposition provided evidence that the accident occurred while S was driving on behalf of Z, P would have met her burden production on summary judgment (i.e., a rational finder of fact could have found for P). Under these circumstances, the burden would have shifted to Z to contest one or both of the elements of P's claim. On the other hand, if P did not produce evidence on the latter point, the burden would have shifted to Z only with respect to the question of causation (i.e., the failure of the brakes).

Assuming the burden of production shifted, to meet its burden of production (i.e., to demonstrate the existence of a genuine issue of material fact), Z would be required to provide evidence that refuted those facts on which P met her burden of production. As to the failure of the brakes, Z could meet its burden of production by providing proof that there was another cause for the accident (e.g., eyewitness testimony that P jumped in front of the truck). As to Z's vicarious liability, and assuming P provided evidence that the accident occurred while S was driving on Z's behalf, Z could meet its burden of production by providing proof that S was not driving on Z's behalf or under circumstances for which Z would be vicariously liable. Similarly, if the substantive law provided a defense premised on the recent inspection of the brakes, Z could introduce proof of that fact. It, however, would not be sufficient for Z to speculate or argue about these possibilities. The burden on Z is to produce evidence.

At the very least, P was entitled to a partial summary judgment on the question of causation since it does not appear that Z provided any evidence that would create a genuine issue of material fact on that point. As to liability, the information is not sufficient to establish whether P met her burden of production on that issue and, if so, whether Z responded through the introduction of evidence.

Z's motion for a judgment notwithstanding the verdict ("JNOV") (now called "judgment as a matter of law" in federal court):

A JNOV (which results in the entry of judgment for the party who lost the trial) is proper where there is no legally sufficient basis for the determination reached by the jury. Z could have contended that while there was uncontradicted testimony that S was employed by Z and that P had suffered personal injury as a consequence of Smith's conduct, there apparently was no proof that S was acting within the course and scope of his employment (or at least with Z's knowledge). Thus, even if S was responsible for the accident, P failed to introduce any proof that Z was vicariously liable for S's conduct. However, if the accident occurred during regular business hours, it is possible that the jury could have inferred that S was employed by Z and was acting within the scope of his employment at the time of the accident. Thus, the court properly denied Z's motion for a JNOV.

P's motion for a new trial:

A federal court may grant a new trial if the verdict (1) is against the clear weight of the evidence or (2) will result in a miscarriage of justice, even though there may be substantial evidence that would prevent a judgment as a matter of law from being granted. The trial judge's determination that $85,000 does not adequately represent the pain and suffering probably would not be reversible. This is because the judge had the opportunity to personally observe the witness's testimony and evidence. However, granting a new trial unless the defendant agreed to raise the damage award was improper since *additur* (a judicial order for a new trial unless the defendant consents to higher damages) has been held by the Supreme Court to be a violation of the Seventh Amendment for federal trial purposes. *Dimick v. Schiedt,* 293 U.S. 474 (1935) (1935). Thus, the trial court probably could grant a new trial solely on the issue of damages, but could not condition it upon Z's agreement to pay P an enhanced verdict.

Answer to Question 18

Given the tolling provision in 28 U.S.C. §A, how should the district court rule on Derrida's ("D") motion to dismiss?

The motion should be denied. The issue presented is whether the statute of limitations was tolled when Plato filed his complaint in a federal court. Since there is a potential conflict between a federal statute and state law, we must first determine if the statute is sufficiently broad to control the issue presented. It seems to be. Section A provides that the filing of a complaint in a U.S. district court tolls "any applicable statute of limitations." It would be difficult to get around this language. Hence, despite the obvious conflict with State X law, which premises tolling on service of the complaint, the federal statute applies. The question then is whether §A represents a valid exercise of congressional power. If so, it trumps all state law to the contrary, that is, it preempts the State X tolling provision. The measure of validity in this context is whether the federal enactment is rationally capable of being classified as procedural. Under this relatively low bar, §A will pass muster since it provides a precise method for determining whether a case has been timely filed, at least one could rationally so conclude. The fact that the operation of the statute might abridge a substantive right created by State X law is irrelevant. Since §A is valid as an exercise of federal power, the district court must deny D's motion.

Would the answer to the preceding question change if the federal tolling provision had been embodied in federal rule as opposed to a federal statute?

It might. Assuming the federal rule used the same language as §A, we would have to conclude, as we did with §A, that the federal rule is sufficiently broad to control the issue presented—tolling the statute of limitations—and that the rule conflicts with State X law. The measure of the validity of a formal federal rule is found in the standards imposed by the Rules Enabling Act ("REA"). Under the REA the rule must be rationally capable of being classified as procedural (just like a federal statute) and may not abridge, enlarge, or modify any substantive right. In this latter respect, the validity measure for a federal rule is quite different from the statutory standard described in the preceding answer. In essence, with a federal rule we must examine the substantive reach of the rule. There is at least an argument that the federal rule would violate the REA's substantive limitation, for the rule operates modify the state statute of limitations by stopping the running of that statute when the state would not. In these sense, a federal court might be able to enforce a state-created right that is not otherwise enforceable as a matter of state law. From this perspective, the district court should grant D's motion. In response, one might argue that any alteration of the state statute of limitations would be de minimus since even under the federal rule the case would have to be filed within the statute of limitations and, typically, service would be required within 120 days. *See* FRCP 4(m).

Would the answer to the preceding question change if the federal tolling principle was a product of judge-made common law?

Again, it might. Here we are dealing with federal common law, which is subject to refined outcome-determinative test established by the Supreme Court in *Hanna v. Plumer*, 380 U.S. 460 (1965). Under this approach, once we determine that the federal principle applies—essentially the same "sufficiently broad" inquiry that is used for federal statutes and formal federal rules—we must ask whether application of the federal principle would violate the "twin aims" of *Erie*; specifically, would application of the federal principle lead to forum shopping and to the inequitable administration of the laws. To apply this standard we must view the case from the forum shopping stage and ask whether the difference between the federal principle and the state law would be such that one would pick the federal forum over the state forum in order to obtain a significant substantive advantage. As with the previous answer, there is at least an argument that the difference between the federal and state standards might have a substantive impact and, hence, affect the choice of forum. Certainly, if the statute of limitations is about to run and it would be difficult to serve the defendant in a timely fashion, the choice of a federal forum would be advantageous since it would give the plaintiff a little more time to effect service of process. This would not be as strong a case as one in which at the time of filing the state forum was foreclosed while the federal forum remained available. But the argument is stronger than one in which, for example, the federal and state courts simply permitted different methods of service.

Answer to Question 19

The FRCP 12(b) motion to dismiss the case:

Since U.S. district courts "borrow" the long-arm statute of the state in which they are located, it is assumed that the State B legislature has enacted a law that gives its courts all personal jurisdiction consistent with due process.

Salco ("S")'s FRCP 12(b)(2) motion probably asserted that it does not have the minimum contacts with State B necessary to satisfy due process (i.e., S does not have sufficient minimum contacts with the forum as to avoid offending traditional notions of fair play and substantial justice). S would contend that it has not availed itself of the benefits of the forum because (1) it employs no agents or salespersons within State B, (2) its advertising is purchased in magazines published outside State B, and (3) the amount of business done with citizens of State B ($75,000) is relatively small.

Poe ("P") could argue in rebuttal, however, that S should have reasonably foreseen being haled into the forum because it was aware (via its employees who received the orders and sent the items) that numerous persons from State B were purchasing its clocks. If the facts are as P alleges—that is, that S's employees accepted orders from State B residents and sent the products to those purchasers in State B—then, given that the claims arise out of those transactions, there would be a strong presumption that the assertion of jurisdiction was reasonable. On the other hand, the facts do not indicate where the purchases were made. If the purchases were made by citizens of State B while they were in State A, for example, the key element of purposeful contacts by S with State B would be lacking.

Hence, whether S's motion to dismiss for want of personal jurisdiction should have been granted depends on a consideration of additional facts.

S could have also asserted that the notice that it received was constitutionally defective (i.e., not reasonably calculated under the circumstances to give it notice of the action against it). (The fact that service of process was made in accordance with State B law presents no problem because the service took place while the case was still pending in a State B court; and, in any event, FRCP 4(h)(1)(A) permits service in accord with law of the state where the federal court sits.) S probably contended that service by mail (even a registered mailing) in the first instance is impermissible where the summons and complaint could probably have been personally served upon the defendant (i.e., presumably, the names and addresses of S's officers or directors could have easily been obtained from the State A corporate records). Registered mailing is always fraught with the possibility that someone could sign for the item and yet (not appreciating the legal significance of the document contained inside) fail to read it or deliver it to the appropriate person.

However, P could argue that the president of a corporation is likely to appreciate the potential importance of registered mail. Moreover, if the president of S actually received the notice, as it appears from the question, any potential defect in the method will be ignored since actual notice satisfies due process. Since courts generally have accepted registered mail as consistent with due process and since it seems that the president of S received actual notice, the motion to dismiss on this grounds was properly denied.

The motion to remand the case back to the state court:
An action cannot be removed to a U.S. district court unless the case could have been filed in a federal court originally. S's motion to remand was probably based upon the assertion that the case could not have been filed in a federal court because subject matter jurisdiction was lacking. S is correct. Since the claims do not arise under federal law, the only potential basis for subject matter jurisdiction would be diversity. While the standards of diversity are satisfied—the named class representative, P, and the sole defendant are from different states—the amount in controversy requirement is not. However, in a class action premised on diversity, the claims of the named plaintiff must satisfy the amount in controversy requirement or the aggregate claims of the class must exceed $5 million. As to the first point, P's amount in controversy is $250, well below the jurisdictional minimum. As to the second point, as explained below, the aggregate damages of the class are also well below the required minimum. 28 U.S.C. §1332(a) and 1332(d)(2).

P could contend in rebuttal that if the $25 million in punitive damages were distributed among each of the members of the plaintiff class, the claims of each person would exceed $75,000. P would also point out that the "amount in controversy" requisite should be considered satisfied, unless the court determines "to a legal certainty" that the damages sought by the plaintiff could not be recovered. It is, however, legally certain that neither P nor any individual class member will be entitled to sufficient punitive damages to satisfy the amount in controversy. Under the due process clause, any award of punitive damages must bear a reasonable relationship with the actual damages, usually something below a 4-1 ratio. To satisfy the amount in controversy here, the ratio would have to be 300-1, an outcome that would clearly violate due process. This same reasoning would apply to the measure of the $5 million aggregate claim. Thus, the motion to remand was improperly denied.

The motion for a more definite statement:

If a complaint is so vague or ambiguous that the defendant cannot reasonably be required to frame a responsive pleading, he may move for a more definite statement. FRCP 12(e). S could have contended that since allegations of fraud must be stated with particularity (FRCP 9(b)), its motion for a more definite statement is appropriate. P's complaint apparently alleged only that the clocks were purchased as a consequence of S's misrepresentations, without any description of the allegedly fraudulent statements. While P could contend in rebuttal that the exact wording upon which the complaint is predicated could be developed during discovery, the court's denial of S's motion for a more definite statement was probably improper.

Was Jones ("J") barred from suing S?

If, as discussed above, subject matter jurisdiction was lacking because each class member's claim did not exceed $75,000, the district court judgment could be subject to rescission on the ground that it is void. FRCP 60(b)(4). To accomplish this, J would have to file a Rule 60 motion for relief from judgment in the original U.S. district court. Alternatively, J could collaterally attack that judgment, but under the modern approach to collateral attack, the general rule is that such attacks are not allowed, the presumption being that the prior court correctly decided the question of its subject matter jurisdiction. This is particularly so where, as here, the prior court actually decided the question.

Assuming J could not prevail on the subject matter jurisdiction issue and that the U.S. district court in *P v. S* certified the action as a class action, more facts would have to be ascertained to determine whether J's claim was barred. Under FRCP 23(b)(3) actions, which this class action would fall under, each member of the class must be given notice and an opportunity to "opt out" of the action if she desires to do so. FRCP 23(c)(2)(B). Assuming J received adequate notice of the action, his claim would be barred. If adequate notice had not been received by J, his present action against S could be maintained.

Answer to Question 20

A default judgment is valid when it is statutorily and constitutionally sound. We'll assume that the Calvada state court is competent to hear the matter upon which Paula ("P") sued Glassco ("G") for $100,000.

Did P comply with the statutory requirements of the Calvada long-arm statute?

G could contend that the Calvada long-arm statute does not apply to it because (1) it is not a "person"; and (2) since the defective manufacture of the glasses occurred in State White, the cause of action did not arise out of "a tortious act" in Calvada. P would argue in rebuttal that (1) a corporation should be deemed a "person" since it is an independent legal entity and the word "natural" would have been inserted before the word "person" by the legislators if they had intended the statute to pertain only to individuals; and (2) the action arose when P was injured, and that "act" occurred in Calvada. On the first point, P is likely to prevail since the word "person" is typically used to encompass artificial entities such as corporations. On the second point, the resolution depends on how the state court interprets the phrase "tortious act." Some courts have construed this phrase to focus on the location of the act itself, and others have it interpreted it broadly to include any element of the tort. If the former definition is adopted, G will prevail since the "act" took place in the location of manufacture. If the latter definition is adopted, P will prevail.

Can the Calvada court constitutionally exercise personal jurisdiction over G?

To establish personal jurisdiction over G, P must establish that G engaged in purposeful activity directed toward the state of Calvada and that her claim arises out of those purposeful contacts. If P satisfies this burden, there will be a strong presumption that the exercise of jurisdiction would be reasonable and would comport with due process. G, however, will have an opportunity to rebut that presumption.

As to purposeful contacts, P will cite the fact that G, through the agency of the Krispy promotional campaign, solicited the sale of its glassware within the state of Calvada. In addition, G intentionally sent the allegedly defective product into the state as part of a commercial exchange with P. P will further assert that her claim arises directly out of the latter contact since she is claiming that the shipped product was the cause of her injuries. As such, P would have established the presumptive reasonableness of the exercise of personal jurisdiction over G. G might attempt to rebut that presumption by asserting that the contract for sale was completed in State Black and that the amount of the sale was marginal. However, given a state's strong interest in protecting its consumers from dangerous products, G's arguments would be insufficient to rebut the presumption of reasonableness. P will prevail.

Was there statutory compliance with the notice (i.e., service of process) statute of Calvada?

A default judgment is not valid if service was not accomplished in conformity with the applicable statute and in a constitutionally valid manner. G would argue that the statutory words "its place of business" should be construed to mean its "principal place of business" since the word "its" suggests a single place, and therefore only the primary place of business would suffice. While P would contend in rebuttal that "its place of business" means the place where the plaintiff conducted her business with the corporation, it is unclear who should prevail on this issue since the question is one of statutory construction. A state court would be free to adopt either interpretation; however, service of process statutes are usually construed liberally to validate process, and substantial compliance with the terms of the statute is typically considered adequate. Given that G used the State Black address as a business address for purposes of engaging in business in the state of Calvada, it is possible that a Calvada court would find substantial compliance here. On the other hand, there is a presumption in favor of allowing a party to defend on the merits, and the court may construe the statute narrowly to void the default.

Assuming, however, there was compliance with the Calvada notice statute, is the statute constitutionally valid?

Notice must be "reasonably calculated" under the circumstances to apprise the defendant of the action. G would contend that mailing a registered or certified letter to a corporation should not suffice since relatively low-level personnel in a mailroom could either (1) lose a certified letter; or (2) if unhappy with management, deliberately misplace such an item.

P could argue in rebuttal that a registered or certified mailing should suffice since people ordinarily recognize that important documents come by such means. Therefore, there is little likelihood that documents mailed in this manner would *not* come to the attention of the proper persons.

Whether service by registered mail satisfies due process is an open question. Most courts addressing the issue have affirmed the use of registered mail under most circumstances, including the type of circumstances presented here. If the mail is returned "not accepted," some courts treat the nonacceptance as proof of service, while others require the plaintiff to engage in additional efforts to serve. Thus, whether service would be considered adequate here, where the defendant refused the mail, is an open question.

If the judgment is valid, should it be overturned?

G may seek to set aside the default judgment under the appropriate provisions of state law. Typically a default judgment may be set aside for good cause shown, including mistake, inadvertence, surprise, or excusable neglect. Using these principles, G might argue that its failure to respond was due to the excusable neglect of its employees in State Black who were not accustomed to receiving service of process. Whether to grant this motion would be within the discretion of the trial court and would depend largely on the evidence produced by G regarding the nature of its State Black operations.

Is P likely to prevail on the same evidence?

G could also contend that there was insufficient evidence for the court finding it liable since P failed to show that G was negligent in the manufacture of the glasses. However, P could argue that under the theories of products liability—breach of the implied warranty of merchantability or negligence (via use of the *res ipsa loquitor* doctrine)—there was adequate evidence to prove the default judgment. It is unclear, however, as to how the court determined that P's damages were $25,000. Without proof of medical bills or lost income, there was arguably insufficient proof for this aspect of the judgment. While P could contend that the trier of fact could infer that she suffered pain and suffering in the amount of $25,000, more evidence probably would have to be introduced to sustain this aspect of the judgment.

Answer to Question 21

The FRCP 12(b) motion to quash:

It is assumed that Peter ("P") claimed damages in excess of $75,000 in good faith, for if he did not, subject matter jurisdiction would be lacking, there being no federal question presented.

Although service within a jurisdiction has been a traditional basis for obtaining personal jurisdiction over an out-of-state citizen, Stanford James ("SJ") could have contended that service here was ineffective since he was "lured" into the jurisdiction. If a defendant is "lured" into a jurisdiction by means of trickery or fraud, a court, in its discretion, may quash the service of process. FRCP 12(b)(5).

In response, P would assert that there was no evidence of trickery or fraud. He "invited" SJ into State White to discuss his claim and made no representation that service of process would not be made. If SJ was concerned about being served in State White, he could have (1) refused P's offer, or (2) required P to stipulate in advance that no attempt to serve him would be made. In the absence of some showing of trickery or fraud by P, a court might not quash service under these circumstances. Some courts, however, follow a bright-line rule that requires no proof of trickery or fraud; instead, these courts would quash service unless P could show that he warned SJ that the latter might be served while in the state or gave SJ a reasonable opportunity to leave the state before effecting service of process.

As to personal jurisdiction, P could also assert that the Supreme Court has held service of process within a forum is still a valid means of obtaining personal jurisdiction over an individual. *Burnham v. Superior Court*, 495 U.S. 604 (1990).

SJ's motion to transfer:

An action commenced in a U.S. district court may be transferred to another federal court in a different judicial district if (1) the action could have been commenced in the latter district court, and (2) the "convenience of the parties and witnesses" would be accommodated by the transfer. Since P's action is based upon diversity, it could have been initiated in State White (the jurisdiction in which the defendant resides and in which substantial events giving rise to the claim occurred; 28 U.S.C. §1391(b)(1) and (2)). Since venue was not proper in State Red (the defendant does not reside there, no events giving rise to the claim occurred there, and there is a district—State White—where venue would be proper), the motion to transfer would be pursuant to 28 U.S.C. §1406(a). Under this section, the U.S.

district court would have discretion to either dismiss the case or transfer it to a federal district court in State White. While the court could dismiss the case for lack of proper venue, in the absence of a showing of injustice to either party, the court is more likely to transfer the case to a State White district court. In no event, however, may the court retain jurisdiction over the case since venue is clearly improper in State Red.

P's motion to amend his complaint:

Under the FRCP, a party may amend a pleading "once as a matter of course: (A) 21 days after serving it, or (B) if the pleading is one to which a responsive pleading is required, 21 days after service of a responsive pleading or 21 days after service of a of a motion under Rule 12(b), (e), or (f), whichever is earlier." FRCP 15(a)(1)(A)-(B). Since P filed his motion prior to SJ filing a responsive pleading and within 21 days of SJ's Rule 12(b) motion ("two weeks after"), P was entitled to amend his complaint as of right.

SJ's motion for a judgment on the pleadings:

SJ apparently contended that since the amendment (which correctly stated SJ's name) was not made until the applicable statute of limitations had expired, he was entitled to a judgment on the pleadings. P could point out that the FRCP provides that an amendment *changing the party* relates back to the date of the original pleading if the party named in the amended pleading (1) has received such notice of the action that it will not be prejudiced in defending itself; and (2) knew (or should have known) that, but for the mistaken identity, the action would have been brought against him. FRCP 15(c). These conditions appear to be satisfied. Nothing in the facts indicate any prejudice suffered by SJ and given that SJ filed a timely Rule 12(b) motion after having been served with the unamended (JS) complaint, it seems clear that he knew that the action was brought against him.

The facts are silent as to whether there is a State Red rule of law that specifically precludes relation back for statute of limitations purposes in a situation such as that posed by the present case. If there were such a rule, SJ would argue that application of the FRCP under these circumstances would violate the second requirement of the Rules Enabling Act, which provides that the federal rules may not abridge, enlarge, or modify a substantive right. The argument in favor of this position is that application of the federal rule appears to extend the statute of limitations and, hence, to permit the vindication of a state substantive right that is otherwise barred as a matter of state law. The contrary argument is that state substantive policy is fully served since the case was filed within the state statute of limitations and SJ received timely notice of that proceeding. (This presumes that the state statute of limitations would have been tolled by the filing of the suit had SJ been properly identified in the complaint.) The resolution of this conflict is not obvious, though the strong presumption of the validity of the federal rules may tip the balance in favor of the federal rule given that the case was filed within the statute of limitations, the only error being that SJ's first and last names had been inverted. Certainly, in the absence of any State Red rule of law specifically stating that a name change may not relate back to the original pleading, as indicated above, P should prevail.

Answer to Question 22

Silley's and Bobb's procedural alternatives:

The defendants could appear in the U.S. district court in Oklahoma and make a motion to dismiss the action for want of personal jurisdiction pursuant to FRCP 12(b)(2). In determining whether the minimum contacts standard (i.e., an out-of-state citizen has minimum contacts with the forum as not to offend traditional notions of fair play and substantial justice) is satisfied, a court will ordinarily weigh (1) the extent to which the defendant has purposefully availed him of the benefits of the forum or purposefully directed activity toward the forum, and (2) the relationship between the wrong allegedly committed by the defendant and any such purposeful contacts with the state. As to Bobb ("B"), Paul ("P") would contend that the limited partnership activities in Oklahoma constitute purposeful availment; however, even if these activities are sufficient to establish purposeful availment, they have no relationship with P's claim against B. Similarly, although Silley's ("S") does have some business contacts with Oklahoma, none of those contacts are related to P's claim against S. As a consequence, P would be unable to satisfy the standards of the minimum contacts test. Nor would P be able to assert *quasi in rem* jurisdiction over B by attaching B's limited partnership assets. There being no relationship between those assets and P's claim against B, due process could not be satisfied under these circumstances. Finally, the relatively limited contacts of the defendants are not sufficient to establish general jurisdiction over either of them.

In the unlikely case that their 12(b)(2) motion were to fail, B and S could also make (simultaneously with their 12(b)(2) motion) a 12(b)(3) motion to dismiss for lack of proper venue. Under the general federal venue statute, venue is proper in the judicial district where one of the defendants resides if all defendants reside in the same state; where substantial events giving rise to the claim occurred; or, if there is no other district available under the first two standards, where personal jurisdiction could be established over one of the defendants. 28 U.S.C. §1391(b)(1)-(3). None of these alternatives establishes proper venue in Oklahoma. Neither defendant resides there, no events giving rise to the claim occurred there, and since venue would be proper in the district embracing Austin, Texas, the third alternative is not available. The district court would grant this motion.

Alternatively and in conjunction with the 12(b)(3) motion to dismiss for lack of proper venue, B and S could file a motion to transfer to the U.S. district court that encompasses Austin, Texas. 28 U.S.C. §1406(a) (motion to transfer where venue improper in the originating court). Venue for a diversity action would be satisfied in the district embracing Austin because substantial events giving rise to the claim occurred in that judicial district. In support of this motion, the defendants could argue that all witnesses to the incident probably live in that area. In lieu of dismissing, the court in Oklahoma could transfer the case to Texas. Given the lack of personal jurisdiction in Oklahoma and the fact that venue was improper in Oklahoma, the court could not retain the case. Its only options are to dismiss or transfer.

Can Paul join all parties in a single action?

Joinder of claims against multiple defendants is permissible where (1) the claims asserted against them arise out of the same transaction or occurrence, and (2) there is common question of law or fact. FRCP 20(a)(2)(A)-(B). Most federal courts adhere to the view that claims arise from the same occurrence if they are "logically related." Since all of P's claims arise from the incident that occurred outside S's store, the initial condition is probably satisfied. As to the second condition, a factual issue that must be resolved in both actions would be whether P had actually taken something from S. If he had, then B's conduct may have been privileged (assuming he had not used excessive force) and the arrest would not have been "false." Thus, the claims probably could be joined.

Would the U.S. district court in Texas have subject matter jurisdiction over Paul's claim?

The court would have subject matter jurisdiction over P's claims. First, the claim against B is predicated upon a federal statute (i.e., a federal claim). The U.S. district court would have jurisdiction over this claim as a case arising under federal law pursuant to 28 U.S.C. §1331 (federal question jurisdiction). Next, the court would have supplemental jurisdiction (28 U.S.C. §1367) over P's factually related assault and battery claim since it arises out of the same common nucleus of operative facts as his federal claim. Finally, the claims against Mary ("M") and S also arise out of the same transaction or common nucleus of operative facts as the federal claim against B. Hence, the U.S. district court would have supplemental jurisdiction over these claims as well. 28 U.S.C. §1367. Note that §1367 specifically permits the exercise of supplement jurisdiction over parties in federal question cases. The claims against M and S may also come within the court's diversity jurisdiction if the amount in controversy is satisfied as to each.

Answer to Question 23

Was the court correct in denying P's motion for summary judgment?

When a summary judgment motion is supported by an affidavit based upon personal knowledge that describes facts that are admissible into evidence at trial, the adverse party may *not* rest upon the allegations contained in his pleadings. The latter must respond with affidavits or other factual matter showing a genuine issue for trial. FRCP 56(e). Thus, Pam ("P") probably contended that, because D's attorney relied solely on the allegations in the complaint, summary judgment on the question of breach of duty was appropriate.

However, while the failure to install a smoke detector in a patient's room constitutes *negligence per se*, it does *not* establish liability. It establishes only that one element of negligence (i.e., the defendant failed to have acted reasonably) is present. In this case, D might still be able to successfully contend that causation is absent (i.e., even with a functioning smoke detector, P would have suffered exactly the same injuries).

Thus, the court was correct in denying P's summary judgment motion, although the court could have, and perhaps should have, entered a partial summary judgment with respect to D's breach of its duty of due care (i.e., its failure to act reasonably). FRCP 56(a).

Was the court correct in ordering D to produce the fire investigator's report?

A party may ordinarily obtain discovery of documents prepared by another party in anticipation of litigation or trial only upon a showing that the former (1) has a substantial need for the item; and (2) is unable, without undue hardship, to obtain the equivalent by other means. FRCP 26(b)(3). P probably argued that (1) there is a substantial need for the report since it greatly assists in establishing an important fact (i.e., P's room did not have a smoke detector in it), which D has denied; and (2) this fact can no longer be verified by P since the home has been demolished.

D might have contended in rebuttal that the appropriate corporate officer had already admitted in an interrogatory that there was no smoke detector in P's room. Therefore, there was no substantial need for the report. However, the court was probably correct in ordering D to produce this item since a statement made in an interrogatory may be contradicted by that party at trial (as occurred in this case).

Was the court correct in holding D in contempt for refusing P's discovery request?

When a party does not furnish information sought to be discovered, the party seeking discovery must ordinarily seek an FRCP 37(a) order compelling discovery. If such an order is obtained *and* the party *persists* in his refusal, the court may order a variety of sanctions (including holding the disobedient party in contempt). FRCP 37(b). However, since the court in this instance held D in contempt *at the same time* that it issued the Rule 37(a) order compelling production of the inspection, the contempt ruling was probably improper.

Was the court correct in denying P's motion to disallow Mac ("M")'s testimony?

There is no rule that precludes testimony simply because it is inconsistent with an answer to an interrogatory. The statement made in the interrogatory may be used (1) to impeach M, and (2) as substantive evidence against D (under the Federal Rules of Evidence, the corporate official's response is *not* hearsay; FRE 801(d)(2)). The court, therefore, was correct in denying P's motion.

Answer to Question 24

Borrow's ("B") motion to remand:

Yes. When the plaintiff's complaint is premised upon a federal claim, the defendant (regardless of citizenship) can have the action removed to the federal district court that encompasses the place where the action is pending. Since B's claim is based upon a federal statute (the TLA), Finco ("F") was entitled to have the action removed to the applicable U.S. district court. 28 U.S.C. §1441(a).

B's motion to amend her complaint:

Dealer ("D") probably contended that, since (1) it is a citizen of State A (where it is incorporated and conducts all of its business), and (2) B is a resident of State A, diversity subject matter jurisdiction is *not* satisfied for the state law claim that B is asserting against Dealer. Additionally, only $20,000 in damages is being asserted (far short of the necessary jurisdictional amount of "in excess of" $75,000). Thus, in D's view, the federal court was required to deny the motion to amend.

However, under *supplemental party jurisdiction* principles, where a valid federal claim has been asserted, a federal court may hear a claim against a party over whom it otherwise would *not* have subject matter jurisdiction, if that claim arises out of a common nucleus of operative facts with the underlying federal claim. D could contend that the claims do not so arise since B is contending that D provided B with erroneous information while the claim against F asserts complete failure to disclose required data. However, since both of B's claims pertain to the circumstances surrounding her signing of the papers with regard to her vehicle purchase, it is likely that the "common nucleus" requirement is satisfied. Thus, the court incorrectly ruled that it lacked subject matter jurisdiction over B's action against D.

B's motion for partial summary judgment:

Summary judgment is proper when there is no "genuine issue of material fact" with respect to one or more aspects of the lawsuit.

B is apparently contending that F should be precluded from relitigating the issue of its violation of the disclosure provisions of TLA. Under the doctrine of issue preclusion (collateral estoppel), where the identical issue was actually litigated in a prior lawsuit by the party, a court may preclude relitigation of that issue in a subsequent proceeding. The question is whether B may rely on issue preclusion in the present proceeding.

To satisfy the basic elements of issue preclusion, B would have to show that an issue that actually litigated, decided and necessary to a prior judgment is the same as the issue presented in his case, namely, Finco's failure to make the required TLA disclosure. That does appear to be the case, though we would need a little more information to resolve the question.

The key difficulty here is that B was not a party to the prior suits. Should B nonetheless be able to benefit from the judgments in those cases? To answer that question we must determine whether the doctrine of mutuality must be followed. Since the previous lawsuits were "brought by other borrowers in federal courts," the district court must apply the federal law of preclusion. Under that law, the doctrine of mutuality has been completely abandoned. Thus, a non-party to a previous suit may use issue preclusion to advantage in both defensive and offensive contexts. B's use of preclusion would be "offensive" since B is attempting to establish an element of his claim by the use of issue preclusion. In determining whether to allow a non-party to a prior proceeding to assert offensive issue preclusion, the court must determine whether it would be fair to do so. Two factors will be considered: whether B could have intervened in the prior proceedings and whether there would be any unfairness to F in permitting B to benefit from the prior judgments. As to the first point, there are no facts that suggest that B was even aware of any of these earlier proceedings; hence, it is unlikely that B would have been expected to intervene in them. Second, as to fairness to F, the use of the issue in the present case cannot be a surprise and one can assume that F had a complete incentive to litigate this issue in the prior proceeding. Moreover, the facts at least suggest that F has had several opportunities to litigate this issue.

Quite likely, the district court erred in denying summary judgment to B on the question of Finco's failure to disclose.

Answer to Question 25

Motions for judgment on the pleadings:

A motion for judgment on the pleadings challenges only the sufficiency of the adversary's pleadings (i.e., it does not assert defects that do not appear on the face of the pleadings). In federal court, a complaint need only adequately inform the defendant of the nature of the action against her and state the relief requested.

Dave ("D") might have argued that the complaint (1) failed to describe the basis of his negligent conduct (i.e., it merely stated he was "negligent" as a legal conclusion), and (2) prayed for an amount ($250,000) far in excess of Paul ("P")'s alleged injuries (i.e., $25,000). However, P probably successfully asserted in rebuttal that (1) it should have been obvious to D that P was contending that the former had not operated his vehicle in a reasonable manner, and (2) the mere fact that the prayer did not coincide with the injuries set forth in the body of the document does not cause a complaint to fail (damages must always be proved).

An answer must effectively deny the plaintiff's allegations for those assertions to be put into issue. Failure to adequately deny allegations contained in a complaint constitutes an admission of those assertions. However, damages are always deemed to be in issue (even if not adequately denied). FRCP 9(d). Since D's answer does not unequivocally "deny" the assertions contained in P's complaint, P probably argued that D, in effect, admitted them (except for damages). D could have argued that, since his answer stated that he did not "admit" the assertions contained in P's complaint, he impliedly denied them. This argument probably would fail, however, since D's answer stated that the allegations in P's complaint were not denied. Thus, the district court could have granted P's motion for a judgment on the pleadings (exclusive of his prayer for damages). However, under such circumstances, a court might well allow the defendant to amend the answer, imposing costs on the defendant for any expenses incurred by the plaintiff.

Al ("A")'s motion to dismiss:

Under the FRCP, an amendment of a pleading relates back to the date of the original pleading when (1) relation back is permitted by the law that provides the statute of limitations applicable to the action; (2) the claim or defense asserted in the amended pleading arose out of the conduct, transaction, or occurrence set forth or attempted to be set forth in the original pleading; or (3) in the case of an added party, that party knew (or should have known) that, but for a mistake pertaining to the identity of the proper party, the action would have been brought against him. FRCP 15(c)(1)(A)-(C). These provisions are disjunctive; hence, satisfaction of any one will permit relation back. The second provision, relating only to added claims or defenses, does not apply since this amendment applies to an added party. The third provision arguably applies but, since A had no notice of P's action prior to the expiration of the statute of limitations, it would not permit relation back under these facts. The first provision, however, does apply and mandates the application of relation back. Since the accident occurred in State Y, State Y law provides the relevant statute of limitations. Accordingly, since the law that provides the relevant statute of limitations mandates relation back, under FRCP 15(c)(1)(A), the district court was correct in denying A's motion (i.e., in allowing the amendment to relate back to the date of the original filing). Importantly, FRCP 15(c)(1)(A) was designed to avoid conflicts with state law under precisely this type of situation.

A's motion to compel an answer to his interrogatory and the production of documents:

A party may obtain relevant papers that were prepared in anticipation of litigation by (or for) another party, or her representative, only upon a showing that the party seeking discovery (1) has a substantial need for them, and (2) is otherwise unable to obtain those materials without undue hardship. FRCP 26(b)(3). The work product privilege, however, prevents discovery of opinions, legal theories, or mental impressions of another party's attorney.

P might have asserted that A's demand does not meet the requirements of FRCP 26(b)(3) because (1) Wilma ("W") was acting pursuant to his direction in anticipation of litigation when she obtained the statements from the two witnesses, and (2) A could obtain this information by directly questioning those persons. However, there was no indication that W was acting pursuant to P's instructions or under his direction; therefore, she may not have been acting in anticipation of litigation. Second, and more important, there is a substantial need for this information because, even if A's attorney questioned those witnesses directly, there is no other means of determining if their answers were consistent. Moreover, given that the statements were made contemporaneously with the accident, there is no way that A can now re-create the circumstances surrounding those initial impressions. Thus, P should be required to answer A's interrogatory and provide the statements. (Interestingly, P could have possibly answered D's interrogatory in the negative, since W, rather than P, took the statements in question.)

If, however, the notes that P's attorney made on these statements contain legal theories, impressions, or conclusions, they are protected by the work product privilege. A can obtain the statements, but Len's notes must be redacted.

Answer to Question 26

Was the denial of Danielle ("D")'s motion to make Trucko ("T") a party proper?

Under FRCP 19(a)(1), a person must be joined if it is feasible to do so and if "(A) in that person's absence, the court cannot accord complete relief among existing parties; or (B) that person claims an interest relating to the subject of the action and is so situated that disposing of the action in the person's absence may: (i) as a practical matter impede or impair the person's ability to protect the interest; or (ii) leave an existing party subject to a substantial risk of incurring double, multiple, or otherwise inconsistent obligations because of the interest." FRCP 19(a)(1)(A) and (B). If such a "required party" is not subject to service of process, or if his joinder will deprive the court of subject matter jurisdiction—that is, if that person's joinder is not feasible—the court must determine whether in "equity and good conscience" it can proceed with that party. FRCP 19(b).

Price ("P") would contend that T was not a required party since complete relief can be given to him (i.e., he can obtain a judgment for the full amount of his injuries against D) and since T's absence would prejudice neither D nor T. Specifically, D's interests would not be prejudiced by T's absence since that absence would *not* in any manner hinder D's ability to assert her defenses or to protect her interests (i.e., to show there was no causal relationship between D's conduct and P's injuries). As to any prejudice to T, nothing decided in the *P v. D* litigation would be binding on T as a nonparty or cause T any practical harm. Hence, the failure to join T will not prejudice T in any manner, and the court was correct in denying D's motion to join T.

Was the order approving an examination of D's physical capabilities proper?

Under FRCP 35(a), upon a showing of good cause, the court may order a physical examination of a party when his condition is in controversy. D can argue that, since P has alleged that the accident was caused by the former's failure to use carburetor heat, D's physical condition is *not* in controversy. P can respond that, while the lack of carburetor heat may have caused D to land the plane, a pilot possessing ordinary physical attributes would have nevertheless been able to avoid the accident.

The court's decision was probably incorrect. It should have awaited discovery by P of evidence that tended to show that D's physical impairment contributed, in some manner, to the accident. Once this was established, P's FRCP 35 motion would be proper.

***Was the court's instruction to the jury that it could consider evidence of
P's contributory negligence proper?***

Affirmative defenses ordinarily must be specifically pleaded by a defendant.
FRCP 8(c). However, when issues not raised by the pleadings are litigated
at trial, those issues are treated "as if raised in the pleadings." FRCP 15(b)
(2). Since D introduced evidence at the trial showing that P's truck lacked
lights without objection by P, the pleadings are deemed to be amended to
contain an assertion of P's contributory negligence.

Thus, the court's instruction permitting the jury to consider P's possible
contributory negligence was proper.

Answer to Question 27

To satisfy the standards of federal question jurisdiction, the plaintiff's claim must satisfy either the creation test or the essential federal ingredient test. 28 U.S.C. §1331. Since the cause of action here is breach of contract, a state-created claim, the creation test is not satisfied (i.e., the claim is not one created by federal law). As to the essential federal ingredient test, two preliminary aspects of that doctrine are satisfied. This is a state-created cause of action (element one) that includes an essential federal ingredient (element two). As to the latter, the question of whether there is a breach of contract depends on whether Daz is in compliance with the CWA, a federal statute. However, there must be some showing that there is a strong interest in providing federal jurisdiction over the claim, as would be the case with issues of constitutional law or with respect to such quintessentially federal matters as the collection of federal taxes. Moreover, the court must be convinced that the exercise of jurisdiction over this particular claim will not open the floodgates of litigation in federal court. The federal element here does not pertain to constitutional law; nor is there anything about it that implicates federal policy in the same manner or to the same degree as, for example, the collection of federal taxes. Moreover, given that Congress has provided no private right of action, which suggests the absence of an interest sufficient to invoke federal jurisdiction, the court is unlikely to exercise jurisdiction over this claim. The district court is likely to grant the motion to dismiss. *Grable & Sons Metal Products, Inc. v. Darue Engineering & Manufacturing*, 545 U.S. 308 (2005).

Answer to Question 28

May Bob ("B") implead Carl ("C")?

Yes. This represents a classic example of impleader. FRCP 14(a). C, as a surety, is a person who is or may be liable to B if B is found liable to Abe ("A") under the primary claim. The U.S. district court would have jurisdiction over the impleader since it is part of the same constitutional case or controversy as A's claim against B—by definition, the impleader (i.e., the claim for indemnity) is factually and legally related to A's claim. 28 U.S.C. §1367(a). In addition, nothing in §1367(b) precludes a defendant (B) from bringing in an additional party pursuant to FRCP 14. The fact that C is not diverse from A is irrelevant. One could also assert an independent basis of jurisdiction over the impleader since B and C are diverse from one another and the amount in controversy exceeds $75,000.

May C file a claim against A related to the construction project?

Yes. FRCP 14(a)(2)(C) specifically allows the third-party defendant (C) to file a transactionally related claim against the original plaintiff. Section 1367(a) creates the jurisdictional premise for doing so (same constitutional case or controversy), and §1367(b) imposes no limits on claims filed by third-party defendants such as C. The fact that C is not diverse from A is irrelevant.

May C file a claim against A unrelated to the construction project?

Perhaps, but unlikely. If C files a transactionally related claim against A under FRCP 14(a)(2)(C) as discussed in the previous section, he may attach other unrelated claims against A pursuant to FRCP 18(a). However, those unrelated claims must have an independent basis of jurisdiction—by definition, they are not transactionally related to the 14(a) claim and therefore would not likely satisfy §1367(a). Since A and C are from the same state, diversity cannot be satisfied. If, however, the unrelated claim arises under federal law within the meaning of §1331, C may file it along with the FRCP 14(a) claim.

May A file a claim against C related to the construction project?

Yes, but only if the claim presents a transactionally related federal question. FRCP 14(a)(3) allows a plaintiff to file a transactionally related claim against the third-party defendant, and this standard would seem to be satisfied here. However, in a diversity case such as this one, there is no supplemental jurisdiction over such a claim since the text of §1367(b) excludes from the coverage of §1367(a) any claim by a plaintiff against a nondiverse person joined pursuant to FRCP 14—precisely the problem presented here—when doing so would be inconsistent with the jurisdictional requirements of §1332. This scenario basically replicates the situation in *Owen Equipment and Erection Co. v. Kroger*, 437 U.S. 365 (1978), in which the Supreme Court held that §1332 would preclude the exercise of jurisdiction over a plaintiff's FRCP 14 claim against a nondiverse third-party defendant. Thus, even though §1367(a) would be satisfied, §1367(b) would bar the exercise of supplemental jurisdiction in this diversity case. Hence, A can file this claim only if there is an independent basis of jurisdiction over it. Since A and C are not diverse from one another, the only potentially independent basis of jurisdiction would be §1331.

If B does not attempt to implead C, may C intervene?

C could attempt to intervene as a defendant relying on FRCP 24. Assuming his application has been timely (no facts indicate otherwise), under FRCP 24(a)—intervention as of right—he would have to claim (1) an interest in the transaction that is the subject matter of the suit (the breach of contract claim as it relates to his obligations as a surety); (2) that the disposition of the case may, as a practical matter, impair his ability to protect that interest (if a breach were found, he would have to indemnify B); and (3) and that his interest is inadequately represented by B (B has little incentive to fully defend the suit given that C will pay the judgment). Under subsection (b), C could also seek permissive intervention by showing a common question of law or fact between the primary action and any claim or defense he might have. If FRCP 24 is satisfied, jurisdiction would be established pursuant to §1367(a)'s same case or controversy test, with no limitations imposed by §1367(b) since C most likely would be aligned as a defendant. In addition, as a surety, it is unlikely that C would be considered an indispensable party, that is, a party without whom the court could not proceed; that being the case, most federal courts would find that C's intervention would be consistent with the jurisdictional requirements of §1332—as they would have been prior to the adoption of §1367.

May B file a counterclaim against A, joining Donna ("D") as a defendant on that counterclaim?

The claim against A would be a compulsory counterclaim within the meaning of FRCP 13(a). If the amount in controversy were satisfied, it would have an independent basis of jurisdiction since A and B are diverse from one another. It would also satisfy the supplemental jurisdiction standards of §1367(a), given the close factual relationship between this claim and A's claim against B. Section 1367(b) would impose no limits on the exercise of supplemental jurisdiction since B is not a plaintiff. Next, the claim against

D could be brought pursuant to FRCP 13(h) since doing so would satisfy the requirements of that rule, including the permissive joinder standards of FRCP 20. As to jurisdiction, although B and D are not diverse from one another, supplemental jurisdiction could be exercised over this factually related claim under §1367(a); moreover, subsection (b) imposes no limitations on defendant B's use of this joinder device.

May D intervene?

First, the standards of FRCP 24 would have to be satisfied, and it is not entirely clear how D's tortuous interference claim would be impaired by this suit. Permissive intervention is a possibility, though a court might conclude that D's intervention would change the basic contours of the lawsuit (a breach of contract suit). Assuming the court allows D to intervene—presumably as a pefendant—the jurisdictional issue is a bit tricky. D's claim is not created by federal law; nor does her claim include an essential federal ingredient. Diversity is also lacking since D and B are both from Arizona and D would line up as a plaintiff against B. Yet, there may be supplemental jurisdiction over D's claim. D's claim does arise out of a common nucleus of operative facts with A's claim against B. In addition, although §1367(b) provides that supplemental jurisdiction may not be exercised over a claim by a party intervening under FRCP 24 when doing so would be inconsistent with the jurisdictional requirements of §1332, the apparent inconsistency with those standards—no diversity between D and B—is only skin deep. Prior to the adoption of §1367, courts deemed it quite consistent with §1332 to permit a nondiverse party to intervene so long as that party would not have been deemed indispensable—a party without whom the court could not proceed—within the meaning of FRCP 19. D is not an indispensable party. Therefore despite the lack of diversity between D and B, the court could exercise supplemental jurisdiction over D's intervention.

May A file a claim against D related to the underlying dispute between A and B?

FRCP 13(g) might allow A to do this depending on how one interprets the scope of that rule. Assuming, as it appears to be the case, that the claim is transactionally related to the primary claim (i.e., to the breach of contract claim), some courts would treat the co-plaintiffs as co-parties and allow the filing of the claim. Other courts, however, would not treat co-plaintiffs as co-parties unless both co-plaintiffs were made defendants on a counterclaim, which is not the situation here. Assuming the rule is satisfied, subject matter jurisdiction must be satisfied as well. Since A and D are diverse, §1332 would be satisfied if the amount in controversy were met. If the amount is not met, the claim would appear to satisfy the standards of §1367(a), but then appears to run afoul of §1367(b) since it would be a claim by a plaintiff (A) against a party (D) joined under FRCP 24 under circumstances that would be inconsistent with the jurisdictional requirements of §1332. Yet, the same not-an-indispensable-party argument discussed in the previous answer, might eliminate the jurisdictional inconsistency.

Answer to Question 29

Surety ("S")'s 12(b)(7) motion requires an application of FRCP 19(a) and (b). That inquiry is divided into three parts. First, is Delmore ("D") a required party, that is, one who should be joined if feasible? Second, assuming an affirmative answer to that question, is D's joinder feasible? And third, assuming that his joinder is not feasible, may the action, in equity and good conscience, proceed without him? As to the first inquiry—the 19(a) inquiry—D is a required party. He has an interest in the performance bond, and that interest may be impaired by an adverse judgment against S. For example, a finding that S is liable to Patricia ("P") might require D to indemnify S, or it might reduce the amount of protection available to D with respect to other subcontractors. In addition, S may be subjected to inconsistent obligations if P prevails against D (triggering S's payment obligation) but loses against S (nullifying S's payment obligation). There is also a type of "inefficiency" prejudice to the judicial system. Next, as to feasibility of joinder, if D is joined as a defendant, complete diversity would be destroyed, and although the claim against D would be part of the same constitutional case within the meaning of §1367(a), the principles of §1367(b) would be violated since P, the plaintiff, would now be asserting a claim against a party joined pursuant to FRCP 19 where complete diversity is lacking. On the other hand, S could file a counterclaim for declaratory relief and join D as a 13(h) defendant on that counterclaim. With this approach, there would be no violation of §1367(b). Alternatively, S might file a counterclaim in interpleader against P and D or an impleader against D, which would also avoid the §1367(b) problems. (Note that these alternative approaches could also be discussed under the "shaping the relief" principle.) Finally, assuming joinder is not feasible, one must reconsider the prejudice to P (minimal since she chose to split her claims), S (potential inconsistent obligations), D (diminution of his security bond), and the courts (inefficiency), and then determine whether this prejudice can be avoided or lessened by shaping the relief. Among other things, the court simply could withhold any judgment in this proceeding pending the outcome of the state court lawsuit between P and D. Alternatively, the court could stay this proceeding until such time as S had an opportunity to intervene in the state court proceeding. In general, since there are alternative ways of bringing D into the suit and ways of shaping the relief that would avoid any prejudice to S, the motion should be denied.

Answer to Question 30

Is A bound by the finding in the first proceeding that the contract allowed B to make the delivery within four months of July 1?

No. The decision on that issue was not necessary to the previous judgment. Excise that decision from the judgment, and the judgment would still stand.

If B raises a defense of claim preclusion, how should the court rule? Does it matter whether the breach at issue in the first proceeding was considered material?

The claim preclusion defense should be denied since the temporal scope of the claim in the first proceeding was limited to 2003. If the breach had been "material," then, in some jurisdictions, A would have been required to sue for both past and future damages. Under this scenario, the claim preclusion defense would prevail. Under these facts, however, there is no basis on which to conclude that the breach was material.

Since the court in the first proceeding made several findings, is B bound by the finding of no fraud?

Yes, B is bound. That issue was actually litigated, decided, and necessary to the previous judgment. As to the latter point, the court could not have found in A's favor in the absence of this finding.

If in the first case the court found for B, would A be precluded from bringing the second suit?

It depends. Under the Restatement (Second) of Judgments, neither issue would be binding unless A appealed and both were affirmed on appeal. Under the original Restatement, however, both would have been binding even in the absence of an appeal. Finally, under an approach adopted by some states, the issue would be binding so long as it was "squarely addressed and specifically decided." (Note this presents a problem of issue preclusion, not claim preclusion. It is the "issue" of fraud that will potentially bar the subsequent suit.)

If A attempts to sue B for damages to the loading dock, may B rely on the prior judgment in favor of D as bar to that suit?

Yes. Under the substantive standards of vicarious liability, B (employer) and D (employee) would be deemed to have been in privity with one another for purposes of claim preclusion. B, therefore, may assert claim preclusion as a defense in the second suit.

If the judgment in the A v. D proceeding was against D and in favor of A, would B be bound by that judgment?

No. Under these circumstances, the substantive policies of vicarious liability would not be advanced by creating a privity relationship between B and D. B, therefore, would be treated as a nonparty. As a nonparty, and consistent with the due process clause, B is not bound by the prior judgment.

Answer to Question 31

May D rely on FRCP 4(k)(2) to establish personal jurisdiction over TV?

In cases involving federal claims, FRCP 4(k)(2) allows a federal court to exercise long-arm jurisdiction over a defendant who is "not subject to jurisdiction in any state's courts of general jurisdiction" so long as the defendant has minimum contacts with the United States. This rule would not be available to assert jurisdiction over TV. First, D's indemnity claim against TV is not a federal claim. Next, there is at least one state court of general jurisdiction that could assert jurisdiction over TV in this matter. Specifically, since TV is a State Z corporation, TV would, as a "citizen" of the state, be subject to jurisdiction in State Z under traditional notions of fair play and substantial justice. It is also quite likely that TV would be subject to jurisdiction in State Y since D's indemnity claim arises out of business transacted by TV with D in State Y, including shipments by TV of its valves into that state. The fact that Titan is not subject to jurisdiction in State X (or might not be) is not in itself adequate to trigger FRCP 4(k)(2). Hence, Rule 4(k)(2) simply does not apply here.

Would the exercise of personal jurisdiction over TV comport with due process?

D's strongest due process argument would be that TV placed its valves into the stream of commerce ("SOC") by shipping them to D in State Y with the awareness that these valves would be fabricated onto radiators in State Y and shipped into other states for retail sales nationwide, including in State X.

The facts fit the basic model for SOC: a manufacturer ships its product from the state of manufacture to another state with the expectation that the product will be sold at retail in a state other than the one to which it shipped its product. The SOC ends in the state where the retail sale is made. Here TV shipped the valve from State Z, the state of manufacture, to State Y, where the valve was fabricated onto a radiator, with the expectation that the radiator and its component part would be sold at retail in a state other than State Z.

There are basically two approaches to SOC. Under the first, the "pure" model, it is sufficient that the nonresident manufacturer place its product in the SOC aware that the product will be sold at retail in the forum state. The fact that TV has engaged in a regular course of sales with D over the past four years (15K valves per year) and given that D distributes its radiators nationwide and particularly in State X, a court is likely to conclude that TV either knew or should have known that its valves would be placed on radiators to be sold at retail in State X. Willful blindness would not be a defense.

Under the second approach, mere awareness is not enough to establish purposeful availment. Instead, purposeful availment will be satisfied only if the nonresident manufacturer has engaged in some other activity directed toward the forum state indicative of an intent to benefit from the market in that state—for example, designing the product for that state, advertising the product in that state, procuring an agent to promote the product in that state. The facts here do not reveal any "plus" engaged in by TV and directed toward State X. TV's activities, therefore, would not satisfy this more rigorous test.

Importantly, many lower courts apply the SOC "plus" test in cases involving component parts on the theory that in such cases the manufacturer has little control over where the product that contains the component part will be sold at retail. This case does involve a component part (the valve).

Assuming D satisfies purposeful availment, it must also satisfy relatedness or general jurisdiction. The strongest argument here is for relatedness since the case for general jurisdiction is virtually nonexistent under these facts. As to relatedness, the purposeful contact with the forum state is the shipment of the radiator/valve into the state. The question is whether the claim of indemnity arises out of that contact—that is, the shipment. If one applies the strictest tests—proximate cause or substantive relevance—the answer would be no. The shipment is not the legal cause of D's right to indemnification; nor is it the legal cause of the P's injuries. The legal cause of the injuries is the explosion. Similarly, the shipment itself is not substantively relevant to the claim of indemnity since that claim is premised on tortious liability incurred by D and not by the fact of an interstate shipment of goods.

Most courts, despite protestations to the contrary, will find relatedness satisfied under the somewhat looser "substantial connection" and "lies in the wake" tests, both of which would seem to be satisfied here. Indeed, these tests are virtually identical. The shipment of the valve in SOC led to the foreseeable possibility of an injury being incurred in the state of retail sale should the valve prove defective. In other words, the shipment created the wake—that is, the foreseeable possibilities—within which the explosion (and indemnity claim) occurred. One could also say that from a "but for" causation perspective the causal chain is not tenuous, but relatively direct.

In short, if the court applies the standard SOC test, jurisdiction will be satisfied; if it applies the "plus" test, it will not. It remains an open question as to which is the proper test.

Should the U.S. district court quash service of process on TV?

FRCP 4(h)(1)(B) provides that service on a corporation may be effected "by delivering a copy of the summons and of the complaint to an officer [or] a managing or general agent . . . . " In this case, service was effected when Macduff, a process server, served Hecate, the receptionist seated in TV's main lobby.

The parties have submitted contradictory affidavits, neither of which is inherently implausible. From a policy perspective, however, the court will likely adopt the D's version of the events (Macduff's affidavit) since that narrative is most likely to lead to an adversarial hearing on the merits (as opposed to a dismissal). Note, however, that if TV were seeking to reopen a default judgment entered against it, the court would likely rely on Hecate's version of the events since her version would likely lead to an adversarial resolution of the controversy by rescinding the default.

Nothing in the facts suggests that Hecate was "an officer or a managing or general agent" of TV. There is no dispute over her claim that she was a newly hired receptionist. Hence, if a court were to apply the text of the rule strictly, one would have to conclude that service was not properly made. The actual service on the CEO would not alter this technical deficiency.

Most federal courts, however, require only substantial compliance with the text of FRCP 4(h). This standard of substantial compliance will be satisfied if the person served is situated such that it is fair, reasonable and just to imply her authority to receive service. According to Macduff's affidavit, he told Hecate, who was seated in the main lobby of TV's headquarters, that he was handing her legal process and that she then affirmed that she was authorized to accept process on behalf of TV. In addition, consistent with her affirmation, Hecate did deliver the papers to the Titan CEO that day.

Given the foregoing facts, it seems likely (fair, just, and reasonable) that the court would deny the motion to dismiss. Essentially, the facts support the conclusion that Macduff acted reasonably in treating Hecate as TV's agent for purposes of service of process, and, given that actual notice occurred on that same day, there is no unfairness or injustice in affirming the effectiveness of service.

Answer to Question 32

Was service of process on D effective?

No. FRCP 4(e)(1) provides that an individual may be served in accord with the law of the state in which the U.S. district court sits, here the law of State Y. Hence, P might argue that service by certified mail, as permitted by State Y law, should satisfy FRCP 4(e)(1) given that D signed the return receipt as required by State Y law. However, the mailing that was sent to D was not service of process but a Request for Waiver of Service of Process made pursuant to FRCP 4(d). Such a request will not be treated as proper service even if the method through which the request is served would otherwise comply with the service provisions of the state in which the federal court sits. In fact, a Request for Waiver will never be treated as actual service since it does not purport to be service and will be effective as a waiver of service only if the defendant signs and returns the waiver.

Assuming effective service of process, did the U.S. district court sitting in State Y have personal jurisdiction over D?

FRCP 4(k)(1)(A) allows a U.S. district court to exercise personal jurisdiction over an out-of-state resident if that person would be "subject to the jurisdiction of a court of general jurisdiction in the state where the district court is located." This means that the exercise of jurisdiction must comport with the local state's jurisdictional statute and the due process limitations imposed by the Fourteenth Amendment due process clause. The facts state that State Y has a "due-process-style" jurisdictional statute, which means that the statutory analysis and the due process analysis are identical. Hence, the question is whether the exercise of jurisdiction would satisfy the minimum contacts test. That test breaks down into three elements: (1) purposeful availment of the forum or activity purposefully directed toward the forum, (2) relatedness between any purposeful contacts and the claim, and (3) reasonableness. (There is no basis on these facts for arguing "general" jurisdiction over D in State Y.)

Purposeful availment:
Has D purposefully directed any activity toward State Y?

Short answer: Yes, but in a manner that is qualitatively inadequate to satisfy the minimum contacts test. Most notably, D placed an advertisement on the Internet (eWay) promoting the sale of his car throughout the world, which, naturally, would include placement of the ad in State Y. In addition, as a consequence of the ad, D entered into a contract of sale with a resident of State Y. On the other hand, as far as we can tell from these facts, this was a "one shot" sale. There is no claim that D uses eWay as a platform for wide-ranging retail sales. Nor is there any allegation that D has made any other sales to residents of State Y. From these facts, all we know is that D entered into a single contract with a single resident of State Y. While a single contract can be sufficient to establish purposeful availment, whether that standard is satisfied depends on the nature of the contract and the obligations it imposes. For example, if the contract imposes continuing forum-state-directed obligations on the out-of-state resident, one might conclude that the purposeful availment requirement has been satisfied. Here, however, this contract imposes no such future obligations. Rather, it is nothing more than an isolated and fully consummated sale. Under these circumstances the purposeful availment requirement is not likely to be met. It is difficult to conceive what benefits D purposefully derived from State Y.

The fact that the ad was placed on the Internet does not alter this conclusion. The defendant is not eWay; nor do the facts suggest that the defendant uses eWay as a general platform for his retail sales. Hence, there is no need to determine whether eWay is a passive or active Web site.

Purposefully directed:

P might argue that the standards of the "effects test" have been satisfied here—that is, that D has purposefully caused an effect in State Y through activity undertaken outside of the state. However, the effects test requires that the D aim his or her activity at the forum state. Here, D aimed at the world. The fact that his ad "hit" State Y is insufficient to satisfy this standard.

Relatedness:

If D's contacts were sufficiently purposeful to satisfy due process standards, the relatedness requirement would likely have been satisfied. The claims of fraud arise directly out of the content of the ad, and the ad itself is substantively relevant to these claims. Stated somewhat differently, the allegedly false content of the ad is the proximate cause of the harm suffered by P. However, in the absence of purposeful availment, this relatedness is inadequate to establish jurisdiction.

Reasonableness:

Once purposeful availment and relatedness are satisfied, there is a strong presumption that the exercise of jurisdiction is reasonable. The defendant can rebut this presumption by presenting compelling evidence to the contrary. Given the failure of the purposeful availment prong, however, there is no need for rebuttal here. One can, however, sense the unfairness that would inure to one-time eWay sellers forced to defend in whatever state (or country) a purchaser happens to reside.

Conclusion:
Even assuming effective service of process, the U.S. district court lacked personal jurisdiction over D.

In what court may or must D raise his challenges to service of process and personal jurisdiction?
D has two options. He could collaterally attack the default judgment in the State X enforcement proceeding by raising his service and jurisdiction challenges as a defense in that proceeding or he could directly attack the default in the State Y U.S. district court by filing a motion for relief from judgment pursuant to FRCP 60(b)(4) ("the judgment is void"). Alternatively, D could proceed to raise his challenges simultaneously in both courts. Whatever route D takes, the judgment of the court that rules first will be determinative, for the other court will be required to give that judgment full faith and credit.

Answer to Question 33

How should the U.S. district court rule on BC's motion to dismiss?

BC's motion challenges the court's subject matter jurisdiction. Whether the district court has subject matter jurisdiction depends on an application of three statutes: 28 U.S.C. §§1331 (federal question jurisdiction), 1332 (diversity jurisdiction), and 1367 (supplemental jurisdiction).

Federal question:

There are two ways in which a case can arise under federal law for purposes of establishing federal question jurisdiction: either federal law creates the cause of action or federal law operates as an essential ingredient in a state-created cause of action. In this case, federal law creates neither of the claims filed by Alice and Bernice. First, as given, the FTWCA does not create a private right of action. Second, the claims asserted by Alice and Bernice, negligence and negligence *per se*, are classically state-created. Hence, the creation test is not satisfied. That brings us to the essential federal ingredient test. The facts state that the negligence *per se* claim is premised on BC's breach of the duty created by the FTWCA. Hence, the federal ingredient is clearly embedded in this claim. Since BC denies responsibility under the FTWCA, it would appear that there is an actual dispute over a nontrivial—that is, substantial, federal question. The question is whether recognizing jurisdiction under these circumstances would open the floodgates of litigation in a manner that Congress would not have intended. In this sense, the case is similar to *Merrill Dow Pharmaceuticals Inc. v. Thompson*, 478 U.S. 804 (1986), which involved an effort to use a federal regulatory standard as part of a state-created negligence *per se* claim. In that case, the Court concluded that the essential federal ingredient test was not satisfied. In so ruling, the Court relied in part on the potential expansion of federal jurisdiction that would have been generated by a finding of jurisdiction. Federalizing the negligence *per se* claim asserted here might have similarly large consequences for the allocation of judicial authority between state and federal courts. In addition, the fact that the FTWCA does not create a private right of action is indicative of a congressional intent to keep such cases out of federal court. This case is, therefore, unlike *Grable & Sons Metal Products, Inc. v. Darue Engineering & Manufacturing*, 545 U.S. 308 (2005), where the Court upheld the exercise of federal jurisdiction, finding a federal tax law issue embedded in a property dispute was not likely to operate as a precedent for federalizing a large number of state-law claims.

In short, neither the creation test nor the essential federal ingredient test is satisfied here.

Diversity:

Diversity jurisdiction requires complete diversity and satisfaction of the "exceed $75,000" amount in controversy requirement. Alice, a citizen of California, and BC, a citizen of New York and New Mexico, are diverse from one another, and Alice's claimed $100,000 in damages satisfies the amount in controversy requirement, assuming that the amount is claimed in good faith. Unless BC can show to a legal certainty that the actual amount in controversy does not satisfy the jurisdictional minimum, Alice's good faith assertion of the amount will control. Bernice, also a citizen of California, is completely diverse from BC, but her potential claim for $2,500 falls short of the jurisdictional minimum. Thus, §1332 would be satisfied with respect to Alice but not with respect to Bernice.

Supplemental jurisdiction:

Supplemental jurisdiction over a claim or party can be established if the claim is part of the same constitutional case as claim over which there is an independent basis of subject matter jurisdiction and if other requisites of the supplemental jurisdiction statute are satisfied. 28 U.S.C. §§1367(a)-(b). Bernice's claims are potentially supplemental to Alice's claims in the sense that Bernice's claims arise out of a common nucleus of operative facts as Alice's claims—BC's disposal of toxic wastes at Happy Acres—making both sets claims part of the same constitutional case for purposes of §1367(a). In addition, subsection (a) specifically provides for supplemental jurisdiction over additional parties, which is the case here. Since this is a diversity case, however, the potential exercise of supplemental jurisdiction may be restricted by §1367(b), which imposes specific limitations on the exercise of supplemental jurisdiction over claims by plaintiffs in diversity cases. However, none of those limitations applies here. While Bernice is a plaintiff, she is not suing a party joined pursuant to Rules 14, 19, 20, or 24. Nor did she enter the case as a plaintiff under either Rule 19 or 24. Rather, she joined under Rule 20(a)(1)—permissive joinder of plaintiffs. As a consequence, the limitations imposed by §1367(b) do not apply to Bernice's claims against BC and the district court has discretion to exercise subject matter jurisdiction over Bernice's claims.

Should the district court allow BC to join PTU as a third-party defendant?

Yes, this appears to be a proper impleader under Rule 14(a) as BC is seeking indemnity from PTU on the claims asserted against BC by Alice and Bernice. Hence, the joinder of PTU falls squarely within the rule. In addition, supplemental jurisdiction is satisfied since, by definition, a claim seeking indemnity for liability imposed in the original action is part of the same constitutional case or controversy as the initiating claim. Moreover, since the joinder is being asserted by a defendant (BC), §1367(b) would not bar the exercise of supplemental jurisdiction. It is irrelevant that BC and PTU are from the same state. Of course, under §1367(c) the district court would retain discretion as to whether to exercise that jurisdiction; nothing in these facts, however, suggests that jurisdiction should not be exercised.

May GH be joined as a co-defendant with BC in the amended complaint?

No. The joinder of GH would be proper under FRCP 20(a)(2) since the claim against GH arises out of the same transaction as the claims against BC—the pollution of Happy Acres—and since the claims share the common question of fact as to whether Happy Acres is polluted. However, there is no jurisdiction over this claim against GH. It is not a federal question and, at least with respect to Bernice, the amount in controversy is not satisfied. As to supplemental jurisdiction, while the standards of §1367(a) are satisfied (same common nucleus or same transaction), the limits imposed by §1367(b) are triggered by this configuration of joinder. Contrary to the specific text of §1367(b), Bernice, a plaintiff, is now suing a party (either BC or GH) joined under Rule 20 and under circumstances that are inconsistent with the jurisdictional requirements of §1332, namely, failure to satisfy the amount in controversy requirement. This result is anomalous, but it is an unintended consequence of the literal text of §1367(b).

Answer to Question 34

To answer this question, we must apply the two-step approach to the assessment of pleadings described by the Supreme Court in *Ashcroft v. Iqbal*, 129 S.Ct. 1937 (2009). Under that approach, we must first excise "legal conclusions" from the complaint and, second, we must determine whether the remaining "factual" allegations are sufficient to support a claim on which relief can be granted. As to the first step, paragraph 20 alleges that Paula was fired "because of her sex and in retaliation for her having filed charges with the EEOC." Both of these assertions would appear to be "legal conclusions" under *Iqbal*. While these allegations would likely have been deemed sufficient under pre-*Iqbal* standards, that is no longer the case. Now, consistently with *Iqbal*, these "legal conclusions" must be excised from the complaint for purposes of assessing the Rule 12(b)(6) motion. As to the second step, the remaining allegations in Paula's complaint appear to be sufficiently factual, including the three "information and belief" allegations, to warrant consideration in the Rule 12(b)(6) motion. The question then becomes whether this remaining "factual matter" is sufficient to state claims of sex discrimination and retaliation. As to the former, there would appear to be sufficient factual allegations of Frederick's sexist behavior and of the "male" culture at the Desk from which to draw an inference that the treatment of Paula, including her termination, was premised on her sex. The same can be said of the factual allegations pertaining to the retaliation claim. Thus, the allegations with respect to Frederick's hostile behavior immediately after the filing of the EEOC report, including his termination of Paula's employment with DBA, would support an inference of unlawful retaliation. Hence, even without the excised allegations, Paula's complaint appears to state an employment discrimination claim and an unlawful retaliation claim within the scope of Title VII. In addition, the complaint may also have stated a hostile work environment claim. The district court should deny the motion.

Answer to Question 35

Does Paula's ("P") discovery request satisfy FRCP 26(b)(1) and 34(a)(1)(A)?

Yes. Putting privilege aside, the request is reasonably calculated to lead to the discovery of admissible evidence pertaining to the question of sexual discrimination and retaliation—who at DBA said what regarding Paula to whom and when. Moreover, the fact that e-mail represented an important means of communication among the relevant parties during this time frame lends strong support to the discovery relevance of the request. In short, FRCP 26(b)(1) appears to be satisfied. As to FRCP 34(a)(1)(A), which permits a party to seek the production of discovery-relevant documents and things, the text of the rule expressly permits the discovery of electronically stored information. See FRCP 34(b)(2)(E) (outlining procedures for the production of electronically stored information).

What should DBA do with respect to communications between Frederick and in-house counsel?

Any discussions between Frederick and in-house counsel regarding Paula's EEOC charges would fall within the scope of the attorney client privilege. *See Upjohn Co. v. United States*, 449 U.S. 383 (1981). With respect to any such these e-mails, DBA may withhold them for production, but must "expressly" make a claim of attorney-client privilege and "describe the nature of" of the withheld e-mails without disclosing their privileged content.

How should the district court rule on P's motion to compel DBA to search its backup tapes?

Rule 26(b)(2)(B) & (C) are particularly relevant to this inquiry. Following the text of (b)(2)(C), the facts do not suggest that this discovery request is "unreasonably cumulative or duplicative, or can be obtained from some other source." Rule 26(b)(2)(C)(i). Nor is there any showing that Paula had "ample opportunity" to obtain this information through previous. Subsection (C)(ii). As to proportionality—subsection (C)(iii)—under a "needs of the case" rationale, this materials may go to critical elements of plaintiff's claims (sex discrimination and retaliation), the amount in controversy is significant—somewhere between $1.2 and $13 million, and the defendant clearly has more resources. More generally, the request is specific and limited, the e-mails may provide a unique source of relevant information (especially give the role e-mails played on the Desk), the information may be quite useful in establishing a pattern of sex discrimination and in support of the retaliation claim (though at this point there is probably not enough information to be definitive), the request is designed to elicit information on critical issues in the case, and DBA has relatively more resources to fund the search. Since we can only guess as to the content of the e-mails, the court should probably order some limited form of "focused" discovery to get a better sense of relevance and materiality.

What should DBA do if privileged e-mails were inadvertently disclosed in its initial production of documents? How should P respond to the action taken by DBA?

DBA should notify P that privileged materials were inadvertently produced and request a return of those documents pursuant to FRCP 26(b)(5)(B). Once notified, P must "promptly return, sequester, or destroy the specified information and any copies it has" and "must not use or disclose the information until the claim is resolved." DBA would also have a duty to preserve the information until the claim of privilege is resolved.

Why would a district court order a limited examination of the backup files?

The district court might order "focused" discovery in order to assess whether the balance of the equities actually favor discovery. As noted in the previous answer, the actual value of the e-mails can only be measured at an abstract level until we have a better sense of their likely content. A focused inquiry should give a better overall sense of that content and of the potential relevance of the stored e-mails to Paula's claims. For example, if the focused inquiry reveals very little of relevance to Paula's claims, the district court might well conclude that further expense is unwarranted or that Paula should shoulder the greater burden of that expense.

Should the district court grant P's request to order the restoration of the remaining backup tapes?

The district court should grant the request. The retrieved e-mails show that the backup tapes contain substantial information relevant to P's claims and there is no showing that this information would be available from any other source. In addition, one can now predict with a degree of confidence that this information will be useful in establishing key elements of P's claims. In addition, the fact that Frederick deleted e-mails from online sources further supports the conclusion that a more complete search is in order.

Multiple-Choice Questions

Personal Jurisdiction, Service of Process and Due Process—Questions

1. P, a citizen of Minnesota, sued D, a citizen of Wisconsin, in a Minnesota state court seeking $50,00 for breach of contract for services rendered by P to D in Wisconsin. At the commencement of the suit, the sheriff attached a $1,000 pig belonging to D that was on exhibit at the Minnesota State Fair. D, who did not attend the fair, was personally served with the summons and complaint at his farm in Wisconsin. D ignored the Minnesota proceedings. The Minnesota court entered a default judgment against D for $5,000 and awarded the pig to P. The pig subsequently escaped from P and found its way back to D's farm in Wisconsin. P has filed an action against D in a Wisconsin state court seeking return of the pig. Which of the following statements is correct?

    A. The Wisconsin court is not required to give full faith and credit to the Minnesota judgment since a *quasi in rem* proceeding cannot be enforced beyond the territory of the issuing court.

    B. The Wisconsin court is required to give full faith and credit to the Minnesota judgment but only if the standards of the minimum contacts test were satisfied in the Minnesota proceeding.

    C. The Wisconsin court must give the Minnesota judgment full faith and credit to the full extent of the $5,000 award since D's property was attached at the commencement of the lawsuit.

    D. The Wisconsin court must give the Minnesota judgment full, faith, and credit to the full value of the pig since the pig was attached at the commencement of the lawsuit.

2. D operates a car repair shop adjacent to an interstate highway in State X. This past summer, D did some quick repair work on the brakes of P's car. P was traveling through State X on her way home to State Y, which borders State X. Just after P crossed the border into State Y, the brakes failed and P's car crashed into a highway barrier, causing significant damage to the car. P sued D in a State Y court for the tort of negligent repair. State Y's tailored jurisdictional statute authorizes the exercise of personal jurisdiction over a non-resident as to any claim that arises out of the non-resident's "commission of a tortious act within the state." D has filed a motion to dismiss, arguing a lack of statutory jurisdiction. (Assume that the above quoted provision is the only provision arguably applicable to this case.) What should the trial court do?

A. The trial court must grant D's motion since the "tortious act" at issue was committed by D in State X (the place of repair).

B. The trial court should deny D's motion since the text of the statute clearly permits the exercise of jurisdiction over D.

C. Whether the trial court should grant or deny the motion depends on how broadly the courts of State Y interpret the phrase "tortious act."

D. Whether the trial court should grant or deny the motion depends on whether the effects test has been satisfied.

3. D created a website titled "P_is_a_murderous_scoundrel.com." The only item on the website is a photograph of P looking somewhat ominous, with the following caption, "This man murdered his family and buried them in California's Mojave Desert on January 1, 2009." The website is not in any fashion interactive. D is a citizen of Arizona and aside from the website has no other contacts with California. P, as D well knows, is a popular radio show host who lives in and broadcasts from his home in California. P sued D for defamation, based solely on the content of D's website, in a California state court. D has filed a motion to dismiss for lack of personal jurisdiction. Which of the following statements is correct?

A. The court must grant D's motion since the website is *Zippo* passive.

B. The fact that the website is *Zippo* passive is not determinative of whether the court should grant D's motion.

C. The effects test would not provide an appropriate measure of jurisdiction in this case.

D. The court must grant D's motion unless the website is to some degree interactive.

4. P sued D in a U.S. district court sitting in State X on a federal statutory claim, over which the district court has subject matter jurisdiction under 28 U.S.C. §1331. D is a non-resident of State X and was personally served in State Y, his home state. Which of the following statements is correct?

A. The district court may borrow the State X long-arm statute in determining whether it may exercise personal jurisdiction over D.

B. The district court may borrow either the State X long-arm statute or the State Y long-arm statute in determining whether it may exercise personal jurisdiction over D.

C. If the applicable state's long-arm statute is not satisfied, the district may not, under any circumstances, exercise personal jurisdiction over D.

D. If a federal statute provides for nationwide service of process in the type of case filed by P, the district court may rely on that statute so long as doing so is consistent with Fourteenth Amendment due process.

5. P is a citizen of New York who works in New Jersey. D and E are citizens of New Jersey who work in that state. One day, D borrowed E's car, advising E that he intended to use it to pick up his sister in Trenton (the capital of New Jersey). However, D drove to New York to take his new girlfriend to Coney Island (which is in Brooklyn, New York). Unfortunately, D became involved in a traffic accident with P while driving in New York City. P brought an action against E in the proper U.S. district court in New York for personal injuries and property damages in the amount of $80,000. A New York statute permits an action against the owner of a motor vehicle who has loaned the car to the person who was driving it when the incident occurred. E has filed a timely FRCP 12(b)(2) motion to dismiss for lack of personal jurisdiction. How should the district court rule on that motion?

A. The district court should grant the motion since, in the absence of additional facts, it appears that the exercise of jurisdiction would violate the Due Process Clause of the Fourteenth Amendment.

B. The district court should grant the motion since, in the absence of additional facts, it appears that the exercise of jurisdiction would violate the Due Process Clause of the Fifth Amendment.

C. The district court should deny the motion under the standards of FRCP 4(k)(2), which permits the exercise of nationwide service of process in such cases.

D. The district court should deny the motion since E caused an effect in New York.

6. P commenced an action against D in a State X court of general jurisdiction. D is a citizen of State Z, and P is a citizen of State X. D owned a boat that he kept at a pier in State X. Pursuant to State X law, P obtained an attachment against D's boat. When properly served with notice of the attachment, D moved to quash it. The boat is probably worth $20,000. P's action is for breach of contract and alleges damages in the amount of $15,000. Which of the following statements is correct?

A. The attachment should be quashed if a State X court could not constitutionally assume personal jurisdiction over D.

B. Prejudgment attachments are *per se* unconstitutional.

C. If D's motion was denied, P could retain all of the proceeds from the sale of the boat.

D. Choices (A) and (B) are correct, but (C) is not.

7. In a state court of general jurisdiction, Pete sued the Big Time Corporation for personal injuries he received in an auto collision with a truck driven by a Big Time truck driver. Doris was the president of Big Time when the accident occurred. Pete personally served Big Time Corporation by handing the summons and complaint to Doris the day before she retired. In the excitement of her retirement, Doris neglected to deliver the papers to anyone else at Big Time. A default was entered against Big Time. Other than service upon Doris, Big Time never received notice of the pending lawsuit prior to the entry of a default judgment. Big Time has filed a motion to rescind the judgment based on the inadequacy of service. You may assume that applicable state law pertaining to service of process is identical to those in the Federal Rules of Civil Procedure. Which of the following statements is correct?

A. Big Time's motion should be granted because it did not receive actual notice of the pending lawsuit.

B. Big Time's motion should be granted because Doris was not an officer of Big Time at the time an answer was due.

C. Big Time's motion should be granted because Pete served the summons and complaint.

D. Big Time's motion should be denied.

8. Pherenike sued Daria in a breach of contract diversity action filed in a federal district court in State X. Under the applicable statute of limitations, the complaint was required to be served within one year of the breach that gave rise to the claim. Pherenike filed her complaint within one year of the breach and on that same day mailed a copy of the complaint to Daria along with a "Notice of a Lawsuit and Request to Waive Service of Summons" and two copies of a "Waiver of Service of Summons." The mailing was in full compliance with FRCP 4(d) and was sent to Daria by certified mail. Daria received and signed for the certified mailing within the statute of limitations. She did not sign or return the Waiver of Service of Summons. The statute of limitations has now expired and Pherenike has not otherwise attempted to serve Daria. Daria has filed an FRCP 12(b)(6) motion to dismiss premised

on Pherenike's failure to perfect service of process within the statute of limitations. The district court should:

A. Grant the motion even if Daria had actual notice of the lawsuit.

B. Deny the motion since Daria has waived service of process by failing to respond to the complaint.

C. Deny the motion if State X law allows service by certified mail.

D. Deny the motion because Daria had actual notice of the lawsuit.

9. Phuong sued Destino in a federal district court. In conjunction with that proceeding, Phuong filed an affidavit of service with the court purporting to establish that Destino had been properly served. Although Destino received actual notice, he did not appear and a default judgment was entered against him. Destino has now filed a motion to vacate the judgment under Federal Rule 60(b)(4), claiming that the purported service of process on him failed to comply with the federal rules. The parties' respective versions of the events surrounding Phuong's attempt to serve Destino conflict with one another. Under Phuong's version, service would be deemed proper, while under Destino's version, it would not. Both versions are plausible and neither is more credible than the other. The district court will most likely:

A. Deny the motion since doing so would advance the policy preference for litigation on the merits.

B. Grant the motion since doing so would advance the policy preference for litigation on the merits.

C. Neither grant nor deny the motion, but hold a mini-trial to determine the credibility of the witnesses.

D. Deny the motion since Destino received actual notice.

10. Petronius owned a house in the San Fernando Valley ("SFV house"), which he purchased in 1975. He lived there with his wife until they separated in 2001. Petronius then moved into a nearby apartment, and his wife continued to live in the SFV house. Petronius paid his mortgage each month for 30 years, and the mortgage company paid his property taxes. After Petronius paid off his mortgage in 2005, the property taxes went unpaid, and the property was certified as delinquent. On April 1, 2007, the state treasurer attempted to notify Petronius of this tax delinquency by mailing a certified letter to him at the address of the SFV house. The packet of information stated that unless Petronius paid his taxes, the property would be subject to public sale two years later on April 1, 2009. Nobody was home to sign for the letter and the letter was

eventually returned to the state treasurer marked "unclaimed." Two years later, and just a few weeks before the public sale, the Treasurer published a notice of public sale of the property in a local newspaper. Prior to selling the property, however, the treasurer mailed another certified "notification" letter to Petronius at the SFV house address. Like the first letter, the second letter was also returned and marked "unclaimed." The property was then sold to Dora. Immediately after the 30-day period for post-sale redemption had passed, Dora had an unlawful detainer notice delivered to the property. The notice was served on Petronius's daughter, who contacted him and notified him of the tax sale. Petronius then filed a lawsuit against the state treasurer and Dora, alleging that the treasurer's failure to provide adequate notice of the sale violated the Due Process Clause. Which of the following statements is correct?

A. There was no violation of due process since an unclaimed certified letter will be deemed actual and valid service under all circumstances.

B. There was no violation of due process so long as the certified mail was properly addressed.

C. There was a violation of due process since personal service is the preferred method of service under such circumstances.

D. There was a violation of due process in the absence of additional measures being undertaken to notify the landowner.

11. Dan, a farmer who resides in State Y, purchased an expensive tractor from Paula under an installment sales contract that included a cognovit clause. Dan agreed to the clause since he was sure he could make the payments and since in exchange Paula agreed to an interest rate below current market rates. The contract was entered in State X, where Paula's business is located and which recognizes the validity of cognovit clauses. After Dan fell behind on the payments, Paula filed breach of contract action against him in a State X court. The State X court, relying on the cognovit clause, entered a default judgment against Dan. Dan was served only after the default judgment had been entered. Paula has now filed an enforcement action against Dan in a State Y court. In response, Dan filed a motion to dismiss the enforcement action based on State Y law, which does not recognize the validity of cognovit clauses. How should the court rule on Dan's motion?

A. His motion should be granted because a judgment enforcing a cognovit clause is not entitled to full faith and credit in those states in which such clauses are deemed invalid.

B. His motion should be denied because judgments enforcing cognovit clauses are entitled to full faith and credit regardless of the circumstances under which the clause was signed.

C. His motion should be granted because while a confession of judgment is entitled to full faith and credit, a cognovit clause is not.

D. His motion must be denied if his agreement to sign the cognovit clause was voluntarily, knowingly and intelligently made.

12. On one of her occasional visits to State X, which is located on the east coast, Witness ("W"), a citizen of State Y, located on the west coast, observed an automobile accident between a yellow cab ("YC") and a pedestrian ("P"). She has now returned to State X under subpoena to testify in a personal injury case filed there by P against YC. W arrived in State X on the day before her scheduled testimony. She spent that evening—a Sunday—with a friend, and together they attended a play. On Monday, when W arrived in court, the attorney for P informed W that her scheduled testimony had been postponed until Thursday of that week. W decided to remain in State X and spent the better part of the next three days doing research in the city library on a project involving her State Y business. As W was leaving the library on Wednesday evening, a process server served W with process in a case having nothing to do with *P v. YC*; neither did that case arise out of any contacts W had with State X. This case was also filed in a State X court. W's attorney has filed a motion to quash service of process on grounds of witness immunity. On the assumption that the courts of State X recognize the witness immunity doctrine, which of the following statements is correct?

A. W's attendance at a play on the night before her scheduled testimony waived her immunity from service.

B. W would be entitled to witness immunity since she was not warned that she might be served if she entered the state.

C. W would not be entitled to witness immunity since the service at issue involved a completely separate case from the one in which she was scheduled to testify.

D. Under the above facts, most courts following the witness immunity doctrine would find that W had not waived her right to immunity from service.

13. Dilbert, the former holder of the title "King of Donkey Kong," lives in a small cabin hidden somewhere in California's Mojave Desert. His only known address is a rented post office box from which someone occasionally retrieves his mail. Dilbert recently received a letter inviting him to attend a Donkey Kong convention to be held at the Convention Center in Los Angeles as an "honored and all-expenses-paid guest." The letter also informed Dilbert that the current holder of "King of Donkey Kong" title has been exposed as a fraud and a cheat and that the title will be returned to Dilbert at a lavish awards ceremony to be held at the convention. Dilbert, who has been severely depressed since his loss of the title, accepted the invitation. When he arrived at the convention, he was immediately served with process; worse yet, he discovered that the invitation was a complete fake and that he will not be reinvested with his title. Dilbert's attorney has filed a motion to quash service as a product of trickery or fraud. What would the majority of courts do?

   A. Uphold service of process regardless of the trickery.

   B. Uphold service of process since Dilbert was guilty of evading service of process.

   C. Quash service since Dilbert was tricked into attending the convention for the sole purpose of subjecting him to service of process.

   D. Quash service since he was not warned that he might be served while attending the convention.

14. P, a citizen of California, was involved in an automobile accident with D, a citizen of Arizona. The accident took place in California while D was visiting there on a vacation. D has since returned to Arizona. P has now sued D in a U.S. district sitting in California. To effect service of process on D in Arizona, P may:

   A. Serve D by properly delivering a copy of the summons and complaint to D personally.

   B. Serve D under the standards of California law.

   C. Serve D under the standards of Arizona law.

   D. All of the above.

15. After P slipped and fell in a parking lot owned by D, she sued D in an appropriate state court. D suffers from Alzheimer's disease. While D's wife handles all of his business affairs under a power of attorney, no one has been appointed as D's legal guardian. When the process server attempted to serve D at the latter's home, D's wife was out-of-state.

Frank, a family friend who was caring for D, answered the door and told the process server that D was mentally incompetent, that his wife was away, and that he, Frank, was staying with D until she returned. The process server left the papers with Frank who said he would see that D's attorney received them. Assuming service complied with the applicable statute or rule, did the method of service satisfy the notice requirements of the Due Process Clause?

A. No, personal service on D's wife would be more likely to provide actual notice.

B. Yes, under the circumstances, the method of service was reasonably calculated to provide actual notice.

C. No, additional measures such as posting on D's door, would be required.

D. Yes, so long as statutory requirements are satisfied, due process is satisfied.

16. P's car was ticketed seven times for being illegally parked in the City of Denver. Each ticket, which consisted of a summons and complaint, was placed under the windshield wiper of his car and warned that unless he responded within 30 days, a fine would be imposed and the car could be immobilized or impounded. A notice of violation was also mailed to P's home a week after each ticket was written. After he failed to respond to any of the tickets in a timely fashion, his car was immobilized by attaching a large metal clamp known as a "Denver Boot" to one of the front wheels. A notice placed on the car explained that to have the boot removed, P would have to go to the court clerk's office and pay the accumulated fines plus a $10 boot fee. P did so but later sued the city. He claimed that it had violated the Due Process Clause by failing to give him prior notice and an opportunity to be heard before immobilizing his car, and by forcing him to pay the fines and the boot fee to get the car released with no chance to contest the amount of the fines allegedly owed. Which of the following statements is correct?

A. The method used to notify P of his parking fines was inadequate since there were other methods available that were more likely to provide actual notice.

B. The method used to notify P of his parking fines was inadequate since this method was substantially less likely to work than other feasible and customary alternatives.

C. The method used to notify P of his parking fines was adequate since P knew or should have known that he was illegally parked and had been ticketed on several occasions.

D. The method used to notify P of his parking fines was reasonably calculated, under all the circumstances, to apprise P of the pending action against him.

17. Same facts as above. Which of the following statements is correct?

A. P waived his right to a hearing to contest the legitimacy of the individual parking fines when he failed to respond to the summons and complaint within 30 days as to each of those fines.

B. By placing a "boot" on his car prior to giving P an opportunity to be heard on the issue of immobilization, the City of Denver violated P's due process right to a pre-deprivation hearing.

C. The City of Denver's failure to provide P a post-deprivation hearing with respect to the immobilization of his car violated due process.

D. The City of Denver was not required to provide P with a hearing pertaining to whether his car was properly immobilized.

18. Panda Sonic Corporation has engaged in price fixing, causing persons who purchased their stereo equipment to pay $50 per item over the fair market price. Marcia Music sued Panda Sonic for a violation of federal antitrust laws. She filed her suit in an appropriate U.S. district court for a federal antitrust violation and sought to proceed as the representative of the class of persons who brought Panda Sonic stereo equipment within the applicable statute of limitations. The district court certified the class under FRCP 23(b)(3), and the following notice was prepared for mailing to all class members (approximately 125,000 persons):

> You are hereby notified that a class action has been brought in U.S. district court under Rule 23(b)(3) of the Federal Rules of Civil Procedure by Ms. Marcia Music on behalf of all persons who have purchased Panda Sonic stereo equipment. You may opt out of the class within one month of this notice. If you choose to remain in the action, you may appear through an attorney.

Which of the following is correct?

A. If Marcia is unable to pay the costs mailing the notice, the court may, in its discretion and for good cause shown, order Panda Sonic to pay these costs.

B. If a class member opts out and Panda Sonic prevails at trial, Panda Sonic may assert collateral estoppel against that individual in a subsequent lawsuit.

    C. The notice to class members was inadequate.

    D. None of the above.

19. ABC Corporation, a relatively new Illinois entity, manufactures high-powered motors that are installed in yachts manufactured by XYZ, Inc., an Ohio corporation. ABC knew that XYZ sold most of its yachts in California and Florida. Paul, a resident of Florida, purchased an XYZ yacht with an ABC motor at a Florida dealership. As result of a defect in the motor, the yacht capsized during its first Florida "run." Paul was seriously injured. Paul sued XYZ in the appropriate U.S. district court in Florida. Four months later, after discovery, Paul sought to add ABC as an additional defendant. Florida's long-arm statute permits jurisdiction over nonresidents when the person or entity involved has done business in Florida or sold personal property to a Florida domiciliary or entity. Under these circumstances, can the U.S. district court assume personal jurisdiction over ABC? (Assume that ABC has never sold any of its motors directly to a Florida citizen or entity.)

    A. Yes, if ABC could reasonably foresee that its motors might eventually be used in Florida.

    B. Yes, because ABC did business with Defendant, who sold the yacht in question to a Florida entity.

    C. No, because ABC never did any business in Florida or sold personal property to a Florida citizen or entity.

    D. No, because ABC clearly lacks sufficient minimum contacts with Florida.

20. Pat is domiciled in Los Angeles. While driving her car in Chicago, Pat collided with a car driven by Dan, a Bar Review lecturer who lived in Chicago. Settlement discussions took place but were not successful. Four months later, while Dan was giving a lecture in Los Angeles, he was personally served by Pat's process server. The lawsuit, filed in a U.S. district court in California, alleges that Dan's negligence caused the accident and claims damages exceeding $75,000. Assuming Dan has no contacts with California other than lecturing there four days each year for the Bar Review course, may the court assert personal jurisdiction over Dan?

    A. Yes, because Dan was personally served within California.

    B. Yes, because Dan had adequate minimum contacts with California.

    C. No, because Dan lacked sufficient minimum contacts with California.

    D. No, because Dan's presence in California was unrelated to Pat's claim.

21. Same facts as the preceding question, except assume that Dan does not object initially to personal jurisdiction. He answers (denying liability) and counterclaims against Pat for his own injuries that were sustained in the accident. After some discovery, however, it appeared that Pat would probably prevail. Can Dan now contest personal jurisdiction?

    A. Yes, because a lack of personal jurisdiction can be raised at any stage of a federal litigation matter.

    B. Yes, because a lack of personal jurisdiction can be raised at any time prior to trial.

    C. No, because an objection to personal jurisdiction must be raised at the first available opportunity.

    D. No, because Pat, as the domiciliary-plaintiff, has the right to choose the forum.

Venue, Transfer and Forum non Conveniens—Questions

22. P, who lives in Nevada, sued D in the U.S. district court in Nevada alleging that D, P's former employer, fired P in violation of the federal Age Discrimination Act. The incident in question took place at D's BBQ restaurant in Tyler, Texas, which is located in the Eastern District of Texas ("E.D."). D, who lived in Tyler all her life, has since sold her business and moved to Los Angeles, California, which is located in the Central District of California ("C.D."). After being served with the complaint, D filed a motion to dismiss or transfer to either the E.D. or the C.D.

    A. The action may be transferred only to E.D. since that is where substantial events giving rise to the claim occurred and where D resided at the time of those events.

    B. The action may be transferred to either the E.D. or the C.D. in the district court's discretion.

    C. The action must be dismissed since it was commenced in an improper venue.

    D. The action may not be dismissed or transferred since P has a right to file an action in his state of residence.

23. Dermot and Paddy entered into a contract in Los Angeles under which Dermot agreed to remodel Paddy's cabin in Missoula, Montana. Although the contract was negotiated and signed in Los Angeles, the entire performance of the contract was to take place in Missoula, including the payments by Paddy to Dermot. Unfortunately, Dermot completely botched the job, rendering Paddy's cabin uninhabitable. Paddy has now sued Dermot in the U.S. district court for the Central District of California, which includes Los Angeles, claiming breach of contract and seeking $100,000 in damages. Paddy is a citizen of California, his primary residence being in Los Angeles, and Dermot is a citizen of Arizona. Which of the following statements is correct?

    A. Venue in the Central District is improper since the claim arose in Montana.

    B. Venue in the Central District is improper because substantial events giving rise to the claim occurred in the Montana.

    C. Venue is proper in the Central District because substantial events giving rise to the claim occurred there.

    D. Venue would not be proper in Arizona since none of the events giving rise to the claim occurred in that state.

24. Pontus, a resident of Manhattan, claims to have been kidnapped by Dag, a retired police officer and resident of South Orange, New Jersey. The incident began in Manhattan where Dag falsely identified himself to Pontus as a police officer enforcing a New Jersey warrant for Pontus's arrest. To that end, Dag produced a fraudulent document purporting to be a New Jersey arrest warrant. Dag took Pontus into custody and transported him to a warehouse in Newark, New Jersey, where the latter was bound and blindfolded with duct tape. Pontus was left in the New Jersey warehouse until the Newark police freed him three hours later. Pontus has filed a diversity suit against Dag in the federal district court for the Southern District of New York (SDNY), which includes Manhattan, claiming false imprisonment and other related state-law torts. Assume that personal and subject matter jurisdiction are satisfied. Dag has moved to dismiss the case on grounds of improper venue, or in the alternative to transfer it to the District of New Jersey (DNJ) pursuant to either §1404(a) or §1406(a). Which of the following statements is correct?

    A. Venue is not proper in the SDNY since only the plaintiff is a resident of that district.

    B. Venue is proper in the SDNY under §1391(b)(3) since a court in the SDNY could assert personal jurisdiction over Dag.

    C. If the case is transferred to DNJ, the transferee court must apply the substantive law that a New Jersey state court would apply to plaintiff's state-law claims.

    D. If the case is transferred to DNJ, the transferee court must apply the substantive law that a New York state court would apply to plaintiff's state-law claims.

25. Pia, a resident of New York, and Diva, a resident of Illinois, both of whom are experienced businesswomen, entered a sale-of-goods contract under which Pia was given the exclusive right to market Diva's fashion products in the State of New York. Under the contract Diva was required to ship 1000 units of the specified products to Pia's warehouse in New York City. The contract included the following clause: "Any dispute arising out of or related to this agreement shall be filed only in a court located in Cook County, Illinois." After Diva failed to deliver the specified products in accord with the contract, Pia sued her for breach of contract in a federal district court located in the Southern District of New York ("SDNY")—the location of Pia's warehouse. Diva has filed a timely motion under §1404(a) to transfer the case to the

federal district court for the Northern District of Illinois ("NDIL"), which embraces Cook County, Illinois. Which of the following statements is correct?

A. Given the wording of the forum selection clause, the federal district court may, but need not, transfer the case to the State of Illinois circuit court in Cook County, Illinois.

B. The forum selection clause will be treated as a factor in the determination of whether to transfer the case to the NDIL.

C. Since the forum selection clause includes no federal option, the court must dismiss Pia's lawsuit.

D. Since the forum selection clause includes a federal option, the USDC must transfer the case to the NDIL.

26. Pacifica owns a commercial avocado farm in San Diego County. She claims that as a result of practices undertaken by Desiree Foods, an Arizona corporation with its principal place of business in Arizona, cash markets for avocados have been destroyed, competition among food distributors has been dramatically reduced or eliminated and prices paid for avocados have plummeted. She sued Desiree in the U.S. district court for the Southern District of California, which encompasses the location of her farm, claiming a violation of the federal Free Trade in Avocados Act. The specific actions of which Pacifica complains include Desiree's acquisition of several avocado ranches, its purchase of numerous food distribution plants, and its having entered long-term contracts for supplying avocados to its subsidiaries. Most of these activities took place in Arizona; however, several of the ranches owned by Desiree are located in the San Joaquin Valley of California (i.e., in the Eastern District of California). Is venue proper in the Southern District?

A. No. For purposes of venue in federal courts, the residence of a corporation is determined by its state of incorporation and its principal place of business. Desiree, therefore, cannot be sued in the Southern District.

B. No. Under the given facts and applicable law, Desiree is not a resident of the Southern District for purposes of venue and substantial events giving rise to the claim did not occur there.

C. Yes. Desiree will be treated as a resident of California for purposes of venue because it is subject to personal jurisdiction in that state.

D. Yes. Substantial events giving rise to Pacifica's claim occurred in the Southern District.

27. Lars, a citizen of Oregon, was injured in a skiing accident that occurred in Mammoth Mountain, California. He claims that his injury was caused in part by the faulty design of his bindings, which were manufactured by Zen Bindings, a Colorado corporation with his principal place of business in Denver, Colorado. Zen does business throughout the United States. Lars purchased his bindings at a Mammoth Mountain ski shop. Lars also claims that the accident was attributable to the negligence of Buster Hill, a snowboarder, who rammed into Lars while cutting across a ski slope. Buster was born and raised in Fort Collins, Colorado and still makes his home there. Lars, who has been recuperating in a Los Angeles hospital, filed a products liability and negligence suit against Zen Bindings and Buster Hill in a Superior Court in Los Angeles County. The defendants properly removed the case to the U.S. district court for the Central District of California, invoking that court's diversity jurisdiction. Mammoth Mountain is located in the Eastern District of California. Los Angeles County is located in the Central District. Is venue nonetheless proper in the Central District?

    A. No. Substantial events giving rise to the claim did not occur in the Central District.

    B. Yes. Venue is proper because the case was properly removed to the Central District.

    C. No. Neither defendant is a resident of the Central District.

    D. Yes. Venue is proper under §1391(b)(3) since both Zen and Buster would be subject to personal jurisdiction in California.

28. A Norwegian cruise ship sunk off the coast of Norway. Several passengers drowned. One of the decedents was from State X. Her estate filed a lawsuit against the cruise line in a State X state court. All of the evidence of the incident, including the salvaged ship, is in Norway, and the parties agree that liability must be established under Norwegian law. The estate filed suit in State X partly because juries there tend to grant larger damage awards than do courts in Norway. After the case was filed, the defendant properly removed the case to federal court based on diversity (alienage) jurisdiction. The defendant then moved to dismiss under the doctrine of forum non conveniens, arguing that a forum in Norway was available and substantially better suited to resolve the controversy given the location of the evidence and the relevant witnesses. State X law, however, prohibits application of the doctrine of forum non conveniens whenever the plaintiff is a citizen of State X. Which of the following statements is correct?

A. The State X law of forum non conveniens should play no role in the district court's application of the federal doctrine of forum non conveniens.

B. The district may take into account State X policy in applying the federal doctrine of forum non conveniens.

C. The plaintiff's choice of a State X forum is entitled to no weight given that the incident occurred in Norway.

D. The district court should order the case transferred to an appropriate court in Norway.

29. An automobile accident occurred in State Y involving P, Q (P's passenger), and a vehicle driven by an employee of D. The car in which P and Q were riding was a Ferrari, which they had just purchased together for $79,000 (P contributing $40,000 toward the purchase price, and Q the remaining $39,000). The car was destroyed in the collision. P and Q are citizens of State X, and D is a corporation organized under the laws of State Z, with its principal place of business in State Y. It does business in all 50 states. Within one year after the accident, P and Q sued D to recover a total of $79,000 in damages for the loss of their car. Which of the following statements is correct?

A. If this suit was properly commenced in a state court in State Y, D could have the action removed to a federal court.

B. If this action was filed in the U.S. district court in State W, D probably could have the action transferred to a U.S. district court in State Y, and the federal court in State Y would then apply the statute of limitations that a state court in State Y would apply.

C. Subject matter jurisdiction does not exist because neither P nor Q had invested a sum in excess of $75,000 in the car.

D. None of the above.

30. P, a citizen of State X, and Q, a citizen of State Y, sued D, a citizen of State Z for breach of contract occurring completely in State Z. The action was filed in the U.S. district court for State Y. D was improperly served in State Z. Upon learning of the suit, D filed a motion to dismiss or transfer the case to the U.S. district court for State Z. Which of the following statements is correct?

A. It would be within the district court's discretion to transfer the case to State Z

B. It would be within the district court's discretion to retain the case.

    C. The district court must dismiss the case since D was not properly served.

    D. Under no circumstances may the district court transfer the case to State Z since Q if the policy of State Y is to provide a forum for its citizens.

31. P, a citizen of Oregon, sued D, a large Colorado corporation doing business only in Colorado. The action asserted that D failed to provide training, support, and service for a computer system that D had sold to P. P sued D in the U.S. district court in Oregon. Assume the amount in controversy is satisfied. Although the contract was accepted and signed in Colorado, there was a provision that stipulated that in the event of litigation, D would be amenable to suit in Oregon. D has moved for transfer of the action to the U.S. district court in Colorado, claiming that its training, support, and service personnel, who would be witnesses, are domiciled in Colorado. The Colorado damage remedies are more favorable to D than the corresponding rules in Oregon. Which of the following statements is correct?

    A. If a transfer is made, it will be pursuant to 28 U.S.C. §1406(a).

    B. If D's motion is granted, the district court in Colorado will apply law of Oregon regarding damages.

    C. The forum selection clause is unconstitutional unless D had "minimum contacts" with Oregon.

    D. None of the above.

Subject Matter Jurisdiction—Questions

32. Penny claims that agents of the Bucolic Valley Police Department violated her federal constitutional rights when they seized her computer as part of a search for illegal music downloads. Assume that Penny's allegations state a colorable claim under the Fourteenth Amendment. She has filed suit against the officers under 42 U.S.C. §1983 in a U.S. district court, seeking monetary and injunctive relief. Which of the following statements is correct?

    A. Neither the constitutional nor the statutory standards for "arising under" is satisfied by Penny's claim.

    B. While the constitutional "arising under" standard is satisfied by Penny's claim, the statutory "arising under" standard is not.

    C. While the statutory "arising under" standards is satisfied by Penny's claim, the constitutional "arising under" standard is not.

    D. Both the constitutional and the statutory standards for "arising under" are satisfied.

33. Acme brought an action against the Steamroller's Union ("Union") in an appropriate U.S. district court, claiming $75,000 in damages as a consequence of Union's alleged harassment of nonunion workers in violation of the National Labor Relations Act and applicable state law. Acme is an Indiana corporation, and the Union, an unincorporated association with its principal place of business in Washington, D.C., has members domiciled throughout the United States. The Union has filed a motion to dismiss for lack of subject matter jurisdiction. How should the district court rule on that motion?

    A. The district court should grant the motion if any members of the Union are domiciled in Indiana.

    B. The district court should grant the motion since Acme has not claimed monetary damages in excess of $75,000.

    C. The district court should deny the motion but only if Acme would be entitled to attorneys' fees under the National Labor Relations Act.

    D. The district court should deny the motion.

34. Polutesalot has filed a breach of contract action against Discharge in a U.S. district court, alleging that Discharge failed to transfer to it certain "emission allowances" issued to Discharge by the federal Environmental Protection Agency (EPA) as part of the Acid Rain Program. The allowances are extremely valuable because they permit

their owner to emit air pollutants that would otherwise exceed federally imposed limits. According to Polutesalot, it agreed to buy electrical power from Discharge's generating plant, in exchange for which Polutesalot agreed to pay a proportionate share of the plant's operating and maintenance expenses. Polutesalot complaint alleges that since it was paying a share of the plant expenses, it was entitled under the Clean Air Act to a proportionate share of the emission allowance that the EPA had issued to Discharge for that plant. Polutesalot further alleged that the failure to convey these emission allowances was a breach of the underlying contract. Discharge asserts that neither the Clean Air Act nor the contract requires it do so. The Clean Air Act does not provide an express private right of action for assertions such as that made by Polutesalot. What is Polutesalot's strongest argument that its breach of contract claim arises under federal law within the meaning of §1331?

A. The claim is created by federal law and does not fall within any exceptions to the creation test.

B. Proof of Polutesalot's state-based claim will require a fact-specific resolution of a substantial and contested federal issue.

C. The Clean Air Act creates the emission allowances and thereby satisfies the creation test.

D. Its claim includes an actual federal ingredient, thus easily satisfying Article III.

35. Pablo, a citizen of State X, owns the patent for the software program "Joinder Template 2.0." The program is designed to resolve joinder problems under the federal rules. Joinder Template 2.0 is marketed by Distributor, Inc., a State X corporation under a contract with Pablo that requires Distributor to make the "best effort" to promote sales of the product. Pablo believes that Distributor failed to satisfy its best-effort contractual obligation. Therefore, Pablo has sued Distributor in a U.S. district court, claiming that Distributor's breach of contract has diminished the value the patent. Which of the following statements is correct?

A. Since the claim involves a federal patent, the federal district court has exclusive jurisdiction over Pablo's claim.

B. Since the claim involves a federal patent, the validity of which is dependent of federal standards, the claim satisfies the creation test and thus satisfies statutory arising under standards.

C. Since the claim is neither created by federal law nor includes an essential federal ingredient, it does not fall within federal question jurisdiction of a federal district court.

D. Since the claim satisfies the essential federal ingredient test, the case arises under federal law for purposes of both Article III and statutory jurisdiction.

36. **Paula, a citizen of State X, sells fans and heaters that feature a spiral grill. Danny, also a citizen of State X, manufactures patented fans and heaters that feature similar grills. Danny has accused Paula of infringing Danny's patent. In response, Paula filed an action in a U.S. district court seeking declaratory relief to the effect that her fans do not infringe Danny's patent. Danny filed an answer, along with a counterclaim alleging that Paula's fans do in fact infringe his patent—a federally created claim. Which of the following statements is correct?**

A. Since federal law creates Danny's counterclaim, the standards of statutory arising under jurisdiction have been satisfied.

B. Since federal law creates Danny's counterclaim and since the counterclaim is one over which federal courts have exclusive jurisdiction, the standards of statutory arising under jurisdiction have been satisfied.

C. Paula's suit for declaratory relief arises under federal law for purposes statutory arising under standards.

D. Under the given facts, statutory arising under jurisdiction has not been satisfied.

37. **Pazzo, a citizen of State X, owns and operates public telephones in that state. When someone uses one of Pazzo's phones to make an "800" call, there is no need to deposit coins. As a result, Pazzo receives no direct compensation for such calls. However, the exchange carrier that provides the "800" service does benefit financially from such calls. State X law requires that such exchange carriers compensate the operators of public telephones at a rate of $0.50 per "800" call. On the other hand, regulations of the Federal Communications Commission (FCC) require compensation for such usage at $0.25 per call. Ditzo, a citizen of State X, is an exchange carrier operating in that state. Four thousand "800" calls have been made through Ditzo's exchange on Pazzo's phones. Pazzo, therefore, claims that Ditzo owes him $2000 under State X law ($.50 x 4,000 = $2,000). Ditzo**

contends, however, that State X law is preempted by the federal regulation and that she owes Pazzo only $1,000 ($.25 x 4,000 = $1,000). Ditzo has paid Pazzo the latter amount. Pazzo sued Ditzo in a state court in State X seeking to recover the additional $1000 it claims under State X law. Ditzo defended by arguing that the higher rate of compensation under State X law was preempted by the FCC regulation. The state trial court rejected this federal defense, and the highest court of the state affirmed. Ditzo now seeks review in the United State Supreme Court. May the Supreme Court grant Ditzo's petition for review?

A. Yes, the jurisdiction of the Supreme Court is derivative of the jurisdiction of the state courts.

B. No, because neither 28 U.S.C. §1331 nor 28 U.S.C. §1332 would have been satisfied in this case.

C. Yes, because the scope of the Supreme Court's appellate jurisdiction is broad enough to encompass this case.

D. No, because the federal issue in this case arose only as a defense and not as a part of the plaintiff's claim.

38. Peter, a citizen of State X, has filed a state-law claim in a U.S. district court against Dan, Daryl and Duncan. Dan and Daryl are citizens of State Y, but Duncan is a citizen of State Z. Assume that the amount-in-controversy requirement is satisfied as to each defendant. Which of the following statements is correct with respect to subject matter jurisdiction under 28 U.S.C. §1332(a)(1)?

A. The complete diversity standard is not satisfied since Dan and Daryl are citizens of the same state.

B. The complete diversity standard is satisfied.

C. Although the Article III standard of minimal diversity is satisfied, the statutory standard of complete diversity is not.

D. Unless the state law claim includes an essential federal ingredient, the standards of subject matter jurisdiction have not been satisfied.

39. Same facts as above except that Duncan is a citizen of the United States, domiciled in Florence, Italy. Which of the following statements is correct with respect to subject matter jurisdiction under 28 U.S.C. §1332(a)(1)?

A. Jurisdiction is satisfied since Peter is not domiciled abroad.

B. The statutory standards of diversity are satisfied since Duncan will be treated as an alien for purposes of diversity.

C. For purposes of diversity, the domicile of a defendant who is a United States citizen living abroad is presumptively diverse from that of the plaintiff.

D. The standards of 28 U.S.C. §1332(a)(1) have not been satisfied.

40. **Paula was injured in a collision between her car and a truck driven by an employee of Delivery, Inc. The accident occurred in Florida, near Paula's home in Miami. Delivery is incorporated in Delaware with corporate headquarters located in New York, but the vast majority of Delivery's operational activities take place in Florida. Paula sued Delivery in a U.S. district court located in Florida. The suit alleged that she suffered personal injuries in excess of $75,000. Delivery moved to dismiss the case for lack of subject matter jurisdiction. How should the district court rule on Delivery's motion?**

   A. The district court should grant the motion since a resident of the forum state cannot invoke a federal court's diversity jurisdiction.

   B. The district court should grant the motion since Delivery's principal place of business is Florida.

   C. The district court should deny the motion since the accident took place in Florida and Delivery is amenable to suit there.

   D. The district court should deny the motion since the parties are diverse and the amount in controversy is satisfied.

41. **Same facts as in the previous question, except that prior to filing her lawsuit, Paula married and moved to Delaware to live with her spouse in their new home. How then should the district court rule on Delivery's motion?**

   A. The district court should deny the motion since Paula's citizenship must be measured as of the date of the accident.

   B. The district court should grant the motion since Paula's citizenship must be measured as of the date of the filing.

   C. The district court has discretion to either dismiss or retain jurisdiction.

   D. The district court should deny the motion since Paula is diverse from Delivery's principal place of business, whether that place is New York or Florida.

42. Pierrot, a citizen of France, and Pierrette, a citizen of State X, were injured while passengers in a taxicab owned by Deluxe Taxi, a State Y corporation. At the time of the accident, Duha was driving the cab. Duha is a citizen of Algeria with permanent legal resident status in the United States. He is employed by Deluxe and lives in State X. Pierrot and Pierrette have sued Deluxe and Duha in a U.S. district court located in State X on a theory of negligence and vicarious liability. Assume that the amount-in-controversy requirement is satisfied and that the district court has personal jurisdiction over both defendants. Deluxe and Duha have filed a Rule 12(b)(1) motion to dismiss for lack of subject matter jurisdiction. How should the district court rule?

   A. The district court should grant the motion since Duha resides in State X.

   B. The district court should deny the motion since there are citizens of different states on each side of the controversy.

   C. The district court should deny the motion since the standards of complete diversity have been satisfied.

   D. The district court should grant the motion since there are aliens on both sides of the controversy.

43. Pearl, a citizen of State X, was injured when the balcony of her apartment collapsed. Dilapidated, Inc., a Delaware corporation headquartered in State X, owns the apartment building. Dilapidated owns and manages apartment units in several states, but 85 percent of its properties and rentals are located in State Y. Pearl has sued Dilapidated in a U.S. district court in State X, invoking that court's diversity jurisdiction. Assume the amount in controversy is satisfied. Which of the following statements is correct?

   A. Subject matter jurisdiction is lacking since Pearl and Dilapidated are both citizens of State X.

   B. Subject matter jurisdiction is satisfied since, under the place of operations test, D's principal place of business is State Y.

   C. Subject matter jurisdiction is satisfied since Dilapidated is a citizen of Delaware and since the Supreme Court in *Hertz v. Friend* eliminated the principal place of business test.

   D. Subject matter jurisdiction is lacking because Dilapidated will be treated a citizen of every state in which it does substantial business, including State X.

44. Same facts as the previous question, except that Dilapidated is a partnership with the bulk of its partners domiciled in State Y (22 partners), which is also the location of the partnership's headquarters, and with one partner domiciled in each of State X and State Z. Which of the following statements is correct?

    A. Subject matter jurisdiction may be exercised since the standards of minimal diversity are satisfied.

    B. Subject matter jurisdiction is lacking since Pearl and Dilapidated are not diverse.

    C. Subject matter jurisdiction is satisfied since State Y will be treated as the Dilapidated's principal place of business.

    D. Subject matter jurisdiction is lacking since a partnership with partners living in multiple states cannot be sued in diversity.

45. Padma, a citizen of State X, has sued Dagmar, a citizen of State Y, in a U.S. district court under a federal civil rights act (FCRA) that expressly creates a cause of action for private parties injured under the terms of the act. FCRA also provides that a prevailing plaintiff in a suit filed under the act is entitled to "reasonable attorneys' fees." Padma claims actual damages of $55,000 and attorneys' fees of $20,000. Assume that Padma's claims are not frivolous and that the amounts claimed by her are objectively reasonable. Dagmar has filed a Rule 12(b)(1) motion to dismiss for lack of subject matter jurisdiction. Which of the following statements is correct?

    A. Dagmar's motion should be granted since the amount in controversy does not exceed $75,000, exclusive of interest and costs.

    B. Dagmar's motion should be granted because P's allegations are insufficient to establish subject matter jurisdiction.

    C. Dagmar's motion should be granted if she can establish to a legal certainty that the true amount in controversy was less than the required minimum at the time of filing.

    D. Dagmar's motion should be denied.

46. Petal, a citizen of State X, and Daisy, a citizen of State Y, were roommates at a college in State Z. During their four years together, Petal loaned Daisy $10,000 that was never repaid. In their sophomore year, Daisy caused $25,000 in damages to Petal's car after borrowing it for a weekend. In their junior year, Daisy destroyed Petal's $5,000 computer while performing an interpretive dance titled, "Five Ideas about Jurisdiction." By the time the two graduated and parted

company, Daisy also owed Petal $40,000 for damages to Petal's high-fashion polythene wardrobe. Petal has sued Daisy in a U.S. district court asserting claims to recover for the unpaid loan, the damage to her car, the destroyed computer, and the wardrobe damages. Daisy first filed an answer denying each of Petal's claims. Thirty days later, Daisy filed a Rule 12(b)(1) motion to dismiss for lack of subject matter jurisdiction. Assume that all of Petal's claims are plausible and that the amounts claimed are alleged in good faith. How should the district court rule on Daisy's motion?

A. The district court should deny the motion since both diversity and the amount in controversy are satisfied.

B. The district should grant the motion since Petal may not aggregate her unrelated claims against Daisy.

C. The district court should deny the motion since Daisy waived her challenge to subject matter jurisdiction by making a general appearance.

D. The district should grant the motion since Petal's claims against Daisy do not arise out of a single right, title or privilege.

47. Diner, Inc., a State Z corporation, operates a highly popular restaurant—Sandy Clams—near the beach in State X. Sandy Clams recently expanded its outdoor eating area, adding a dozen new spotlights to illuminate the area at night. Eight nearby property owners have sued Diner in a State X court, alleging that the restaurant failed to comply with a local zoning ordinance. Plaintiffs seek to enjoin defendant from using the new lights until the expansion project is submitted to and approved by the zoning board. Once such an application is submitted, it will take the board at least 60 days to review the restaurant expansion. Plaintiffs are all citizens of State X. Each owner claims that the use of the new spotlights has reduced the value of his or her property in an amount ranging from $10,000 to $50,000, for a collective reduction in property value of $175,000. Without use of the new spotlights, Diner reasonably estimates it will lose an average of $1,500 per day. Diner has removed the case to a U.S. district court, based on diversity of citizenship. Which of the following statements is correct?

A. Under the plaintiff-viewpoint rule, the amount in controversy is satisfied.

B. Under the party-with-the-most-to-gain-or-lose rule, the amount in controversy is satisfied.

C. Under the party-invoking-jurisdiction rule, the amount in controversy is not satisfied.

D. None of the above.

48. Pamela brought suit in a Minnesota state court against her employer, Dairy Made, Inc., claiming that the company failed to pay her overtime in violation of the federal Fair Labor Standards Act (FLSA), and that it breached an implied contract of employment by firing her. She does not allege any relationship between her overtime claim and her contract claim. Dairy Made is a Delaware corporation with its principal place of business in Bemidji, Minnesota. Pamela is a citizen of South Dakota. She seeks $60,000 in damages. Within thirty days of receiving service of process, Dairy Made filed a notice of removal in the proper U.S. district court. Which of the following statements is correct?

A. Dairy Made's attempted removal was untimely.

B. Removal would satisfy the standards of §§1441(a) & (b).

C. Removal would satisfy the standards of §1441(c).

D. All of the above answers are correct.

49. Same facts as the previous question. Assume for purposes of this question only that the case was properly removed. Which of the following statements is correct?

A. The federal district court will retain jurisdiction over the FLSA claim but must dismiss the breach of contract claim.

B. The federal district court has discretion to retain jurisdiction over the entire case.

C. The federal district court will retain jurisdiction over the FLSA claim but must remand the breach of contract claim.

D. The federal district court must remand the entire case since the standards of §1367(a) have not been satisfied.

50. P, a citizen of Idaho, brought a multimillion-dollar diversity action for wrongful death in the proper U.S. district court against his wife's employer, D Construction Company, a Washington corporation. He alleged that D negligently allowed scaffolding to collapse while his wife was walking beneath it. D impleaded T, the manufacturer of the scaffolding, alleging that D would have a right to indemnity from T as a consequence of the latter's negligent manufacture of the equipment. T is an Idaho corporation. The district court granted P leave to file an amended complaint alleging negligent manufacture

against T. Thereafter, T moved to dismiss P's claim against it for lack of subject matter jurisdiction. Which of the following statements is correct?

A. The motion should be denied because the federal rules specifically allow a plaintiff to file claim a third-party defendant.

B. The motion should be granted because the exercise of jurisdiction over the claim would be inconsistent with the jurisdictional requirements of §1332.

C. The motion should be granted in accord with the district court's discretion to decline the exercise of supplemental jurisdiction.

D. The motion should be denied because the claim arises out of the same transaction as P's claim against D.

51. **Acme is a Georgia corporation with its headquarters in Alabama. Polly was employed at the Alabama headquarters for 20 years but was fired in 2010. After being fired, she relocated to Georgia where she landed a good position as a secretary at a law firm in Atlanta. On the advice of her boss, Polly filed a wrongful termination action against Acme in a Georgia state court, asserting a claim under the Wrongful Termination Act, a recently enacted federal statute that creates a cause of action for wrongful termination of "long-term" employees, and under a similarly worded Georgia statute. See seeks $80,000 in damages. After Acme filed a timely petition to remove the case to the proper U.S. district court, Polly filed a motion to remand. How should the district court rule on Polly's motion?**

A. The district court should grant Polly's motion to remand because Acme is a citizen of the forum state.

B. The district court should deny Polly's motion to remand because the case could have been filed in federal court as an original matter.

C. The district court should grant Polly's motion to remand because the standards of diversity are not satisfied.

D. The district court should deny Polly's motion to remand because state courts cannot entertain federal claims.

52. **Bee and Bop are huge Justin Bleeper fans. They went to his 3-D performance at the local cinema and were really, really having fun until someone sitting up front just freaked and caused like a riot and everything went crazy. Bee and Bop were both injured as the frenzied crowd pressed for the doors. Bee's big toe was crushed, and she**

has had to undergo extensive reconstructive surgery. Her medical bills were well over $100,000. Bop was a little luckier. Her little toe was crushed, and the reconstructive surgery cost only $50,000. Bee and Bop, both of whom are true Californians, have joined together as plaintiffs in a suit against Cineplex Inc., a New York corporation and the owner and operator of the theater. The suit, which charges Cineplex with various acts of negligence, was filed in a federal district court. Bee seeks over $100,000 in damages. Bop seeks $50,000. Which of the following statements is correct?

A. The federal district court may exercise diversity jurisdiction over Bop's claim.

B. The federal district court may not exercise supplemental jurisdiction over Bop's claim since Bop is attempting to evade the jurisdictional requirements of §1332.

C. The federal district court may exercise supplemental jurisdiction over Bop's claim.

D. The federal district court may not exercise supplemental jurisdiction over Bop's claim since Bop is a plaintiff joined under FRCP 20 whose claim is inconsistent with the jurisdictional requirements of §1332.

53. Same facts as the previous question, except that Bee and Bop sued both Cineplex and Iolana, the girl they believe to have started the riot. At the time of the incident, Iolana, who is from Hawaii, was visiting her grandmother, who lives near the Cineplex. Bee and Bop claim that Cineplex and Iolana are jointly and severally responsible for the injuries suffered by each of them. Which of the following statements is correct?

A. The presence of Iolana contaminates the independent basis of jurisdiction over Bee's claim.

B. The federal rules do not allow Bee and Bop to join Cineplex and Iolana as defendants since there is no allegation of conspiracy.

C. The federal district court may exercise supplemental jurisdiction over Bop's claims against Cineplex and Alula.

D. Section 1367(b) precludes the exercise of supplemental jurisdiction over Bop's claims against Cineplex and Alula.

54. North America Insurance Company ("NAIC"), an Illinois corporation with its principal place of business in New York, has been sued by two of its policyholders in a class action filed in a U.S. district court in Illinois. The complaint alleged that NAIC overcharged

them and 5,000 other similarly situated policyholders for automobile insurance. The class seeks a refund of the overcharges, which equal slightly over $5 million in the aggregate. The plaintiffs in the action are Adams ("A"), a citizen of Illinois, and Baron ("B"), a student domiciled in New York but attending law school in California. The amounts of the overcharges claimed by the named plaintiffs are $5,000 for A and $8,000 for B. The members of the class are domiciled in roughly equal proportions in ten states, including New York and Illinois. Which of the following statements is correct?

A. The federal court lacks subject matter jurisdiction over the action since the complete diversity requirement is not met.

B. The federal court lacks subject matter jurisdiction over the action because the claims of the named representatives do not satisfy the amount in controversy requirement.

C. The federal court has subject matter jurisdiction since the aggregate claims of the class meet the amount in controversy requirement and since minimal diversity is satisfied.

D. Both A and B.

55. While dining at Dandy Sandwich in State X, Perdido, a citizen of State Y, slipped on a pickle and injured his back. He brought an action against Dagwood, the owner of Dandy Sandwich in a State X state court of general jurisdiction, seeking damages in "an amount to be proven at trial." State X law does not permit a plaintiff in a personal injury action to allege a specific amount in controversy. Dagwood lives with his family in nearby State Z. Dagwood would like to remove the case to the appropriate U.S. district court. Which of the following statements is correct?

A. Dagwood may not remove the action since as the owner of Dandy Sandwich he will be deemed a citizen of the forum state for purposes of removal.

B. Dagwood may remove the action, but only if he establishes by a preponderance of the evidence that the amount controversy exceeds $75,000.

C. Dagwood may not remove the action because the amount in controversy must be satisfied on the face of the plaintiff's complaint.

D. Dagwood may remove the case unless Perdido can establish to a legal certainty that the amount in controversy is not met.

56. **Paul, a citizen of Ohio, was involved in a three-car auto collision with Peter and Mary. Paul sued Peter and Mary in the only U.S. district court in Maine. The defendants are citizens of Maine. Paul's action against each defendant was for personal injuries in the amount of $70,000 and property damage in the amount of $9,000. Which of the following statements is correct?**

   A. Paul will be permitted to assert an unrelated $1,000 breach of contract action against Mary.

   B. Peter will be permitted to assert an unrelated $80,000 breach of contract action against Mary.

   C. Paul's action should be dismissed because no single claim satisfies the "amount in controversy" requirement.

   D. None of the above.

57. **Ten college students in State X filed a class action in U.S. district court. The complaint requested that five specifically named state officials, the defendants, be enjoined from enforcing the state's flag desecration statute, which was alleged to be unconstitutional under the First Amendment to the U.S. Constitution. The class that the plaintiffs sought to represent was all college students in State X. The defendants filed a motion to dismiss for lack of subject matter jurisdiction. Assuming the students have standing to assert their claim, the defendants' motion to dismiss should be:**

   A. Denied, because the claim asserted satisfies the standards of statutory arising under jurisdiction.

   B. Denied, but only if the standards of 28 U.S.C. §1332 have been satisfied.

   C. Granted, because no specific assertion has been made that each plaintiff has suffered damages in excess of $75,000.

   D. Granted, if any member of the plaintiff class and any defendant are citizens of the same state.

58. **P, who had been employed by D, was fired when D learned that P, who was unmarried, was living with Q. P and Q sued D in the appropriate U.S. district court. P sought $58,000 for breach of their employment contract, $10,000 for violation of a federal civil rights statute, and $9,000 for damages that D had caused to P's car after P loaned it to D earlier that year. Q claimed $12,000 in damages as a result of P's wrongful termination since she is now obliged to pay their entire apartment rental by herself. Prior to his discharge, P contributed**

one-half of the rental amount. P and Q are both citizens of State X. D is a citizen of State Y. Which of the following statements is correct?

A. The FRCP do not allow all the claims of P and Q to be joined together in a single action.

B. A U.S. district court would have subject matter jurisdiction over Q's claim.

C. If P failed to assert the claim for damages to his car in this action, it would be barred.

D. None of the above.

59. P brings an action against D, E, and F, asserting (1) infringement of copyright and (2) breach of contract. Copyright actions are exclusively within the subject matter jurisdiction of federal courts. All of the claims arose from the defendants having produced a television show based upon a script that P had written for them. P seeks to recover $80,000 from each of the defendants. All of the parties are citizens of California. Which of the following statements is correct?

A. If this action is filed in a California state court, the defendants could have it removed to federal court.

B. If this action is filed in federal court, dismissal for lack of subject matter jurisdiction would be required.

C. If this case goes to trial in a state court, and judgment is entered against P, P will have waived any lack of subject matter jurisdiction by failing to assert it before or during trial.

D. None of the above.

60. Pluto, a citizen of Arizona, was involved in an auto accident with Daffy, a citizen of New Mexico. The accident occurred in Utah. Pursuant to the applicable Utah long-arm statute, Pluto sued Daffy in a Utah state court of general jurisdiction for $80,000. Pluto also named State Barn, Inc., as a defendant. State Barn is D's insurer. Pursuant to Utah law, this type of direct action against an insurer is permissible. State Barn is incorporated in Delaware and has its principal place of business in Utah. Daffy removed the case to the U.S. district court for the State of Utah. Pluto has now filed a timely motion to remand. What should the district court do?

A. Deny the motion because complete diversity is satisfied.

B. Grant the motion because the State Barn did not join in the petition for removal.

C. Grant the motion because State Barn's principal place of business is in Utah.

D. Both (B) and (C) are correct but (A) is not.

61. Denny, a citizen of Texas, leased an apartment from Polly, a citizen of California, under a one-year rental agreement at $500 per month. The rental agreement states that Denny may not sublet the premises to any person of Asian ancestry. With six months remaining on the lease, Denny sublet the apartment to an individual of Chinese ancestry. Polly sued Denny in a U.S. district court for breach of contract, seeking to evict Denny and recover the remaining six months' rent. The complaint states that Denny violated the terms of the rental agreement and asserts that the clause concerning subletting does not violate the U.S. Constitution. Denny has filed an answer in which he asserts that the terms of the rental agreement violate the Fourteenth Amendment to the U.S. Constitution. He has also filed a motion to dismiss for lack of subject matter jurisdiction. How should the district court rule on Denny's motion?

A. Grant the motion since Polly's claim satisfies neither §1331 nor §1332.

B. Deny the motion since Denny's answer operates as a waiver of his subject matter jurisdiction defense.

C. Deny the motion since the controversy between Polly and Denny is ultimately premised on a question of federal constitutional law.

D. Deny the motion since Denny's answers frames a question arising under the U.S. Constitution.

Erie and Related Doctrines—Questions

62. Penny was struck by David's car while she was somewhat carelessly jaywalking across a busy street. David was driving 10 mph over the speed limit at the time of the accident. The accident occurred in State X. Penny has filed a diversity suit against David in a U.S. district court sitting in State X. Although the overwhelming trend in most states is toward adoption of a comparative negligence standard, State X follows the rules of contributory negligence as a matter of state common law. The legislature is actively considering adopting a comparative negligence standard; the State X Supreme Court, however, has not had occasion to address this issue since 1958, when it last affirmed contributory negligence as the state law standard. Penny has filed a motion asking the district court to instruct the jury on a comparative negligence standard. Which of the following is correct?

A. The district court must adhere to the most most recent decision of the State X Supreme Court on this issue.

B. The district court must adhere to the legislative intent implicit in the pending legislation.

C. The district court must determine what the State X Supreme Court would hold if the question were presented to it today.

D. The district court should follow the arc of the law adopted by a majority of the states.

63. Pablo, a citizen of State X, filed a breach of contract claim in a State X court against Dallas, a citizen of State Y. Under State X law Pablo is entitled to a trial within six months since his claim is for less than $100,000. Dallas successfully and properly removed the case to the appropriate U.S. district court. Pablo now seeks a remand on the grounds that removal is improper since, due to a backlog of cases, trial in the federal court will not be held for at least 18 months from the date of removal. Assuming the case was otherwise properly removed, how should the district court rule on Pablo's motion to remand?

A. Grant the motion since Pablo has a state-created right to a speedy trial that will be violated by 18-month delay in federal court.

B. Grant the motion since federal law is subsidiary to state law in diversity cases.

C. Deny the motion but only if the district court can schedule the trial within six months of the removal date.

D. Deny the motion since the removal statute represents a legitimate exercise of the congressional power to create procedure for federal courts.

64. Patrice filed a proper diversity action against Dr. Doctor in a U.S. district court sitting in State X. Patrice's complaint, which satisfies the pleading standards of FRCP 8(a)(2), alleges that the "negligent medical treatment" he received while under Doctor's care caused permanent damage to Patrice's heart. State X law requires a plaintiff in a medical malpractice case to allege all such claims "with particularity." [*State procedural*] Accordingly, Doctor has filed a motion to dismiss Patrice's complaint, correctly claiming that it fails to satisfy this state-law standard. The goal of the State X law is to cut down on the number of frivolous malpractice claims. How should the district court rule on Doctor's motion?

   A. The district court should deny the motion since FRCP 8(a)(2) is a rule of practice that does not abridge, enlarge or modify a substantive right.

   B. The district court should grant the motion since a federal court sitting in diversity must apply pertinent state law.

   C. The district court should grant the motion since FRCP 8(a)(2) conflicts with a significant state policy, namely, the curtailment of frivolous malpractice claims.

   D. The district court should grant the motion since FRCP 8(a)(2), as applied, abridges the substantial right of Doctor to be subject to a malpractice suit only if a former patient can allege such a claim with particularity.

65. Under State A law, a worker injured on the job may sue her employer for negligence if and only if she first files a report with the State Industrial Commission (SIC). She must file the report within 60 days of the injury. A failure to do so precludes enforcement of the underlying right. The purpose of the report is to assist the state in record keeping. Once the report is filed, the employee has one year from the date of the injury to file lawsuit against her employer. Pandora was injured on the job on January 1, 2010, while in the employ of Delicious Food, Inc. ("Delicious"). Pandora did not file a SIC report. Instead, on June 1, 2010, she filed a diversity action against Delicious in a U.S. district court sitting in State A, claiming damages for her on-the-job injury. Delicious has filed a motion to dismiss, citing Jane's failure to file a SIC report. What should the district court do?

   A. The district court should deny the motion since Pandora's lawsuit was filed within the federal one-year statute of limitations.

   B. The district court should deny the motion since Pandora's lawsuit was filed within the State A one-year statute of limitations.

    C. The district court should grant the motion unless Pandora immediately files a report with the SIC.

    D. The district court must grant the motion since to do otherwise would be to enforce a state-created right that is no longer enforceable in the courts of the state.

66. Under State X law, a state trial court may overturn a civil jury verdict if the judge concludes that the jury's factual findings were "against the weight of the evidence." Federal judges, on the other hand, may overturn a jury verdict only if no reasonable juror could have arrived at the contested verdict, a standard that is significantly more deferential toward the jury's verdict and that is required by the Seventh Amendment. In a diversity case filed in a U.S. district court sitting in State X, may the federal judge follow the state rule?

    A. Yes, since application of the federal rule would be outcome-determinative at the forum shopping stage.

    B. Yes, since application of the federal rule would abridge, enlarge, or modify a state substantive right.

    C. No, since the Seventh Amendment trumps all state law to the contrary regardless of whether that law is deemed substantive or procedural.

    D. No, since application of the federal rule would not violate the refined outcome determinative test.

67. Pakuna sued Dabria in a U.S. district court sitting in State Y, seeking monetary damages for a state-law breach of contract claim. The district court dismissed the suit based on Pakuna's failure to file the suit within the applicable State Y statute of limitations. The dismissal was designated by the court as being "with prejudice and on the merits." Pakuna then refiled the case in a State X state court, relying on that state's longer statute of limitations. Dabria has filed a motion to dismiss the State X proceeding based on claim preclusion. How should the state court rule on Dabria's motion?

    A. The court should grant the motion since FRCP 41(b) would treat the U.S. district court's dismissal as "on the merits" for purposes of claim preclusion.

    B. The court should grant the motion since the uniform federal standard of claim preclusion has been satisfied.

    C. The court should grant the motion, but only if State Y law would treat a statute of limitations dismissal as having full preclusive effect.

D. The court should deny the motion since the uniform federal standard of claim preclusion has not been satisfied.

68. Mark was seriously injured when he swallowed a large marble that was in a jar of olives he had purchased from Wholesome Foods, Inc. ("WF"). This particular jar had been supplied to WF by the Really Good Olive Company ("RGOC"). Mark sued WF in a U.S. district court claiming negligence and products liability. The parties are diverse from one another and the amount in controversy is satisfied. WF would like to implead the RGOC pursuant FRCP 14(a) on a theory of indemnity. State law, however, prohibits indemnity actions from being filed by a defendant until such time as the defendant's primary liability to the plaintiff is established pursuant to a final judgment. Which of the following statements is correct?

A. FRCP 14(a) may be applied despite the state law to the contrary.

B. FRCP 14(a) is not sufficiently broad to control the issue presented.

C. FRCP 14(a) is sufficiently broad to control the issue presented, but to apply it here would impermissibly enlarge WF's right to sue in violation of the Rules Enabling Act.

D. FRCP 14(a) modifies WF's indemnity claim and therefore cannot be applied under these circumstances.

69. Petunia filed a medical malpractice case against Doctor in a U.S. district court sitting in State A, properly invoking the court's diversity jurisdiction. Doctor filed a motion to dismiss Petunia's claim for failure to comply with a State A "affidavit of merit" statute. That statute requires plaintiffs in medical malpractice cases to file an "expert report" as to each defendant physician no later than 180 days after the date on which the action is filed. In terms of content, the mandated expert report must verify that there exists a reasonable probability that the care, skill, or knowledge exercised or exhibited in the treatment that is the subject of the complaint fell outside acceptable professional standards. The expert report may not be used as evidence at trial. If a plaintiff fails to file a timely and satisfactory expert report, the case must be dismissed with prejudice. Assume that Petunia failed to comply with the affidavit-of-merit statute. In response to Doctor's motion to dismiss, Petunia argues that the State A requirement is in conflict with FRCP 26 which provides that "a party must disclose to the other parties the identity of any witness it may use at trial" as an expert witness. FRCP 26 further provides that a "party must make these disclosures at

the times and in the sequence that the court orders." (Assume there are no other relevant federal rules.) Which of the following statements is correct?

A. The defendant's motion should be granted since a district court must conform the federal rules to state procedural law in a diversity case.

B. The defendant's motion should be denied since FRCP 26 supplants State A's affidavit of merit statute.

C. The defendant's motion should be granted since FRCP 26 is not sufficiently broad to control the issue presented.

D. The defendant's motion should be denied since FRCP 26 is sufficiently broad to control the issue presented.

70. Under State A law, in a case involving the tort liability of a state agency brought by an individual who was employed by a contractor working for that agency, the question of whether the plaintiff was a "statutory" employee of the agency, and thus not entitled to file a tort claim against the agency, is decided by a judge. In a diversity case filed in a U.S. district court sitting in State A, this same question—whether the plaintiff was a statutory employee of the agency—would be decided by a jury as a matter of federal common law. Which of the following statements is correct?

A. The choice between the state rule and the federal rule would not be outcome determinative under the approach adopted in *Hanna v. Plumer*.

B. The choice between the state rule and the federal rule would be outcome determinative under the approach adopted in *Hanna v. Plumer*.

C. Whether the choice between the state rule and the federal rule is outcome determinative is a question of state law.

D. Regardless of whether the choice between the state rule and the federal rule is outcome determinative, the district court must apply the state rule.

71. Bill has filed a proper diversity action against Medical Inc. (MI) in a U.S. district court sitting in State X. He claims, in very general terms, that the "negligent medical treatment" he received while under MI's care in State X caused a significant worsening of his disease, including permanent damage to his heart. Assume that Bill's complaint satisfies the notice pleading standards of FRCP 8(a)(2). MI, relying on a State

X law that requires a plaintiff in a medical malpractice case to allege all such claims "with particularity," has filed a motion to dismiss, claiming that Bill's complaint fails to satisfy this state-law standard. The goal of the State X law is to cut down on the number of frivolous malpractice claims. What should the district court do?

A. The district court should deny MI's motion because FRCP 8(a)(2) is a rule of practice that does not abridge, enlarge, or modify a substantive right.

B. The district court should grant MI's motion because FRCP 8(a)(2) conflicts with a significant state policy, namely the curtailment of frivolous malpractice claims.

C. The district court should grant MI's motion because as applied, FRCP 8 abridges the substantial right of MI to receive a complaint that states the claims against it with particularity.

D. The district court should deny MI's motion because the formal federal rules were promulgated pursuant to a constitutional delegation of congressional power.

Pleadings and Discovery—Questions

72. Packer, a New York citizen, purchased a mountainside home in Lake Tahoe, Nevada, from Denton. Packer asked Denton if Denton was sure that the land on which the home is situated was geologically sound. Denton (aware that there was a major fault under the home) nevertheless responded to Packer's question in a positive manner. Two months after Packer occupied the house, it collapsed. Packer brought an action for fraud against Denton in the appropriate U.S. district court. The complaint alleged that "Denton fraudulently induced Plaintiff to enter into the purchase agreement for the house and land." Denton moved for a more definite statement under FRCP 12(e). Which of the following statements is correct?

   A. The motion should be granted since the FRCP requires that circumstances constituting fraud to be stated with particularity.

   B. The motion should be denied since the FRCP requires only that the pleader give a short, plain statement of the claim for relief.

   C. The motion should be denied if the complaint is adequate under Nevada law.

   D. None of the above.

73. Plaintiff brought a claim of discrimination in a U.S. district court against her former employer for being subjected to a sexually hostile work environment and for retaliatory termination. She has now filed a motion to compel responses to Request for Production No. 9, which asks defendant to produce "copies of personnel files, including supervisor files, disciplinary files, formal and informal files, of" 15 specified individuals employed by defendant. Defendant objected to this request on the grounds that it is not reasonably calculated to lead to the discovery of admissible evidence. Plaintiff asserted that the individuals listed either played important roles in the employment decisions affecting Plaintiff or participated in or witnessed the hostile work environment and/or retaliation that gave rise to this litigation. Should the court grant her motion?

   A. Yes. The discovery request is relevant to a claim or defense in the lawsuit and the information gathered would be admissible at trial.

   B. Yes. The discovery request is relevant to a claim or defense in the lawsuit and the information gathered would be reasonably calculated to lead to admissible evidence.

C. No. Although the request meets the standards of discovery relevance, it necessarily calls for information protected by the attorney client privilege.

D. No. Although the request meets the standards of discovery relevance, it calls for information protected by the work product doctrine.

74. Same facts as above. For purposes of this question, assume that the district court granted the motion to compel. Defendant now seeks a protective order to prevent the plaintiff from disclosing the information she discovers within the personnel files for any purpose other than that which is appropriate to the immediate litigation. In other words, under the order, Plaintiff would not be permitted to publish the discovered materials unless those materials have been properly introduced into a public record during the litigation process. May the district court grant this motion?

A. No. The order would violate Plaintiff's First Amendment right to communicate information she has lawfully received.

B. Yes. The district court has unfettered discretion to control the use of materials discovered pursuant to judicially supervised discovery.

C. No. The order would violate the public's right to have complete access to this information.

D. Yes. The district court may issue this order consistent with the First Amendment since the protection of the privacy interests of the employees is both substantial and unrelated to the suppression of free speech.

75. Param, a physician of Indian descent, lost his medical staff privileges at a hospital after an unfavorable peer review concluded that he had created a "life-threatening emergency" during a surgical procedure. Param sued the hospital in a U.S. district court claiming that its peer review process discriminated against Indian physicians, in violation of federal law. As part of discovery, he sought access to peer review records the hospital had compiled over the past 20 years. The hospital claimed that the records were privileged as "medical peer review materials" and sought a protective order to that effect. The hospital argued that such a privilege is necessary to promote the frank "in-house" evaluation of a doctor's performance. Most states, including the one in which this suit was filed, have adopted a medical peer review privilege in the context

of malpractice claims. Which of the follow most correctly describes what the district court should do?

A. If the state in which the federal court sits recognizes the privilege, the district court should grant the motion.

B. The district court should deny the motion since the asserted public good does not outweigh the strong presumption against the recognition of a new privilege.

C. The district court should grant the motion based on the presumption in favor of the recognition of an asserted privilege.

D. The district court should deny the motion since the recognition of a new privilege requires legislative action by Congress.

76. Peabody filed a sexual harassment and wrongful termination suit against his former employer, Dancer, Inc., the owner of the All Night Dance Club. The suit was filed in a U.S. district court. At the time of his termination Peabody was a bouncer at the club. After the termination, but before Peabody filed the immediate lawsuit, in-house counsel for Dance interviewed Peabody's coworker, Hi-Lo. The interview was undertaken to gather information regarding the termination and to prepare for any potential lawsuit. In his mandatory disclosures, Peabody had identified Hi-Lo as his principal witness. Dancer has refused to answer interrogatories asking it to reveal what Hi-Lo said to in-house counsel. In response, Peabody has filed a motion to compel. Should the district court grant the motion?

A. No. The attorney-client privilege applies to the communication between in-house counsel and Hi-Lo.

B. No. Since Hi-Lo is not a party to the lawsuit his communications with in-house counsel are not discoverable.

C. Yes. The material is discovery relevant and not privileged.

D. Yes. So long as the disclosures are relevant to a claim or defense in the lawsuit, they are discoverable since Hi-Lo was not the attorney's client at the time the interview took place.

77. In a personal injury lawsuit involving the collapse of temporary bleachers, the defendant propounded the following interrogatory: "Identify every person who has assisted you in the investigation of this accident, and summarize the information obtained from each person so identified." Which of the following statements is true?

A. The information sought is discoverable so long as the word "identify" has been given a specific definition.

B. The interrogatory may call for work product.

C. Although the interrogatory is compound, it will only count as a single interrogatory since the questions asked are separable.

D. Since the plaintiff has put the collapse of the bleachers at issue, the plaintiff has waived any objections to this interrogatory.

78. A commuter train operated by Metro collided with a car that was stalled on the tracks at a railroad crossing. Although no one was injured, the vehicle was completely destroyed. The owner of the car, Parker, sued both Metro and the train's engineer in a U.S. district court, claiming that his car was visible for at least a quarter of a mile before the collision and that the engineer should have been able to stop the train within that distance. Witnesses on the train claim that they did not feel the train brake until seconds before the crash. Parker claims that either the brakes were defective or that the engineer was negligent. Relying on FRCP 35, Parker has filed a motion to compel the engineer to undergo a neurological exam to determine if a neurological defect may have contributed to the accident. Attached to the motion is the deposition of the engineer in which the engineer states that he was paying attention at the time of the accident, that he saw the car "some distance off," and that he did not hit the braking system immediately because he first thought the car was still moving across the tracks.

A. The court should deny Parker's motion since she has failed to establish that the engineer's neurological condition is really and genuinely in controversy.

B. The court must grant Parker's motion since the examination is reasonably calculated to lead to admissible evidence.

C. The court may grant Parker's motion but only if doing so is consistent with state law.

D. The court must grant O's motion since the "in controversy" and "good cause" requirements would merge under such circumstances.

79. Paul was injured while operating a drill press manufactured by Delta Manufacturing Inc. Paul properly commenced an action against Delta in the appropriate U.S. district court. Prior to trial, Paul sought discovery of a report that had been made to Delta by Brown, a claims investigator hired by Delta's in-house counsel. Brown had inspected the machine and investigated the circumstances of the accident immediately thereafter. The report summarizes the facts gathered by Brown.

The machine was subsequently destroyed in a fire, and Brown has retired and moved, leaving no forwarding address. Which of the following statements is correct?

A. The report is absolutely discoverable since it satisfies the standards of discovery relevance.

B. Delta may refuse Paul's discovery request since the report is subject to the attorney-client privilege.

C. The report is discoverable, but only if Paul can show that there is a substantial need for the information and he is otherwise unable to obtain it without undue hardship.

D. Delta may refuse Paul's discovery request since the report qualifies as work product.

80. Same facts as the previous problem. In addition, suppose that Delta's in-house counsel annotated the only copy of the report, describing her views of the legal consequences of Brown's findings. If Delta refuses to turn over the report on this basis alone, what should the district court do if Paul files a motion to compel?

A. Deny the motion since the annotated report reveals the mental impressions, opinions and legal opinions of Delta's attorney.

B. Grant the motion, but allow Delta to provide a copy of the report that excludes in-house counsel's annotations.

C. Grant the motion since the annotations were voluntarily made and any redaction of them would reduce the probative value of the report.

D. Deny the motion since the report now constitutes opinion work product.

81. The purchaser of a 2010 Prestige mobile home brought suit against the manufacturer and distributor, alleging breach of contract and breach of express and implied warranties based on defects in the motor home's electrical system. The plaintiff submitted a discovery request for information relating to potential electrical-system defects in the 2001-09 models of the Prestige. Which of the following statements is correct?

A. The information sought is reasonably calculated to lead to the discovery of admissible evidence.

B. The information sought is not necessarily admissible at trial and is not, therefore, discoverable.

C. The information sought is not relevant to a claim or defense and is not, therefore, discoverable.

D. The information sought is not discoverable in the absence of a court order.

82. Phil was driving his car in San Diego, California, when he was involved in an accident with Dowd. Phil is domiciled in San Diego. Dowd is a citizen of Alabama. Phil filed and served a timely action against Dowd in the appropriate U.S. district court in California. The complaint contained a proper subject matter jurisdiction allegation. On the merits of Phil's claim, the complaint alleged only that there was a collision between the cars driven by Phil and Dowd and that Phil suffered personal injuries and property damage in the amount of $85,000. Dowd has filed a motion to dismiss for failure to state a claim upon which relief could be granted. How should the district court rule on that motion?

A. The district court should grant the motion without leave to amend.

B. The district court should deny the motion since the allegations of Phil's complaint are sufficient to state a claim on which relief can be granted.

C. The district court should grant the motion since Phil's complaint fails to identify the legal theory upon which his claim is predicated.

D. The district court should grant the motion with leave to amend.

83. Same facts as the previous question, except that Phil's complaint contained a proper subject matter jurisdiction allegation and asserted that (1) the collision was caused by Dowd's negligence in driving into the rear of Phil's car while Phil was lawfully stopped at a red light, or alternatively, (2) the collision was caused by Dowd's negligence in driving through a red light and into Phil while the latter was lawfully driving through an intersection. Dowd has filed a motion to dismiss for failure to state a cause of action upon which relief can be granted. How should the district court rule on that motion?

A. The district court should grant the motion on grounds of inconsistency.

B. The district court should grant the motion, since Phil has pleaded a legal conclusion (i.e., that Dowd was negligent in his conduct).

C. The district court should deny the motion, since alternative grounds for relief are permissible under the FRCP.

D. The district court should deny the motion but require Phil to strike one of the inconsistent claims.

84. Parker properly commenced a diversity action in the appropriate U.S. district court against Danielle. He claimed that he and Danielle had entered a valid contract, that Danielle had repudiated the agreement, and that as a consequence he sustained economic losses in the amount of $90,000. In her answer, Danielle denied the existence of a contractual agreement but asserted no affirmative defenses. At trial, she attempted to introduce evidence that Parker had made an anticipatory repudiation of the alleged agreement prior to the time that her performance was due. If this assertion were correct, the evidence would establish an affirmative defense to Parker's claim. Parker made a timely objection to Danielle's evidence. Which of the following statements most correctly describes the district court's authority under the circumstances?

A. The court must sustain the objection because the evidence falls outside the pleadings.

B. The court may permit Danielle to amend her answer to conform to the evidence.

C. The court must sustain the objection because amendments to pleadings cannot be made after trial has commenced.

D. The court must admit the evidence since it is relevant to Danielle's defense.

85. P sued D for trespass at her Los Angeles residence. The action was properly commenced in a U.S. district court. D defended by claiming that he was in New York at the time of the alleged incident. D intends to call Wanda as a witness to testify that she saw him in New York on the day in question. P believes Wanda is hopelessly nearsighted and could easily have mistaken someone else for D. To impeach Wanda's testimony, P sends Wanda a Notice to Appear for Medical Examination before a licensed ophthalmologist selected by P. Which of the following statements is correct?

A. Wanda must appear, but D is entitled to a copy of the ophthalmologist's findings.

B. Wanda must appear since her eyesight is in issue.

C. Wanda need not appear because she is not a party to the action.

D. Wanda need not appear because the judge must select the physician.

86. Don, while traveling to a nearby relative's house, was injured by a vehicle negligently operated by an Acme employee in the course of Acme business. After initiating an action against Acme (but prior to trial), Don sought to discover if Acme had insurance. Assuming this jurisdiction follows the FRCP, which of the following statements is correct regarding discovery of the insurance policy covering the Acme vehicle?

    A. If the insurance policy is not admissible at trial, the insurance policy is not discoverable.

    B. Insurance maintained by a party is never discoverable.

    C. An insured party must disclose an insurance policy if the insurer may be liable for all or part of a judgment entered against the insured.

    D. Insurance is discoverable only where it is relevant to the *prima facie* issues of the case.

87. P filed an action against D Corporation for material breach of contract and misrepresentation in the sale of a home located in a subdivision. An agent of D allegedly represented to P that the property was in excellent condition and ready for occupancy. In fact, the plumbing was defective, and there were termites in the basement. Prior to filing the action, P's attorney consulted with an economist concerning P's damages. Which of the following statements is correct?

    A. The economist's opinion is discoverable.

    B. The opinion of the economist is not discoverable absent exceptional circumstances.

    C. The opinion of an expert is discoverable only if it is solicited or obtained prior to the commencement of litigation.

    D. Discovery of an expert's opinion is privileged.

88. P, seeking damages from D Inc., for patent infringement, sued D in an appropriate U.S. district court. P's complaint alleged that D's agents knowingly copied P's patented electric generator and purposely made meaningless cosmetic changes to cover up the infringement. D answered by denying all of P's allegations. D's research and development department keeps detailed records as well as models of all of its research projects. Must D disclose the existence of these items as part of its initial disclosure obligations?

    A. No, the documents and models are privileged.

    B. No, unless requested by an opponent, a party need not make such disclosures.

    C. Yes, D is obligated to disclose the existence of these items to the extent that they may be used in support of a defense.

    D. Yes, a party must disclose the existence of documents and tangible things relevant to the disputed facts.

89. Same facts as the previous question. In addition, D retained five experts in anticipation of litigation. D procured reports from each expert but does not plan to call the experts at trial. Can P obtain the identities and opinions of the experts?

    A. Yes, a party must disclose the identity and opinions of an expert it retains in anticipation of litigation.

    B. Yes, a party, through interrogatories, may discover the opinions of any expert the opposing party retains in anticipation of litigation.

    C. No, since the opinions are not admissible at trial they are not discoverable.

    D. No, unless the moving party can show exceptional circumstances that warrant discovery of the expert's opinions.

90. Same facts as the previous two questions. In addition, 20 days before trial, D learned that a retired employee developed the first sketches of D's new generator—the one at issue in the litigation. Must D divulge this information to P?

    A. Yes, since a party has a duty to supplement its initial mandatory disclosures.

    B. No, since the adverse party could find this person through its own discovery devices.

    C. No, unless D intends to use the employee as a witness.

    D. No, since a party is not obligated to supplement its initial mandatory disclosures.

Joinder of Claims and Parties—Questions

91. Harvey, a citizen of Missouri, had a $7,000 savings account with Friendly Bank, a Missouri corporation. Harvey died and in his will he left the savings account to his nephew Sam, a citizen of Texas. On the same day that Sam showed up to claim the money, Jay appeared at the bank and presented a notarized agreement signed by Harvey assigning the entire bank account to Jay. Jay is a citizen of New York. Friendly Bank filed a statutory interpleader action in the U.S. district court for the judicial district of Missouri. Which of the following statements is correct?

   A. This is an improper interpleader since neither Sam nor Jay has instituted an action against Friendly Bank.

   B. The case must be dismissed since the jurisdictional requirements of §1332 have not been satisfied.

   C. The standards of subject matter jurisdiction are satisfied under the facts presented.

   D. Venue is not proper in Missouri since neither of the claimants resides there.

92. Plaintiff, a citizen of California, sued the Bank of Nevada ("Bank"), Nevada corporation, in the U.S. district court for the District of Nevada. Plaintiff sought an order directing Bank to deliver the proceeds of a savings account in the amount of $80,000 to her. She alleges an agreement between her and Krooke, also a California citizen, whereby they each deposited an equal amount of money in the account, to be held solely in the name of Krooke. The Bank answered and alleged that it refused to make the transfer because Krooke claims that Plaintiff assigned her interest in the account to him as repayment for a loan. The Bank then filed a motion to dismiss for failure to join Krooke as a required party under FRCP 19. The district court granted the Bank's motion. Which of the following statements is correct?

   A. Krooke was not a required party within the meaning of Rule 19.

   B. The court should have ordered Bank to interplead Plaintiff and Krooke.

   C. The court could not order Bank to interplead Plaintiff and Krooke because both claimants were from the same state.

   D. The court properly dismissed the suit since the joinder of Krooke was not feasible.

93. Pauline and Declan were classmates in law school many years ago. Declan settled in Los Angeles, where he has a lucrative practice representing the pets of movie stars. Pauline works as a public defender in Phoenix, Arizona. Pauline broke her ankle last fall while staying at Declan's home in Los Angeles. The injury occurred when she slipped on the newly waxed kitchen floor. Pauline has sued Declan in a federal district court in Los Angeles. She seeks $35,000 for her medical bills, $10,000 for damage to her car, which was caused when Declan backed into it on the day before the "slip and fall," $25,000 for money lent by her to Declan while the two were law school roommates, and $1,000 for the value of a valuable first edition civil procedure casebook that Declan borrowed from Pauline but never returned. Which of the following statements is correct? (Assume there are no statute of limitations problems on any of Pauline's claims.)

    A. Pauline may join all of her claims against Declan in a single proceeding even though the claims do not arise out of the same transaction.

    B. Since Pauline's claims against Declan do not arise out of the same transaction, they may not be joined together under the federal rules.

    C. Pauline may not aggregate her unrelated claims for purposes of establishing subject matter jurisdiction.

    D. Under the federal rules, Pauline must join all of her claims against Declan that have matured as of the date she files her complaint.

94. Polina, a citizen of State X, used her credit card with High Tech World ("HTW") to purchase a new flat-screen television set. The set became inoperable after three weeks, but HTW refused to take it back. In response, Polina stopped making payments on the account. HTW assigned her account to Debt Collections R Us, Inc. ("Debt"), a State X corporation known for its high-pressure collection techniques. Polina has now sued Debt in a federal district court, claiming that Debt subjected her to unfair and deceptive debt collection practices in violation of the federal Fair Debt Collections Practices Act ("FDCPA"), which creates a private right of action for persons subjected to such practices. Debt has filed a counterclaim for collection of the debt. Which of the following statements is correct?

    A. The federal district court must exercise jurisdiction over Debt's counterclaim.

    B. Under the majority rule, since the counterclaim is permissive and the parties are not diverse, the federal district court may but need not exercise jurisdiction over the counterclaim.

C. Under the minority rule, since the counterclaim is permissive and the parties are not diverse, the federal district court may but need not exercise jurisdiction over the counterclaim.

D. Debt's counterclaim does not arise out of the same transaction or occurrence as the Polina's claim and, as a consequence, and regardless of the circuit in which the federal district court sits, the court may not exercise supplemental jurisdiction over that counterclaim.

95. Willie and Waylon, both of whom hail from Texas, were on the road again somewhere between here and there. While Willie was driving and Waylon was snoozing in the passenger seat, their truck was rammed by a motorcycle driven by Merle, who hails from Muskogee, Oklahoma. Willie and Waylon have joined together to sue Merle in a federal district court, each claiming over $80,000 in damages. Merle has filed an answer denying his negligence. Waylon has asked leave of court to file a crossclaim against Willie for $80,000 since he figures Willie should have seen that motorcycle coming. Which of the following statements is correct?

A. Under the majority interpretation of FRCP 13(g), Waylon would not be allowed to file a crossclaim against Willie.

B. Under the minority interpretation of FRCP 13(g), Waylon would not be allowed to file a crossclaim against Willie.

C. Under both the majority and minority interpretations of FRCP 13(g), Waylon would be permitted to file his crossclaim against Willie since Merle has filed an answer to the plaintiffs' joint complaint.

D. Waylon's claim against Willie must be filed as an impleader.

96. Same facts as above except assume for purposes of this question that the federal rules allow Waylon to file his claim against Willie. Which of the following statements is correct?

A. The federal district court would have an independent basis of jurisdiction over Waylon's claim against Willie.

B. Waylon's claim against Willie would violate the complete diversity rule.

C. Waylon's claim against Willie would be inconsistent with the jurisdictional requirements of §1332.

D. The federal district court may exercise its discretion and allow the claim to be filed since it arises out of a common nucleus of operative facts with plaintiffs' claims against Merle.

97. Norm, a citizen of California, sells high-end vintage guitars from his Vintage Guitar Shop in the San Fernando Valley. Rocky, a citizen of Nevada, has bought several guitars from Norm. On a recent visit to the shop, Rocky was a little "high" and completely destroyed a 1958 Fender Stratocaster, which had just been appraised at $80,000. Norm sued Rocky in a federal district court seeking $80,000 in damages. In response, Rocky filed an answer and a counterclaim. In the counterclaim, Rocky asserted that a "vintage" 1957 Les Paul guitar that he purchased from Norm the previous year was a fake worth less than $200. Rocky seeks $99,800 in damages (the price Rocky paid for the Les Paul less $200) and he has joined Jennifer as a third party defendant to this claim, as it was Jennifer who inspected the Les Paul and warranted its authenticity. Jennifer is a citizen of Nevada. Which of the following is correct?

    A. Rocky should have used interpleader to join Jennifer to this lawsuit.

    B. Since the counterclaim is permissive, the federal rules do not allow Rocky to add Jennifer as a defendant to that claim.

    C. The claim against Jennifer would run afoul of the limits imposed on supplemental jurisdiction in §1367(b).

    D. The presence of Jennifer in the suit may contaminate the independent basis of jurisdiction over Rocky's claim against Norm.

98. Same facts as the previous problem except that instead of the claim filed against Norm and Jennifer, Rocky filed an answer denying his liability for the damage to the Stratocaster, asserting that Pierre, a California citizen, was completely at fault. Attached to Rocky's answer was a motion to implead Pierre as a third party defendant. Which of the following statements is correct?

    A. The motion must be denied.

    B. The motion may be granted, but only if it was timely filed.

    C. The motion may be granted since Rocky is not a plaintiff.

    D. The motion must be granted.

99. Same facts as the previous problem except assume that Rocky is allowed to implead Pierre. Will the federal district court permit Norm to file a claim against Pierre for the destruction of the Stratocaster?

    A. No, Norm's claim against Rocky precludes Norm from claiming that Pierre is responsible for the damage to the Stratocaster.

    B. Yes, since Norm's claim is transactionally related to the claim against Pierre.

C. No, Norm's claim against Pierre would be inconsistent with the jurisdictional requirements of §1332.

D. Yes, both the federal rules and pertinent jurisdictional statutes would allow this claim to be filed.

100. When Bertha died she bequeathed her estate to Myra, her last surviving relative. Aaron, who was Bertha's caregiver for the last five years of her life, claims that Bertha gifted her savings account to him prior to her death. The account balance was $100,000 at the time of her death. If Aaron were correct, the assets in the account would not pass through the estate to Myra. Myra, of course, disagrees with Aaron and claims that the bank account passed to her through the estate. The account remains in Bertha's name on deposit with the Bank of Seven Flags, a Georgia corporation. Myra and Aaron are citizens of California. Aaron has filed a lawsuit in a federal district court in California against the Bank demanding that it convey the assets in the account to him. The Bank has filed a motion to dismiss for failure to join a required party. Which of the following statements is correct?

A. Myra is not a required party since the only basis for bringing her into the suit is joint and several liability.

B. Myra is a required party because in her absence the Bank could be subject to inconsistent obligations.

C. Myra is a required party because in her absence the Bank could be subject to double liability on a single obligation.

D. Myra is not a required party because her presence would destroy complete diversity.

101. Same facts as above, but assume that Myra is a required party. Which of the following statements is correct?

A. Aaron can be ordered to bring Myra in as a defendant since he and Myra are clearly adverse to one another.

B. Aaron can be ordered to bring Myra in as a defendant since he and Myra both claim an interest in the same stake.

C. The Bank can join Myra as a party to a counterclaim in interpleader.

D. The Bank cannot use interpleader since the standards of statutory interpleader have not been satisfied.

102. Dearborn, Inc., a Michigan corporation, sells its automobiles through independent dealers. Dearborn's principal place of business is Detroit. All dealers have dealership agreements that they

executed with Dearborn at the time they were appointed as dealers. Their agreements entitle them to sell cars manufactured by Dearborn within their respective assigned territories. This year, Dearborn has produced a new electric car that is a "green" departure from its more typical "muscle" cars. Instead of selling its new electric car through existing dealers, Dearborn plans to sell the electric car through a new line of dealers. Twelve current Dearborn dealers in California jointly filed actions for breach of contract against Dearborn in the appropriate U.S. district court. Dearborn has moved to sever the actions for misjoinder of parties. Which of the following statements is correct?

A. The motion should be granted since the plaintiffs are all citizens of the same state.

B. The motion should be denied because plaintiffs are compelled to join their actions if their claims arise out of the same transaction or series of transactions.

C. The motion should be granted if the court finds that the claims arise out of the same transaction or series of transactions, and there are common issues of law and fact to all of the claims.

D. None of the above.

103. Porphyria and Carmella have been roommates for several years. Last summer they went on a vacation together, and unfortunately, they were involved in an automobile accident. Porphyria was driving at the time. The accident occurred on a busy section of an interstate when Porphyria collided with another car while attempting to change lanes. Porphyria and Carmella have joined together and sued Denny, the driver of the other car, in a U.S. district court sitting diversity jurisdiction. The plaintiffs, both of whom are from State X, claim in excess of $75,000 in damages. Denny, who hails from State Y, has filed a counterclaim against Porphyria, asserting that the accident was due to her negligence. He seeks $50,000 in damages. Which of the following statements is true?

A. Denny's claim is permissive within the meaning of the federal rules.

B. Denny's claim is compulsory within the meaning of the federal rules, but he need not assert the claim in this proceeding since there is no independent basis of jurisdiction over it.

C. Denny's counterclaim is permissive and the court may exercise supplemental jurisdiction over it.

D. Denny's counterclaim is compulsory and the court may exercise supplemental jurisdiction over it.

104. Same facts as above. Carmella has now filed a separate claim against Porphyria, asserting that the latter's negligence was a contributing factor in causing the accident. Carmella has also joined an additional claim against Porphyria for breach of contract. This claim is based on an alleged agreement under which Porphyria agreed to hire Carmella to paint Porphyria's portrait. On this claim Carmella seeks $100,000 in damages. Under the majority approach to the federal rules, which of the following statements is true?

A. Carmella's negligence counterclaim against Sofia is compulsory since it arises out of the same transaction as the original claim that is the subject matter of the lawsuit.

B. Carmella's negligence crossclaim against Sofia is compulsory since it arises out of the same transaction as the original claim that is the subject matter of the lawsuit.

C. The federal rules would allow Carmella to file her negligence claim, but not her breach of contract claim.

D. The federal rules would allow Carmella to file both of her claims against Porphyria.

105. Hank, a California citizen, owns a small commercial building that was destroyed when an earthquake caused electrical lines to spark and ignite a fire. Hank had insured the building for losses due to fire with Fire Insurance, Inc., a Delaware Corporation, and for losses due to earthquakes with Shaker, Inc., a California Corporation. Both Fire and Shaker have denied liability. Fire claims that the cause of the damage to the building was the earthquake, and Shaker claims that the cause was the fire resulting from the sparks. Fire has filed a diversity suit against Hank seeking declaratory relief to the effect that the damage was caused by an earthquake. Assume the amount in controversy is satisfied. Hank would like to bring Shaker into the lawsuit. Which statement describes the best method for doing so?

A. Hank should file a crossclaim against Shaker under FRCP 13(g).

B. Hank should file an impleader against Shaker.

C. Hank should counterclaim against Fire and join Shaker to that counterclaim under FRCP 13(h).

D. Hank should counterclaim against Fire and join Shaker to an interpleader action under FRCP 22.

106. Mall Developer (MD), a Minnesota partnership, hired Contractor (CON), a South Dakota corporation, as the prime contractor on the construction of a new shopping mall. CON entered a subcontract with Sub-Con (SUB), a partnership with partners in both Minnesota and South Dakota, for installation of the plumbing. SUB agreed to indemnify CON for any liability incurred by CON pertaining to SUB's installation of the plumbing. The project is complete, and CON has paid SUB the amounts due on the subcontract. However, MD refuses to reimburse CON for those amounts, claiming that SUB negligently performed the job. CON sued MD in a U.S. district court, invoking that court's diversity jurisdiction. Assume that the amount in controversy is satisfied. MD counterclaimed seeking damages for the additional costs incurred in redoing the plumbing. In response to that counterclaim, CON filed an impleader claim against SUB. Which of the following statements is most accurate?

    A. CON's impleader must be dismissed since FRCP 14 permits only defendants to file impleaders.

    B. CON's impleader must be dismissed since a plaintiff in a diversity suit may never file a claim against a non-diverse party.

    C. CON's impleader may be retained if prior to the adoption of 28 U.S.C. §1367, a USDC would have been free to entertain pendent or ancillary jurisdiction over this claim.

    D. CON's impleader must be dismissed because 28 U.S.C. §1367 plainly forbids a plaintiff from filing such a claim under the given circumstances.

107. Bob lives across the street from Carol in State X. They agreed to appear on a new reality show "House Changers," in which neighbors trade homes for a week during which time they remodel their neighbor's kitchen. Unfortunately, as a result of this "trade", both kitchens suffered substantial damage caused by the designers and crewmembers hired by the show's producers, Ted and Alice. Bob got the worst of it with $90,000 in damages, while Carol's home suffered a mere $35,000 loss. Bob and Carol have joined together in a suit filed in a U.S. district against Ted and Alice, both of whom are citizens of State Y, seeking damages based on breach of contract and negligence. Which of the following statements is correct?

    A. The text of §1367(a) precludes exercise of jurisdiction over Carol's claims.

    B. The text of §1367(b) precludes exercise of jurisdiction over Carol's claims.

C. The text of §1367(a) and (b) would permit the exercise of jurisdiction over Carol's claims since Carol is a plaintiff joined under FRCP 20.

D. The text of §1367(a) and (b) would permit the exercise of jurisdiction over Carol's claims since Carol did not enter the case under FRCP 19 or 24.

108. Public School District 909 requires all schools within the district to begin the day with a recitation of the Pledge of Allegiance. Students not wishing to participate may stand silently while the others recite. Bob, a Jehovah's Witness whose daughter attends an elementary school within the district, filed a suit in a U.S. district court against the school district challenging the policy as a violation of the Free Exercise and Establishment Clauses of the U.S. Constitution. The case received an enormous amount of notoriety in both the local and national press and has been the subject of several heated public meetings with the school board. Some 23 months after Bob filed the lawsuit and after extensive discovery and pretrial motions, the district court granted Bob's motion for summary judgment, finding that as a matter of law the district policy violated the Free Exercise and Establishment Clauses. Final judgment was entered. Shortly thereafter, after an acrimonious meeting, the school board voted not to appeal the decision. Bette, a parent of a child who attends a District 909 school, immediately filed a motion to intervene under FRCP 24(a) for the purpose of appealing the district court's decision. She claims that the board's decision not to appeal undermines the right of her daughter to recite the Pledge of Allegiance as part of the school day. Which of the following statements is most correct?

A. Intervention should be granted since Bette has an interest in the subject matter that may be impaired by the board's decision not to appeal.

B. Intervention should be denied since Bette's motion was not timely.

C. Intervention should be denied unless Bette can show that the district court's decision was clearly erroneous.

D. Intervention should be denied since a private party can never intervene in a case that a government body declines to defend.

109. Zeppo was driving his three pals, Groucho, Harpo, and Chico, to the opera. As he exited the highway, he lost control of the car and ended up colliding with a telephone pole. All three of his pals were injured in the accident. Zeppo was insured by Firefly Brokers. His

policy limit for liability in any single accident was $100,000. All of his pals suffered injuries and have filed claims with Firefly Brokers in the following amounts: Groucho for $45,000, Harpo for $25,000, and Chico for $20,000. Firefly Brokers has filed an interpleader action against Groucho, Harpo, and Chico. The interpleader is conditioned on the defendant's first establishing that Zeppo was at fault, a fact that Firefly Brokers denies. Assume jurisdictional elements have been satisfied. Which of the following statements is correct?

A. Interpleader is improper since Firefly Brokers has retained a claim to the fund.

B. Interpleader is proper since a stakeholder may, as Firefly Brokers has done, assert an interest in the stake.

C. Interpleader is improper since there are no adverse claimants to the stake.

D. Interpleader is proper so long as Firefly Brokers deposits the stake with the court or posts an appropriate bond.

110. Early one morning at the St. James Infirmary, Larry found a huge diamond beneath a bench. Larry lives at the infirmary, which is located in State X. The estimated value of the diamond is just shy of $75,000. Carol claims that the diamond is hers and that she lost it while visiting a young cowboy at the infirmary. Carol lives in neighboring State Y. Several heirs of the young cowboy, each of whom lives in State Y, claim that the diamond belongs to the estate of the young cowboy, who was also a resident of State Y. Larry wants to file an interpleader action in a U.S. district court. Which of the following statements is correct?

A. Even if Larry is a claimant, he may file a rule interpleader in federal court since, as the stakeholder, he is completely diverse from the other claimants.

B. Even if Larry is not a claimant, he may file an interpleader in federal court pursuant to 28 U.S.C. §1335.

C. Unless Larry is a claimant, he many not file an interpleader in federal court.

D. None of the above.

111. Tina, who has lived her entire life in New York, decided that she wanted to move to California. As part of her planned move, she placed a $100,000 deposit on an expensive home in a suburb of Los Angeles. The deposit was placed into escrow with Speedy Escrow, a California

corporation. The deal on the house fell through, and Tina has yet to make her planned move, in part because Speedy refuses to return the escrow deposit. Oscar, the owner of the home Tina was going to purchase, claims that the deposit should be forfeited to him because Tina reneged on the sale. Oscar no longer lives in the house but has moved to New York with his family in order to pursue a career on Wall Street. Tina has sued Speedy in a U.S. district court in California, seeking a return of her escrow funds, and Speedy has filed a motion to dismiss under FRCP 12(b)(7). What should the district court do?

A. The court should grant the motion since Oscar's joinder is not feasible.

B. The court should grant the motion since the court cannot in good conscience proceed without Oscar.

C. The court should deny the motion since Oscar is not a required party.

D. The court should deny the motion and permit Speedy to join Oscar to a counterclaim in interpleader.

112. The Coal Company conducted mining operations in Dublin, Virginia and in Orrville, Ohio. Workers at both mines were members of the Teamsters Union. Local 101 of that union, located in southwest Virginia, represented workers at the Dublin facility, while Local 901, based in Ohio, represented workers at the Orrville facility. When the Coal Company shut down its Orrville facility, workers there were free to transfer to the Dublin facility to the extent work was available. A dispute arose between the two Locals concerning seniority for the transferring workers. Local 101 claimed that the transferring workers should lose their seniority and be placed at the bottom of the Dublin seniority list. Local 901 contended that these workers should retain their seniority upon transfer. To resolve the issue, Local 901 instituted a grievance proceeding in Ohio against the Coal Company and Local 101 before a Joint Union-Management Seniority Committee. The Committee found in Local 901's favor, ruling that transferring workers should keep their seniority. Local 101 then sued the Coal Company in a Virginia federal court under the federal Labor Management Relations Act. It sought an order vacating the Committee's decision and ordering the Coal Company to place transferring workers at the bottom of the Dublin seniority list. Local 901 was not named in the suit because it could not be served in Virginia. The Coal Company has moved to dismiss the action under FRCP 12(b)(7) on the ground

that Local 901 is a required party whose joinder is not feasible. How should the district court rule on the motion?

A. The court should grant the motion.

B. The court should deny the motion since Local 901 could intervene and waive personal jurisdiction.

C. The court should deny the motion because the court can in equity and good conscience proceed without Local 901 presence in the lawsuit.

D. The court should deny the motion because Local 901, which operates only in Ohio, will suffer no prejudice by this proceeding in a Virginia federal court.

113. Ten college school students enrolled in a in a State X college filed a class action against the appropriate state officials in U.S. district court seeking to enjoin the enforcement of a flag discretion statute on the campuses of State X colleges and universities. The plaintiffs contend that enforcement of the statute would violate the First Amendment to the U.S. Constitution. Plaintiffs seek to certify a class that consists of all students enrolled in a college or university located in State X. The defendants have filed a motion requesting that the court deny class certification. Assume that the plaintiffs' case does not satisfy the standards of the Class Action Fairness Act. Which of the following represents the defendants' best argument in support of their motion?

A. Plaintiffs' have failed to satisfy the class-action numerosity requirement.

B. Plaintiffs have failed to allege that each member of the prospective class will suffer damages in excess of $75,000.

C. The named plaintiffs do not adequately represent the interests of the entire class.

D. It would be impossible to provide individual notice to each member of the proposed class.

114. Same facts as the preceding question. If the court refused to certify the class, which of the following would be true?

A. The plaintiffs could immediately appeal the court's decision.

B. The plaintiffs could not appeal immediately, but would be obliged to try the action on the merits as a nonclass action.

C. The plaintiffs would waive any right to appeal if they elected to first try the case on its merits.

D. The court would be obliged to dismiss the case.

115. Dr. Dumb, a citizen of State A, performed surgery on Pam, a citizen of State B, for which he charged $5,000. Pam was injured during the surgery. She filed a negligence lawsuit against Dr. Dumb in the appropriate U.S. district court in State A, seeking $90,000 damages. Dr. Dumb filed an impleader against his malpractice insurer, the Insureall Corporation, a State A corporation, for payment on his policy if Pam should win her lawsuit. In response, Pam filed a claim against Insureall for the nonpayment of a $76,000 claim on an insurance policy she had maintained with the company when her car was stolen. Insureall has filed a motion to dismiss Pam's claim for improper joinder. What should the district court do?

A. Deny the motion since FRCP 14(a) specifically allows a plaintiff to file a claim against a third-party defendant.

B. Deny the motion since the court has subject matter jurisdiction over Pam's claim.

C. Dismiss Insureall from the case entirely since Dr. Dumb and Insureall are not diverse from one another.

D. Grant Insureall's motion.

116. Polly, a citizen of Nevada, purchased $7,000 of ABC Corporation securities from her broker, Don, also a citizen of Nevada. However, because ABC was insolvent, the securities were worthless. Polly sued Don in the appropriate U.S. district court for violation of federal securities law. In addition, Polly joined a claim against Don for injuries caused when Don's car rear-ended Polly's car following a party they had both attended. Which of the following statements is correct?

A. The district court may exercise jurisdiction over both claims since FRCP 18(a) permits Polly to join as many claims as she has against Don in a single proceeding.

B. The district court may exercise jurisdiction over both claims since Polly's federal and state law claims are part of the same case or controversy within the meaning of Article III of the U.S. Constitution.

C. The federal rules would not allow Polly to join her claims against Don in a single proceeding.

D. The district court must dismiss Polly's state-law claim.

117. Art and Bob were passengers in a car being driven by Oscar. They were both injured when Oscar last control of the car and crashed into the center divider. Art and Bob are citizens of Illinois, while Oscar is

a citizen of Ohio. Art and Bob commenced a lawsuit against Oscar in a U.S. district court in Ohio (where the accident had occurred). Each claimed damages for personal injuries arising out of the accident. Art, whose injuries were quite severe, sought $80,000 damages. Bob, whose injuries were relatively minor, sought $11,000 in damages. Oscar has filed a motion to dismiss Bob's claim. Which of the following statements is correct?

A. The motion must be granted since Bob's claim does not satisfy the amount in controversy requirement.

B. The motion must be granted since Art and Bob are not claiming injuries to a joint right or title.

C. The motion must be denied since the claims arise out of the same accident.

D. The district court has discretion to exercise jurisdiction over Bob's claim.

118. Same facts as the previous question, except that Bob is a citizen of Ohio who legitimately claims in excess of $75,000 in damages. Oscar has again filed a motion to dismiss Bob's claim. Which of the following statements is correct?

A. The motion must be granted since Bob is not diverse from Oscar.

B. The motion must be granted since the federal rules would not allow joinder of Art and Bob's claims.

C. The motion must be denied since the claims arise out of the same accident.

D. The district court has discretion to exercise jurisdiction over Bob's claim.

119. X, a citizen of Kentucky, entered into a contract to sell a car to Z, also a citizen of Kentucky. However, when Z was late in tendering a prepayment, X advised Z that he was no longer bound to complete the transaction. Z unequivocally informed X that the contract was still binding. Prior to the due date for delivery of the automobile under the original agreement, X entered into a new transaction with Y, whereby X agreed to sell the vehicle to Y. Y is a citizen of Ohio. Y was aware of the outstanding contract that X had with Z, but was assured by the former that Z's right in the automobile had been lawfully terminated. X subsequently repudiated his contract with Y, contending it was entered into under coercive circumstances. Y commenced an

action against X in the appropriate U.S. district court for specific performance and breach of contract. X moved to dismiss on the ground that Z was an indispensable party. Which of the following statements is correct?

A. The district court will grant the motion since Z claims an interest in the vehicle.

B. The district court will deny the motion since Z is not a required party.

C. The district court will grant the motion since Z's joinder would destroy complete diversity.

D. The district court will deny the motion since Z can be brought into the suit in a manner consistent with the court's subject matter jurisdiction.

120. While stopping by the woods on a snowy evening, Robert was rear-ended by a car driven by Wallace, the 17-year-old son of Emily, who also owned the car Wallace was driving. Robert is a citizen of Massachusetts. Wallace and Emily are citizens of Maine. The accident occurred in Massachusetts. Robert sued Emily and Wallace in the U.S. district court in Maine pursuant to a statute that made parents liable for the negligent driving of their minor children. The suit demanded $90,000 in damages. Emily would like to file a claim against Wallace for damages to her car. Which of the following statements is correct?

A. Emily may assert her claim against Wallace as a crossclaim.

B. If Emily fails to assert her claim against Wallace, the claim will be barred in future litigation.

C. Emily may not assert a crossclaim against Wallace.

D. Emily claim against Wallace would be properly characterized as a counterclaim.

121. Paul, a citizen of South Dakota, died in a job-related accident in Colorado when some scaffolding collapsed on a construction project he was working on. At the time of the accident, Paul was employed by Construction Company ("CC"), a Colorado corporation. Big Builders ("BB"), a subcontractor for the job and also a Colorado corporation, constructed the scaffolding. Paul's wife, Mary, as the executrix of his estate, sued CC in an appropriate U.S. district court in Colorado. She claimed that CC had been negligent in failing to inspect the defective scaffolding supplied by Big Builders and she sought $1 million in damages. Colorado law provides that a general

contractor is presumed to have not inspected materials supplied to it by a subcontractor. This presumption is rebuttable. At the time of his death, Paul owed CC $7,000 for wages previously advanced. Which of the following statements is correct?

A. BB has a right to intervene in this proceeding.

B. CC may file an impleader against Big Builders.

C. While the federal rules would allow CC to file an impleader, subject matter jurisdiction would be lacking since CC and BB are both from Colorado.

D. CC could assert a counterclaim against the estate for the advance in wages that it made to Paul.

Adjudication—Questions

122. Basil sued Sybil for breach of contract in a diversity suit properly filed in a U.S. district court in State X. Under the contract, which was signed by both parties, Sybil was to be paid an advance on a novel she agreed to deliver to Basil no later than April 1, 2007. The suit was filed on March 15, 2010, and Sybil was served one month later. After discovery, Basil moved for summary judgment on his claim. He attached a copy of the signed contract, which specified the above payment and delivery obligations, a copy of a check made out to and cashed by Sybil for the contractual advance, and an affidavit signed by Basil asserting that Sybil had not yet delivered the novel. Sybil responded to the motion by attaching a copy of the completed novel to an affidavit in which she explained why it took her longer than expected to complete the novel. Which of the following statements is correct?

    A. Basil met his burden of production on summary judgment.

    B. Basil failed to meet his burden of production since his affidavit is self-serving and will not be admissible at trial.

    C. Although Basil met his burden of production on summary judgment, Sybil's response established the existence of a genuine issue of material fact.

    D. The burden did not shift to Sybil to respond to Basil's motion.

123. Same facts as above. In addition, suppose that Sybil raised the statute of limitations as an affirmative defense and that she filed a cross-motion for summary judgment on that defense. In support of her motion, she included an affidavit from the process server establishing that service took place 15 days after the expiration of the statute of limitations. Which of the following statements is correct?

    A. Regardless of whether Sybil met her burden, Basil must respond to her motion since it pertains to an affirmative defense that may bar his claim.

    B. Sybil's motion is improper since she will bear the burden of proof at trial.

    C. Sybil's motion is improper since it was not responsive to Basil's motion.

    D. Sybil met her burden of production on this motion if the applicable statute of limitations is tolled only by service of process.

124. Bianca claims her employer, Qualex, discriminated against her based on race when it terminated her employment. She has filed a federal

Title VII against Qualex in a U.S. district court. To establish a *prima facie* case under Title VII, Bianca must prove that she is a member of a minority race, that she was qualified for the position she held, and that her employer replaced her with a nonminority applicant. If she meets this standard, the defendant must prove that it had a bona fide, that is, nondiscriminatory, reason for the dismissal. A bona fide justification is a complete defense. After the completion of discovery, Qualex filed a motion for summary judgment. In that motion Qualex admitted that Bianca is a member of a racial minority and that it had filled her position with a nonminority applicant. Qualex denied, however, that Bianca was qualified for the position and argued in its brief that she has no evidence to support a contrary view. In addition, Qualex attached to its motion an affidavit from Bianca's immediate supervisor that detailed the reasons Bianca was fired, including her constant absences, her failure to complete projects in a timely fashion, and her refusal to follow company policy when instructed to do so. Bianca has responded to this motion by filing her own affidavit in which she details her educational and work experience, facts that tend to show she was qualified for the job. How should the court rule on Qualex's motion for summary judgment?

A. Grant the motion since Bianca failed to meet her burden of production.

B. Deny the motion since Qualex failed to meet its burden of production as the party with the burden of persuasion at trial.

C. Deny the motion since Bianca met her burden of production with respect to her job qualifications.

D. Grant a partial summary judgment in favor of Qualex.

125. Same facts as above, but instead of Qualex filing for summary judgment, Bianca filed for summary judgment. Attached to her motion were (1) an official copy of her birth certificate, which identifies her as of Japanese descent; (2) an affidavit signed by Bianca that details her educational and job experience, which, if believed, tends to establish her qualifications for the job; (3) a copy of all of her annual performance reports (3 years) from Qualex, the most recent of which was filed 3 months before her termination, in all of which she is rated as from good to excellent on each criterion reported; and (4) an unanswered Request for Admission that was properly served six months ago asking Qualex to admit that the position had been filled by a nonminority. Qualex responded to Bianca's motion for

summary judgment by filing an affidavit by Bianca's supervisor in which the supervisor explained that Bianca was fired for engaging in sexual harassment of a fellow employee. Supporting documentation was attached to the affidavit. The court should:

A. Deny Bianca's motion because Qualex met its burden of production.

B. Grant summary judgment *sua sponte* for Qualex.

C. Grant partial summary judgment for Bianca on her *prima facie* case except for the question of whether the position had been filled by a nonminority.

D. Grant partial summary judgment for Bianca on her *prima facie* case including on the question of whether the position had been filled by a nonminority.

126. Paige is from California and Daphne is from New York. Paige sued Daphne in a U.S. district court located in California for breach of contract. Although Daphne was properly served with the summons and complaint, Daphne failed to plead or otherwise defend within 21 days. Which of the following statements is correct?

A. Paige is entitled to a summary judgment since there is no genuine issue as to any material fact.

B. Paige is entitled to sanctions under FRCP 11.

C. If Paige shows that Daphne has failed to plead or otherwise defend, the clerk must enter Daphne's default.

D. Daphne must pay the costs of service.

127. Same facts as above. Assume that the judge has entered a default judgment against Daphne. Daphne was not, however, provided a seven-day notice prior to the entry of that judgment. Which of the following statements is correct?

A. The judgment can only be rescinded if Daphne can establish that the judgment was procured through fraud.

B. The judgment must be rescinded since Daphne, having been served on the underlying action, was entitled to a 7-day notice prior to the entry of the default judgment.

C. The federal district court may relieve Daphne of the default judgment on grounds of excusable neglect but only if the motion to do so is filed no more than a year after the entry of the judgment.

D. Under no circumstances may the federal district court rescind the default judgment.

128. P and D were involved in a car accident in Texas. P is a citizen of State X, and D is a citizen of State Y. The State X service of process statute is identical to FRCP 4(e). P sued D in a State X court of general jurisdiction. P served D by sending, via first-class mail, the summons and complaint to D in State Y. D received these documents but failed to respond to them. P then obtained a default judgment and filed an enforcement action against D in a State Y court. D has filed a motion to dismiss the enforcement proceeding, arguing that the State X default judgment is void. What should the State Y court do?

- **A.** The State Y court should deny D's motion and give full faith and credit to the judgment of the State X court.
- **B.** The State Y court should grant D's motion and decline to give full faith and credit to judgment of the State X court.
- **C.** The State Y court must enforce the State X judgment because a default judgment is usually deemed to be "on the merits."
- **D.** Choices (A) and (C) are correct, but (B) is not.

129. Paul was injured while operating a meat and tofu slicer manufactured by Dice and Slice, Inc. ("Dice"). Paul properly commenced an action against Dice in an appropriate U.S. district court. In selecting the jury, the judge conducted the voir dire, but refused Dice's request that the she ask the members of the jury panel whether any of them were prejudiced against corporations. The trial judge's refusal to comply with Dice's request at the voir dire was:

- **A.** Correct, because the question was irrelevant to the issues presented in the case.
- **B.** Correct, because Dice could have exercised a peremptory challenge against the potential juror.
- **C.** Erroneous, because prejudice against a party is a proper subject for inquiry during voir dire.
- **D.** Erroneous, because when the trial judge conducts the voir dire, she must ask any questions requested by counsel.

130. Same facts as above. In addition, after a trial, the jury returned verdict in favor of Paul for $80,000. Dice moved for a new trial. The trial judge agreed to grant Dice's motion unless Paul accepted a reduction in the verdict from $80,000 to $30,000. Paul agreed to the reduction under protest. He then appealed. On appeal, Paul challenged the remittitur. Paul's challenge will be:

A. Successful, since the court's order violated Paul's Seventh Amendment right to a trial by jury on the issue of damages.

B. Successful, if the trial court's order was an abuse of discretion.

C. Unsuccessful, because Paul elected to accepted the remittitur.

D. Unsuccessful, because the Seventh Amendment does not apply to damage issues.

131. Plaintiff, a citizen of Arizona, sued Defendant, a citizen of Oregon, in the U.S. district court in Arizona for breach of contract seeking $78,000 in damages. Defendant answered by denying that a contract had been formed. Plaintiff and Defendant stipulated that the jury would consist of eight persons. Trial was held, and seven jurors voted in favor of Plaintiff. One juror voted for Defendant. The jurors then deliberated on the amount of damages and rendered a verdict in favor of Plaintiff for $18,500. Defendant appealed the ruling. On which of the following grounds would Defendant be most likely to prevail on appeal?

A. The ruling was defective because it was rendered by fewer than 12 jurors.

B. The ruling was defective because it was based on a nonunanimous vote.

C. The court did not have subject matter jurisdiction because the verdict did not exceed $75,000.

D. The court lacked personal jurisdiction.

132. Delbert liked to cut across Pat's land on his way to law school. Pat, however, disliked Delbert because Delbert had become somewhat arrogant since he made Law Review. When Pat asked Delbert to cease using the shortcut, Delbert responded that his time was "extremely valuable" and therefore it was a "private necessity." Pat instituted an action against Delbert in the appropriate U.S. district court, demanding that Delbert be enjoined from using her land. You may assume that jurisdictional requisites have been satisfied. Although Pat's real property had not been damaged by Delbert's constant encroachments, Pat also sought nominal monetary damages. Which of the following statements is correct?

A. Delbert is entitled to a jury trial with respect to the trespass issue.

B. Delbert is not entitled to a jury trial on the trespass claim since the primary relief Pat is seeking is an injunction.

C. As a consequence of the "clean-up doctrine," the court, in its discretion, may decide both the legal and equitable issues.

D. There is no right to a jury trial because trespass was not a "suit at common law" under the Seventh Amendment.

133. Joan was experiencing difficulties with her balance. She visited Dr. Jekyll to determine the cause of her problem. After examining her, Dr. Jekyll put some drops in Joan's left ear. Three weeks after her visit to Dr. Jekyll, Joan lost her balance and sustained serious injuries. Joan sued the doctor and requested a jury trial. The action was properly commenced in a U.S. district court. At trial, Joan testified to the facts as stated above and then called Dr. Robert to the stand. Dr. Robert testified that (1) he had examined Joan and found substantial damage to her inner ear and (2) that the damage was caused by a fluid containing acid. Joan rested her case. Dr. Jekyll took the stand and testified that (1) Joan had been suffering from an infection of her inner ear, and (2) he had put some drops of perforium (an innocuous, nonacidic substance) into her ear canal. He further stated on cross-examination that the bottle containing perforium stood in the vicinity of a bottle containing an acidic substance. He then rested his case. In rebuttal, Joan called Dr. Robert, who stated that the injury to Joan's inner ear is totally inconsistent with Dr. Jekyll's assertion of an infection. All sides then rested. Joan then filed a motion for judgment as a matter of law. How should the district court rule on that motion?

A. The court should grant the motion since Dr. Jekyll admitted that the perforium bottle stood near a bottle containing an acidic substance.

B. Her motion should be granted, but not for the reason set forth in Choice A.

C. Her motion should be denied.

D. None of the above.

134. Same facts as the preceding question, except that instead of Joan filing a motion for judgment as a matter of law, Dr. Jekyll made such a motion and the district court granted his motion. Joan has filed an appeal. Which of the following statements correctly describes how the appellate court should rule?

A. The court of appeals should reverse the judgment and order a new trial.

B. The court of appeals should reverse the judgment and direct that judgment be entered for Joan.

C. The court of appeals should affirm the judgment.

D. None of the above.

135. Same facts as the preceding question, except assume that neither party moved for a judgment as a matter of law prior to the submission of the case to the jury. After the jury returned a verdict for Joan, Dr. Jekyll moved for a judgment as a matter of law (i.e., a judgment notwithstanding the verdict, or "JNOV") and, in the alternative, for a new trial. The district court granted the motion for a JNOV but denied the motion for a new trial. Joan appealed. Which of the following statements correctly describes how the court of appeals should rule?

A. The court of appeals should reverse the judgment since a motion for a new trial cannot be joined with a JNOV.

B. The court of appeals should affirm the judgment.

C. The court of appeals should reverse the judgment, but order a new trial.

D. The court of appeals should reverse the judgment and reinstate the verdict for Joan.

136. Paul, a citizen of South Dakota, died in a job-related accident caused by the collapse of scaffolding at construction project he was working on in Colorado. At the time of the accident, Paul was employed by Construction Company ("CC"), a Colorado corporation. Paul's wife, Mary, as the executrix of his estate, sued CC in an appropriate U.S. district court in Colorado. She claimed that CC had been negligent in failing to warn Paul that the scaffolding was dangerous. She sought $1 million in damages. At trial, CC introduced credible evidence showing that Paul had been warned by his supervisor not to work near the scaffolding until it had been thoroughly inspected because it appeared to be unsafe. Mary then produced a witness who testified that Paul had always objected to working close to scaffolding. If no further evidence was introduced by either side:

A. CC's motion for a judgment as a matter of law would have to be granted.

B. CC's motion for a judgment as a matter of law would have to be denied.

C. Mary's motion for a judgment as a matter of law would have to be granted.

D. If the jury rendered a verdict for CC, Mary's motion for a judgment as a matter of law would have to be granted.

137. Same facts as the previous question, except now assume that the case was tried to a judge and that each side introduced substantial evidence pertaining to whether CC had adequately warned Paul of the danger. Following the trial, the judge entered findings of fact and conclusions of law. The judge found that CC had provided an adequate warning and that, therefore, Mary was entitled to nothing. Which of the following statements is correct?

A. The finding must be set aside because it is clearly erroneous.

B. The finding must be set aside because the evidence was conflicting.

C. The finding must be set aside because there was substantial evidence supporting Mary's contrary view.

D. None of the above.

138. Plaintiff sued Defendant seeking to recover for personal injuries suffered as a result of a battery inflicted on him by Defendant. The suit was filed in a U.S. district court. Assume that the requirements of 28 U.S.C. §1332(a)(1) were satisfied. Trial was held to a jury. Along with the form for a general verdict, the court instructed the jury to answer three specific questions. In answering these questions, the jury found that (1) Defendant hit Plaintiff with a vase, (2) Defendant intended to so hit Plaintiff; and (3) Defendant caused Plaintiff's damages as alleged in the complaint. The jury, however, returned a general verdict against Plaintiff. Which of the following statements is correct?

A. The jury verdict must stand.

B. The court must enter a verdict in conformity with the jury's responses to the questions posed.

C. The judge may order a new trial.

D. The court may not ask the jury to further consider its verdict.

Claim and Issue Preclusion—Questions

139. Pam and Don entered a contract under which Don agreed to deliver certain goods to Pam on July 1, 2000, and certain other goods on July 1, 2002. Don failed to make the first delivery. In response, Pam sued Don for breach of contract, seeking an order requiring Don to make the initial shipment. Don denied the validity of the contract, claiming a lack of consideration. After a trial on this issue, judgment was entered for Pam. Don complied with the court's order to make the delivery, but then failed to make the July 1, 2002 delivery. Pam again sued Don. This time she sought damages for the late 2000 delivery and an order requiring Don to make the 2002 delivery. Which of the following statements is correct?

   A. Neither of Pam's claims is precluded.

   B. Both of Pam's claims are precluded.

   C. The 2000 damages claim is precluded by claim preclusion, but the 2002 delivery claim is not.

   D. Claim preclusion does not bar either of the claims, but issue preclusion might.

140. Pete sued Darla and Rita claiming that both were individually responsible for a three-car pile up that caused severe damage to Pete's truck. Darla and Rita each raised contributory negligence as a defense to Pete's claim; in addition, Darla filed a negligence cross-claim against Rita, claiming that Rita was responsible for injuries suffered by Darla arising out of the accident. Rita asserted contributory negligence as a defense to Darla's claim. After a trial on these claims and defenses, the jury specifically found that all three parties were guilty of negligence in causing the accident. A judgment was entered denying Pete any recovery against Darla or Rita, and denying Darla any recovery against Rita. No party appealed, and the time to appeal has elapsed. Rita has now sued Darla, claiming damages from the same accident based on Darla's negligence. Darla has asserted contributory negligence as a defense. What should a court do if both Darla and Rita seek to enforce issue preclusion against the other? (Assume that the jurisdiction does not have a compulsory counterclaim rule.)

   A. Preclude Rita from denying her negligence.

   B. Preclude Darla from denying her negligence.

   C. Preclude both Darla and Rita from denying their respective negligence.

D. Preclude neither Darla nor Rita from denying their respective negligence.

141. Dr. Holmes is a famous diagnostician employed by Have Mercy! Hospital. He usually figures out what's wrong with a patient but quite often destroys several of the patient's vital organs in the process. Patty, one of Holmes's patients, came to Have Mercy! with a mild concussion and left without one of her lungs. ("My bad," said the doctor.) Patty sued Have Mercy! for medical malpractice, arguing that Holmes was negligent in his diagnosis. After a trial on that issue, judgment was entered for Have Mercy! Patty has now sued Holmes for "diagnostic negligence" based on the same incident. Which of the following statements is correct?

A. Holmes may assert claim preclusion against Patty.

B. As a nonparty to the prior proceeding, Holmes cannot assert claim preclusion as a defense.

C. Since Holmes could have intervened in the prior case, he may not benefit from the prior judgment.

D. Since Have Mercy! did not defend the prior suit in a representative capacity, Holmes cannot benefit from the prior judgment.

142. Same facts as the previous question, except that Patty prevailed in the prior case, the court expressly finding that Holmes was negligent. She has now sued Holmes for negligence. Which of the following statements is correct?

A. Holmes is bound by the prior judgment as a derivative product of his employer's liability.

B. Holmes is not bound by the prior judgment.

C. Holmes is bound by the prior judgment under a theory of mutuality.

D. Holmes is bound by the prior judgment if he testified in the prior case.

143. Joan owns Riverdale, a palatial residence. Bill owns the adjoining property. One day Matt, Bill's butler, started a fire on Bill's estate to burn excess rubbish. Unfortunately, the fire got out of control and destroyed Joan's home. Joan sustained some injuries and was hospitalized for ten days. She filed an action against Bill in which she sought damages in excess of $1.8 million for property loss caused by the fire. If she were to obtain a judgment against Bill, which of the following statements would be correct?

A. Bill cannot sue Matt on a theory of indemnity.

B. Joan may not file an action against Matt arising out of the same incident.

C. The judgment against Bill would not be binding on Matt in a subsequent lawsuit by Joan against Matt.

D. Joan's claim against Bill for personal injuries would not be precluded under the majority approach to claim preclusion.

144. Anne was fired as Chief Financial Officer with BTrade. In conjunction with this action, BTrade issued a press release in which it explained that its action was based on the fact that Anne had "cooked the books" by exaggerating company assets in the last three annual reports. Anne sued BTrade for breach of contract based on her termination. Her suit was filed in a U.S. district court for the Central District of California, properly invoking that court's diversity jurisdiction. After discovery, the court entered summary judgment for Anne. Assume no appeal was taken. Anne has now sued BTrade for defamation based on the press release. This suit was filed in a California state court. California courts follow the "primary rights" theory of claim preclusion. BTrade has filed a motion for summary judgment on grounds of claim preclusion. The trial court should:

A. Deny the motion since Anne's defamation claim is not based on the same primary right as her breach of contract claim.

B. Grant the motion since the defamation claim arises out of the same transaction as the breach of contract claim.

C. Deny the motion since the defamation claim does not arise out of the same transaction as the wrongful termination and breach of contract claims.

D. Grant the motion since all the claims involve pertain to the invasion of a single right or interest in employment.

145. A sued B to recover damages for B's failure to comply with the terms of a contract between them. B defended by claiming that he had not reached majority as of the date on which the contract was signed and, in any event, that the contract was procured by A through fraud. After a trial without a jury, judgment is for B, the court finding that B had not reached majority and that A had procured the contract through fraud. If B later sues A for damages resulting from A's fraud (and there is no compulsory counterclaim rule), in a jurisdiction that

adheres to the Restatement Second of Judgments, may B use issue preclusion against A on the question of A's fraud?

A. Yes, if the record of the initial proceeding established that the trial court fully and fairly considered and decided the question of A's fraud.

B. No. An issue decided defensively may not be used offensively.

C. Yes, if an appeal was taken and the appellate court affirmed on both grounds.

D. No. Alternative findings are not binding under any circumstances.

146. Same facts as the previous question, except that the judgment in the first proceeding was for A by a jury entering no special findings. In a subsequent proceeding by A against B involving a separate claim on the same contract, may A prevent B from raising the fraud defense?

A. Yes, B is bound by the prior judgment.

B. Yes, but only if B appealed and the appellate court affirmed on the question of fraud.

C. No, because no specific finding was made by the jury on the question of fraud.

D. No, because the fraud defense is an alternative holding implicit in the jury's judgment.

147. Martha was indicted by a federal grand jury for engaging in insider trading on stock issued by Martha's Goodies, Inc. While her criminal case was pending, shareholders of Martha's Goodies stock filed a civil action against Martha involving the same facts and on the same grounds. In the criminal proceeding, the jury acquitted Martha. May Martha use that judgment to preclude the shareholder plaintiffs in the civil action from establishing that she engaged in insider trading?

A. No. A criminal finding cannot be used in a civil proceeding because of the different standards of proof.

B. Yes, since the reasonable doubt standard of proof in the criminal proceeding was higher than preponderance of the evidence standard in the civil proceeding.

C. No. Under no circumstances may Martha use the prior judgment to preclude the shareholders from proving that she engaged in insider trading.

D. Yes. An offensive use of issue preclusion is permitted since the plaintiffs in the civil action could not have intervened in a criminal proceeding and since the subsequent use in the civil proceeding would have been reasonably foreseeable.

148. On behalf of herself and the 92 specific students in her class, P brought an FRCP 23(b)(2) class action against D, claiming that D had arbitrarily assigned final grades in a law school course by drawing names and numbers from two different hats. P sought declaratory relief and an injunction, forcing the teacher to withdraw the original grades and submit a new set based upon actually having read the students' papers. While P was a citizen of State Z, all of her classmates and D were citizens of State Y. The suit was filed in a U.S. district court in State Y, which entered judgment for D after the jury found that P had failed to prove that D did not read the exams. The judgment was affirmed on appeal. Thereafter, X, one of the students in the class who had received a grade of 65, brought an action against D in a State Z court, seeking $76,000 in damages for D's alleged failure to actually read X's exam, as a result of which X received his lowest grade in law school. Which of the following statements is correct?

A. The judgment rendered in the first action is not entitled to full faith and credit in the present suit, if the U.S. district court lacked subject matter jurisdiction.

B. The U.S. district court lacked subject matter jurisdiction because members of the plaintiff class and D were citizens of the same state (State Y).

C. Assuming the federal court had subject matter jurisdiction, D can preclude X from seeking to prove that D failed to read the exams, even though X's action seeks to recover monetary damages (rather than injunctive relief).

D. None of the above.

149. Demosthenes borrowed $76,000 from Plato and signed a promissory note in which he promised to repay that sum, plus interest, in six months. Aristotle guaranteed the note and promised to pay the sum due to Plato in the event Demosthenes defaulted. Demosthenes became delinquent under the note, and Plato sued him to recover the amount due. Demosthenes asserted a usury defense to Plato's claim. Which of the following statements is correct?

A. A judgment in favor of Plato will be binding on Aristotle.

B. Aristotle will neither be bound nor benefited by a judgment in *Plato v. Demosthenes.*

C. If Demosthenes won on the issue of usury, Aristotle probably could assert collateral estoppel in an action brought by Plato against Aristotle on the guaranty.

D. None of the above.

150. A sued B, seeking personal injuries and property damage in the amount of $100,000 for B's negligence in causing a collision with a car driven by A. The jury rendered a verdict for B, expressly finding that B was not negligent. C (a pedestrian walking along the street when he saw the accident) suffered back injuries when he attempted to extricate A from the latter's vehicle. C sued B, claiming B negligently caused the accident and was therefore responsible for C's personal injuries. In the latter action, B made a motion to dismiss based upon the decision rendered in A's earlier lawsuit. Which of the following statements is correct?

A. The court has discretion to determine whether C should be bound by the prior judgment.

B. The court must grant B's motion since C's action is barred under principles of claim preclusion.

C. The court must deny B's motion because C is not bound by the prior judgment.

D. The court must deny B's motion if the state has abandoned the concept of mutuality of estoppel.

Multiple-Choice
Answers

Personal Jurisdiction, Service of Process and Due Process — Answers

1. **B** A *quasi in rem* proceeding is entitled to full faith and credit only if the standards of the minimum contacts test have been satisfied. *Shaffer v. Heitner*, 433 U.S. 186 (1977). Choice **A** is not correct; a *quasi in rem* judgment is entitled to full faith and credit to the extent of the property attached—here the pig—but only if the standards of the minimum contacts test have been satisfied. Choices **C** and **D** are both incorrect because they leave out the crucial minimum contacts requirement.

2. **C** Although it may seem counterintuitive, some courts have interpreted similar language to cover the entire tortious transaction from (the faulty repair) to injury (the malfunction). For the foregoing reason, Choice **A** is wrong. Choice **B** is incorrect since the statute is not clear on this issue. Choice **D** is wrong. The effects test is irrelevant to the statutory construction.

3. **B** The website *Zippo* is passive in the sense that it is not interactive, but *Zippo* is not an independent measure of personal jurisdiction. It is simply a framework that outlines the range of possibilities from which to apply the standards of the minimum contacts test. It is true that a passive website is unlikely to operate as a purposeful contact, but "unlikely" does not mean never. It is quite possible that this website will be treated as a purposeful contact under the effects test since P's claim involves an intentional tort that appears to have been aimed at California where the brunt of the harm is most likely to be felt. For these reasons, the other options are all incorrect.

4. **A** This is a correct statement of the legal standard under FRCP 4(k)(1)(A). Choice **B** is incorrect; while the district court could rely on State Y's service of process standards, it cannot rely on the State Y long-arm statute. Choice **C** is incorrect. FRCP 4(k)(1)(C) and (k)(2) provide potential federal long-arm alternatives. Choice **D** is incorrect. Jurisdiction under a federal long-arm statute must comply with the Fifth Amendment Due Process Clause—minimum contacts with the United States.

5. **A** In the absence of a traditional basis for obtaining personal jurisdiction, the assertion of personal jurisdiction over an out-of-state citizen must (1) conform to the applicable long-arm statute, and (2) be consistent with Fourteenth Amendment due process (i.e., the defendant must have sufficient minimum contacts with the forum as not

to offend traditional notions of fair play and substantial justice). Since E (1) could not foresee being haled into New York (D had misrepresented to E that this trip would terminate in New Jersey), and (2) apparently has no other contacts with New York, the assertion of personal jurisdiction over E would violate due process. Choice **B** is incorrect; the measure of a federal court's jurisdiction in a case such as this is the Fourteenth Amendment Due Process Clause, not the Fifth. Choice **C** is incorrect; FRCP 4(k)(2) applies only in federal question cases and only under limited circumstances. Choice **D** is incorrect; the standards of the effects test would not be satisfied under these facts (intentional act aimed at the forum state where the brunt of the harm would be felt).

6. **A** *Quasi in rem* jurisdiction ordinarily will be tested by the due process standard applicable to personal jurisdiction (i.e., the defendant must have had sufficient minimum contacts with the forum as not to offend traditional notions of fair play and substantial justice). *Shaffer v. Heitner*, 433 U.S. 186 (1977). If D does not have sufficient contacts with State X as would support personal jurisdiction over him, the attachment should be quashed. Choice **B** is incorrect because prejudgment attachments are not *per se* unconstitutional. *Mitchell v. W. T. Grant Co.*, 416 U.S 600 (1974). Assuming proper due process safeguards have been provided, a defendant's property can be seized prior to the time a judgment is actually rendered against him. Choice **C** is incorrect because even if the motion to quash was denied and the boat sold, A could retain proceeds only in an amount equal to his obligation. The balance would have to be remitted to D. Choice **D** is incorrect for the reasons described above.

7. **C** Rule 4(c)(2) provides that, "Any person who is at least 18 years old and *not a party* may serve a summons and complaint." Pete is a party. Choice **A** is incorrect; the fact that Big Time did not receive actual notice is irrelevant. Choice **B** is incorrect; there is no such requirement. Choice **D** is incorrect for the reason stated in Choice **C**.

8. **A** Daria was not properly served under the federal rules (as explained below) and actual notice will not cure that failure. Choice **B** is incorrect. While Daria signed for the certified mailing, she did not sign the waiver. Moreover, a failure to respond to a complaint is not a waiver of the right to service of process. **C** is incorrect. A mailing of a request for waiver of service under FRCP 4(d) will not be treated as proper service even if the mailing otherwise complies with applicable state law. Choice **D** is wrong for the reason given in Choice **A**.

9. **B** The court will credit Destino's version because doing so will allow the party's to litigate the merits of their dispute. Choice **A** is incorrect. By denying the motion, the court will foreclose litigation on the merits. Choice **C** is plausible, but unlikely given the time and inefficiencies that would be involved in holding a mini-trial. Choice **D** is incorrect. Actual notice does not cure a failure to comply with rules pertaining to proper service of process.

10. **D** Given the facts within the Treasurer's knowledge—that is, the return of the certified mail, the chosen methods were not reasonably calculated to apprise Petronius of the pending sale. This was the holding in *Jones v. Flowers*, 547 U.S. 220 (2006). Choice **A** is incorrect; there is no such standard. Choice **B** is incorrect; the fact that the letter was properly addressed does not resolve the due process issue. Choice **C** is incorrect; while personal service will usually satisfy due process, it is not necessarily the preferred method and the use of alternative methods will not necessarily violate due process.

11. **D** A state that does not recognize the validity of cognovit clauses must nonetheless give full, faith and credit to a sister state's judgment premised on a cognovit clause so long as the standards of due process have been satisfied—that is, so long as the defendant voluntarily, knowingly, and intelligently agreed to be bound by the clause. Choice **A** misstates the law. Choice **B** fails to incorporate the due process limits on the enforceability of a cognovit clause. Choice **C** misstates the law; there is no such enforceability distinction.

12. **D** These facts present a classic instance to which the doctrine of witness immunity would apply. W was in the state to testify in a pending case and she remained there only due to the delay in her scheduled testimony. Choice **A** is incorrect. Engaging in such casual (and expected) activity the night before the scheduled testimony would not waive the immunity. Choice **B** is incorrect. No warning is required under circumstances such as those presented here. The only question is whether the party has engaged in sufficient non-litigation activities to warrant a finding of waiver. Choice **C** is incorrect. The immunity applies to "completely separate" proceedings.

13. **A** In the absence of outrageous conduct that shocks the conscience, trickery within the jurisdiction is permissible—that is, a party who is in the jurisdiction may be tricked into revealing her whereabouts. Choice **B** is incorrect. There is no evidence of evasion here, nor is there a requirement that evasion be shown. Choice **C** is factually correct, but legally incorrect. Choice **D** is incorrect since Dilbert

was not tricked into the jurisdiction, but tricked into revealing his whereabouts.

14. **D** All of these options are available under the federal rules. *See* FRCP 4(e).

15. **B** A party is not required to adopt the best or most effective method of service. Rather, a party is required to use a method that is reasonably calculated to apprise the defendant of the pending lawsuit. Under the given facts, service on Frank was reasonably calculated to be effective. Choice **A** misstates the due process standard. Choice **C** would only be correct if the plaintiff learned that the initial method of service had been ineffective. Choice **D** is incorrect. Due process is not automatically satisfied by satisfaction of statutory service standards.

16. **D** Given the practicalities, the method adopted by the City was reasonably calculated to give P notice of his parking violations. While other methods, such as personal service, might be more likely to work. The expense of such methods outweighs their superior efficacy. Hence, Choice **A** is incorrect. Choice **B** is incorrect since it relies on a standard that applies only when there are no methods reasonably calculated to work. When there are such methods available, a plaintiff has a degree of latitude to choose among the alternatives. Choice **C** is incorrect. The fact that P should have known he was illegally parked is irrelevant.

17. **C** When a person is deprived of a property interest by the state, that person is presumptively entitled to a pre-deprivation hearing. That presumption is rebuttable, and under the given facts, a court would likely find that City could due away with a pre-deprivation hearing on a theory of exigent circumstances. The City would, however, be required to provide P with a prompt post-deprivation hearing. Choice **A** is incorrect. A failure to appear does not constitute a waiver. Choice **B** is incorrect. Under the given facts, including the mobility of the vehicle, the City was not required to provide a hearing prior to placing the boot on P's car. Choice **D** is incorrect; P was entitled to a prompt post-deprivation hearing.

18. **C** In a FRCP 23(b)(3) class action, the "notice must clearly and concisely state in plain, easily understood language: (i) the nature of the action; (ii) the definition of the class certified; (iii) the class claims, issues, or defenses; (iv) that a class member may enter an appearance through an attorney if the member so desires; (v) that the court

will exclude from the class any member who requests exclusion; (vi) the time and manner for requesting exclusion; and (vii) the binding effect of a class judgment on members under Rule 23(c)(3)." FRCP 23(c)(2)(B). Since the notice fails to indicate the nature of the action and that a final judgment is binding upon all members of the class, it is inadequate. Choice **A** is incorrect because the plaintiff (rather than the defendant) must pay the costs of mailings to class members. Choice **B** is incorrect because a class action judgment has collateral estoppel effect with respect to individuals who opt out of the class. Choice **D** is incorrect because choice **C** is true.

19. **C** Under FRCP 4(k)(1), federal courts generally borrow the long-arm statute of the jurisdiction in which the federal court is located. Although ABC arguably had minimum contacts with Florida as a consequence of its knowledge that its motors were integrated into yachts that were sold in that state, the Florida long-arm statute precludes personal jurisdiction in this situation because ABC neither has sold any products in Florida nor to a Florida domiciliary. Choice **A** is incorrect since Florida's long-arm statute does not permit the assertion of personal jurisdiction in this instance. Choice **B** is incorrect because the fact that ABC did business with the party that sold the item in question does not bring the actions of ABC within the scope of the Florida statute. Choice **D** is incorrect because ABC's knowledge that its motors might be operated in Florida could constitute "sufficient minimum contacts" with Florida is irrelevant to the statutory issue.

20. **A** A court may exercise personal jurisdiction over a defendant who is served while physically present in the jurisdiction. Because Dan was personally served while voluntarily in California, the courts of California may exercise jurisdiction over him. Choice **B** is incorrect because Dan probably lacks adequate minimum contacts with California; he is there only four days per year and at the discretion of his employers. Choice **C** is incorrect because, although Dan probably lacked minimum contacts with California, he was personally served in the jurisdiction. Choice **D** is incorrect. Relatedness is irrelevant under these circumstances.

21. **C** Under FRCP 12(b), "[e]very defense . . . to a claim for relief in any pleading shall be asserted in the responsive pleading . . . except that the following defenses may at the option of the pleader be made by motion: . . . (2) lack of jurisdiction over the person. . . . A motion making any of these defenses shall be made before pleading if a

further pleading is permitted." Since Dan failed to object to personal jurisdiction in his first pleading (his answer and counterclaim), he has waived this defense. Each of the other choices presents an incorrect statement of the law.

Venue, Transfer and Forum non Conveniens — Answers

22. **B** The case may be transferred to a district where it could have been filed, and both the E.D. and the C.D. qualify under this standard — the former, based on substantial events giving rise to the claim and the later based on D's residence there. Choice **A** is incorrect (given the explanation for choice **B**). In addition, the fact that D resided in the E.D. at the time the claim arose is irrelevant for purposes of venue. Choice **C** is incorrect, 28 U.S.C. §1406(a) gives the district court the option to transfer a case that has been filed in the wrong venue. Choice **D** is incorrect; P has no such right.

23. **C** is correct. Since the contract was negotiated and signed in Los Angeles, it is correct to conclude that substantial events giving rise to the claim occurred in the Central District. Choice **A** is incorrect as it relies on an improper standard. Choice **B** is incorrect since substantial events giving rise to a claim can occur in more than one location. Choice **D** is incorrect. Venue would be proper in Arizona based on Dermot's residence there.

24. **D** is correct. Since venue was properly laid in the SDNY under §1391(b)(2)(substantial events giving rise to the claim), on transfer to the DNJ, the law of the initial forum must be followed. Choice **A** is incorrect; venue was proper in the SDNY under §1391(b)(2), not (b)(3). Choice **B** is incorrect to the extent it relies of the venue fallback provision. Choice **C** would be correct only if venue in the SDNY was improper; as previously noted, venue in the SDNY was proper.

25. **B** is correct. This is the somewhat counterintuitive rule established in *Stewart Organization, Inc. v. Ricoh Corp.*, 487 U.S. 22 (1988). Choice **A** is incorrect; a federal court may not transfer a case to a state court under any circumstances. Choice **C** is incorrect; the forum selection clause provides a federal option — that is, a federal court sitting in Cook County, Illinois. Choice **D** may seem like the sensible option; but that is not the rule (as noted in the explanation to choice **B**).

26. **B** In a state with multiple judicial districts, a corporation is deemed to be a resident in any "district in that State within which its contacts would be sufficient to subject it to personal jurisdiction if that district were a separate State, and, if there is no such district, the corporation shall be deemed to reside in the district within which it has the most significant contacts." The facts do not indicate any contacts

between Desiree and the Southern District, though they do reveal contacts with the Eastern District. Hence, Desiree will not be treated as a resident of the Southern District. Similarly, the facts do not indicate that substantial events giving rise to Pacifica's claim occurred in the Southern District. Choice **A** misstates the law. Corporate residence for purposes of venue includes those judicial districts in which the corporation is subject to personal jurisdiction. Choice **C** would be correct only if California had only a single judicial district. Choice **D** is factually inaccurate.

27. **B** Proper removal establishes proper venue regardless of non-compliance with other venue provisions. See 28 U.S.C. §1390(c). For this reason, while choices **A** and **C** are both factually correct, the "no" conclusion of each is incorrect. Choice **D** references the general venue "fallback" provision, which is both irrelevant (the explanation for choice **B**) and unavailable, there being alternate venue available in Colorado.

28. **B** Under the federal doctrine of forum non conveniens, the district court may take into account the relevant law of the forum state. For this same reason, choice **A** is incorrect. Choice **C** is incorrect. Despite the fact that the incident occurred in Norway, plaintiff's choice of forum will remain a factor in the calculus. Choice **D** is incorrect; a federal court has no means of *transferring* a case to a foreign tribunal.

29. **B** Transfer would be appropriate since the case could have originally been brought in State Y and since State W has no connection to the controversy. Indeed, venue was improper in State W. (Note: Although for venue purposes a corporation will be deemed a resident of any district in which the standards of personal jurisdiction can be satisfied, 28 U.S.C. §1391(c), this cause of action has no connection with State W or any district therein. Hence, D would not be treated as a resident of State W under the given facts.) That being the case, the transfer would be pursuant to §1406(a). In a §1406(a) transfer, the substantive law does not travel with the transfer. Rather, the law of the transferee court must be followed. Hence a U.S. district court in State Y would apply the law a State Y court would apply to the controversy. Choice **A** is incorrect because D is a citizen of State Y since its principal place of business is there. Thus, removal is not possible. Choice **C** is incorrect because, where a joint claim is involved, each plaintiff is viewed as asserting the entire sum requested. Choice **D** is incorrect because choice **B** is true.

30. **A** Under the general venue statute, the proper judicial district for venue purposes is one in which (1) any defendant resides, if all defendants reside in the same state; (2) a substantial part of the events or omissions on which the claim is based occurred or a substantial part of the property is located; or (3) if there is no federal venue where the suit may otherwise be brought, a venue in which any defendant is subject to personal jurisdiction. 28 U.S.C. §1391(b). If venue is improper, a U.S. district court may dismiss the case or transfer the action to another U.S. district court in which the matter could have originally been commenced. 28 U.S.C. §1406(a). Although D was improperly served, he apparently waived this error by making a motion to transfer the case to State Z. Since the original venue was improper, the court could transfer the action to State Z where the suit could have originally been commenced. Choice **B** is incorrect since venue is not proper in State Y. Choice **C** is incorrect since D has waived any challenge to service. Choice **D** is incorrect. While the policy of State Y would be a factor to consider if venue had been proper in the State Y federal court, it is not a factor here since venue was not proper in the State Y federal court.

31. **B** The forum selection clause is fully enforceable. Hence, venue in Oregon was proper. A transfer of the case, if one were ordered, would be pursuant to 28 U.S.C. §1404(a) (one proper venue to another proper venue). In such a case, the transferee court will apply the law that would have been applied by the transferor court, here the U.S. district court sitting in Oregon. Choice **A** is incorrect. Section 1406(a) would only be used if venue had been improper in Oregon. **C** is incorrect; there is no such rule. Choice **D** is incorrect because choice **B** is correct.

Subject Matter Jurisdiction – Answers

32. D Penny asserts a federal claim against the BVPD. Since federal law creates her claim, both statutory and constitutional "arising under" standards are satisfied. Satisfaction of the former is premised on the fact that federal law creates the claim; satisfaction of the latter is premised on the presence of an actual federal ingredient in the case, a broader standard that is universally satisfied when the statutory standard has been met. For the reasons given, all the other options are incorrect.

33. D U.S. district courts are competent to hear cases involving a federal claim (i.e., one arising under the Constitution, a treaty, or the laws of the United States). Since Acme is asserting a federal claim against the Union, subject matter jurisdiction exists—even though the amount in controversy does not exceed $75,000. Choices **A, B,** and **C** would only be accurate if jurisdiction were asserted under §1332. Had that been the case, all three would be correct since the parties would not be diverse under choice **A**, for the Union would be a citizen of Indiana by virtue of the residence of its members; the amount in controversy would not be satisfied under choice **B** as it does not exceed $75,000; but the amount would be satisfied under the additional assumption provided in choice **C**.

34. B Plaintiff has asserted a state-law claim that includes an essential federal ingredient. That ingredient is subject to a dispute between the parties, substantial in the sense that a federal forum would be appropriate, and unlikely to upset the jurisdictional balance between state and federal courts given the narrow, fact-specific nature of the disputed issue. Choice **A** is incorrect—P's breach of contract claim was not created by federal law. Choice **C** is a misstatement of the creation test. Choice **D** is incorrect since satisfaction of Article III standards is not, in itself, sufficient to establish subject matter jurisdiction; statutory standards must be satisfied as well.

35. C Pablo asserts a breach of contract claim that includes no federal element. The fact that the case "involves" a patent in some general way is not sufficient to satisfy either the creation test or the essential federal ingredient test. **A** is incorrect; the federal court's exclusive jurisdiction is limited to patent claims and does not encompass all claims that in some manner involve a patent. **B** is wrong for the same reason; patent law does not create Pablo's breach of contract claim.

D is wrong; there is no federal ingredient in Pablo's claim that the Distributor has not used "best efforts" to market Pablo's patent.

36. **C** In an action for declaratory relief, jurisdiction is viewed from the perspective of the party who would have an action for coercive relief—for example, monetary damages or an injunction. Here that would be Danny who would have a patent infringement claim. Hence, federal question jurisdiction is established under the creation test. Choices **A** and **B** are incorrect; a counterclaim cannot be used to establish federal question jurisdiction. Choice **D** is incorrect for the reasons give with respect to choice **C**.

37. **C** The Supreme Court's jurisdiction to review state court judgments is controlled by 28 U.S.C. §1257, which allows the Supreme Court to review state-court decisions ("highest court of a State in which a decision could be had") in which a federal question has been raised and decided. Choice **A** is incorrect; the Supreme Court's jurisdiction over state court decisions is not derivative. Choice **B** is incorrect; neither §1331 nor §1332 have any bearing on the Supreme Court's jurisdiction over a case decided by a state court. Choice **D** is incorrect; there is no such limitation on the Supreme Court's jurisdiction to hear a case decided by a state court.

38. **B** Since no plaintiff is from the same state as the plaintiff, the complete diversity standard is satisfied. Choice **A** is incorrect. The complete diversity requirement does not prevent multiple defendants from being from the same state. Choices **C** and **D** are wrong for the reasons given with respect to choice **B**.

39. **D** Since Duncan is not a citizen of any state, he can neither sue nor be sued in diversity. His presence in the suit is inconsistent with the standards of §1332(a)(1). Choices **A, B,** and **C** each state incorrect legal propositions.

40. **D** Paula is a citizen of Florida (a given) and Delivery is a citizen of Delaware and New York. This conclusion is a product of the Supreme Court's decision in *Hertz v. Friend*, which endorsed the "nerve center" test as the exclusive measure of a corporation's principal place of business. Choice **A** states a false legal proposition. Choice **B** would be correct under the place-of-operations test, but as noted with respect to choice **D**, that is no longer the appropriate test. The facts and proposition stated in choice **C** are irrelevant to the question of subject matter jurisdiction.

41. B Citizenship is measured as of the date of filing. Hence, Paula will be treated as a citizen of Delaware and diversity will be defeated. Choice **A** misstates the law. Choice **C** also misstates the law. If the district court lacks jurisdiction, it has not choice but to dismiss the case. Choice **D** is incorrect. Paula must be diverse from Delivery's state of incorporation and its principal place of business.

42. A Diversity jurisdiction does not extend to suits between a citizen of a state and a permanent resident alien who resides in that same state. Choice **B** is accurate factually, but overlooks the effect of Duha's residence in State X. Choice **C** is accurate legally, but also overlooks the effect of Duha's residence in State X. Choice **D** is not correct; aliens can be on different sides of a controversy filed under §1332(a)(3), which this would be.

43. A Pearl and Dilapidated are both citizens of State X, the later by virtue of its headquarters there. Choice **B** is incorrect; the Supreme Court, in *Hertz v. Friend*, established the nerve center as the exclusive measure of principal place of business. Choice **C** incorrectly describes the holding in *Hertz*. Choice **D** misstates the law.

44. B A partnership is a citizen of every state in which a partner resides; hence, both Pearl and Dilapidated are citizens of State X. Choice **A** is incorrect; that standards of minimal diversity are relevant here. Choice **C** is not correct; principal place of business does not define the jurisdictional citizenship of an unincorporated association. Choice **D** misstates the law. There is no such rule.

45. D Since Padma has asserted a federal claim, the amount in controversy is irrelevant. Choices **A** and **C** are incorrect since each presumes an amount in controversy requirement. Choice **B** is incorrect since Padma has asserted a federal claim and there is nothing in the question to indicate the insufficiency of her allegations.

46. A Diversity is satisfied and Petal may aggregate all of her claims, related or otherwise. Choice **B** misstates the law of aggregation. Choice **C** is not correct; a challenge to subject matter jurisdiction is not waived by a general appearance. Choice**D** is incorrect; there is no such requirement when suing a single defendant.

47. B Adopting the party-with-the-most-to-gain-or-lose approach, the potential loss to Sand Claims exceeds the jurisdictional minimum. Choice **A** is not correct since under the plaintiff-viewpoint rule, no single plaintiff satisfies the amount in controversy and the plaintiffs would not be allowed to aggregate their separate claims. Choice **C**

is not accurate since the party invoking jurisdiction is Sandy Clams and from that perspective the amount in controversy is satisfied (as in choice **B**). Choice **D** is incorrect, but choice **B** is correct.

48. **C** Pamela's claim is a federal question attached to a claim that is otherwise non-removable. Section 144(c) allows removal under these precise circumstances. Choice **A** is incorrect since the removal was timely, that is, within 30 days of the receipt of service of process. 28 U.S.C. §1446(b). Choice **B** is incorrect since the entire cases — a federal claim and an unrelated state-law claim — could not have been filed in a federal district court originally. Choice **D** is wrong because choice **C** is correct.

49. **C** This is precisely the result that §1441(c) requires — a remand of the otherwise non-removable claim. Choice **A** is similar to choice **C**, but incorrect because of the word "dismiss." Choice **B** is wrong; the court does not have discretion to retain the non-removable claim under current standards. Choice **D** is wrong; the court must remand only the non-removable claim.

50. **B** P's claim runs afoul of §1367(b) and the Supreme Court's decision in *Owen Equipment v. Kroger*, 437 U.S. 365 (1978), and as a consequence is inconsistent with the jurisdictional requirements of §1332. Choice **A** is incorrect; while the federal rules would allow such claim, the standards of jurisdiction still must be satisfied and as the discussion of choice **B** indicates, those standards would not be satisfied here. Choice **C** is incorrect. The district court has no discretion under these circumstances. It must dismiss. Choice **D** is accurate factually, but incorrect from a jurisdictional perspective.

51. **B** Polly has asserted a claim under a federal statute, thus satisfying the creation test. Choice **A** is incorrect; the defendant's state of citizenship is not relevant in federal question removals. Choice **C** is incorrect to the extent that this is a federal question case. Choice **D** misstates the law.

52. **C** In accord with 28 U.S.C. §1367(a)-(b), the district court may exercise supplemental jurisdiction over Bop's claim. This was the precise holding in *Exxon Mobil Corp. v. Allapattah Services, Inc.*, 545 U.S. 546 (2005). Choice **A** is incorrect since Bop's claim does not satisfy the diversity amount in controversy requirement. Choice **B** is incorrect for the reasons given in choice **C** above. Choice **D** is incorrect since it is premised on a misconception of §1367(b) standards. That

section imposes no limitations on a plaintiff joined under FRCP 20 when filing a claim against a single defendant.

53. **D** Section 1367(b) precludes a plaintiff from filing a claim against a party joined pursuant to FRCP 14, 19, 20 or 24 when doing so would be inconsistent with the jurisdictional requirements of §1332. Cineplex and Iolana were joined under FRCP 20(a)(2) and Bop's claim does not satisfy §1332's amount in controversy requirement. Choice **A** is incorrect since Iolana is diverse from Bee and Bop. Choice **B** is incorrect. FRCP 20(a)(2) would permit joinder under these circumstances. Choice **C** is incorrect for the reasons given in choice **D** above—that is, §1367(b) precludes the exercise of supplemental jurisdiction over Bop's claims.

54. **C** Under the Class Action Fairness Act of 2005, 28 U.S.C. §1332(d)(2), federal courts may exercise diversity jurisdiction over a class action in which the aggregate amount in controversy exceeds $5 million, exclusive of interests and costs, and in which any member of the class is a citizen of a state different from any defendant. Choice **C** is therefore correct since the aggregate amount in controversy exceeds $5 million and since some of the class members are domiciled in states other than New York and Illinois. Choice **A** is incorrect because complete diversity is not required under these circumstances. Choice **B** is incorrect because aggregation is specifically allowed in class actions so long as the aggregated amount exceeds $5 million. Choice **D** is incorrect because it combines two incorrect answers.

55. **B** Section 1446(c)(2)(A)-(B) permits removal under the given circumstances if the plaintiff can prove by a preponderance of the evidence that the amount in controversy exceeds the statutory minimum. Choice **A** is incorrect. There is not such rule. Choices **C** and **D** are both incorrect based on the standard set in §1446(c)(2)(A)-(B).

56. **A** A party asserting a claim against a single defendant may join any claims she has against that defendant. FRCP 18(a). In addition, a plaintiff may aggregate unrelated claims for purposes of satisfying the amount in controversy requirement. Paul, therefore, may assert an unrelated breach of contract action against Mary. Choice **B** is incorrect because Peter's crossclaim must arise out of the transaction or occurrence that is the subject matter of the original action under FRCP 13(g). In addition, there would be no independent basis of jurisdiction over this claim since Peter and Mary are not diverse and since it does not appear to raise a federal question. Choice **C**

is incorrect because a plaintiff may aggregate personal injury and property claims to satisfy the amount in controversy requirement. Choice **D** is incorrect because choice **A** is correct.

57. **A** A U.S. district court is competent to hear federal claims (i.e., claims arising under the Constitution, a treaty, or the laws of the United States). 28 U.S.C. §1331. Since the plaintiffs are asserting a right under the U.S. Constitution, "federal claim" subject matter jurisdiction exists (regardless of diversity or the amount in controversy). **B** is incorrect because the court would have subject matter jurisdiction regardless of the standards of §1332. Choice **C** is incorrect because §1331 does not impose an "amount in controversy" requirement. **D** is incorrect for the same reason as **B**.

58. **B** The liberal joinder rules principles of FRCP 18(a) (joinder of claims) and 20(a) (joinder of parties) would allow the joinder of these claims and parties. Hence, choice **A** is incorrect. Choice **B** is correct because the court may exercise supplemental jurisdiction over Q's claim. Section 1367(a) permits a federal court to exercise "supplemental party" jurisdiction over claims brought by additional parties so long as those claims arise out of the same transaction or common nucleus of operatives as the claim over which the court has an independent basis of jurisdiction. Section 1367(b), which limits the exercise of such "supplemental party" jurisdiction in diversity cases, would not apply here because the text of that subsection does not limit claims filed by supplemental parties against the original defendant when the supplemental party did not enter the case via FRCP 19 or 24 and when the party against whom the claim was filed was not joined pursuant to FRCP 14, 19, 20, or 24. None of those limits apply here. Choice **C** is incorrect because P's claim for damages to his car is unrelated to dismissal from his job. Thus, no claim-splitting would result from P's failure to assert the damage to his car in the present action, and *res judicata* is not applicable. If P had not asserted the claim for damage to his car, subject matter jurisdiction based upon diversity would not exist for that claim (i.e., P's claim would not exceed $75,000). Choice **D** is incorrect because choice **B** is correct.

59. **A** Where a claim over which the federal courts would have original jurisdiction is brought in a state court, the action may be removed to the U.S. district court that sits in the judicial district that encompasses the state court, if (1) all the defendants join in the petition for removal, and (2) removal is sought within 30 days from the time the

moving party receives service of process. 28 U.S.C. §1446(b). Since federal courts have exclusive jurisdiction over copyright claims, the action is removable; the state court's lack of jurisdiction is irrelevant for removal purposes. 28 U.S.C. §1441(e). Choice **B** is incorrect since subject matter jurisdiction is not lacking because the action is premised on a federal claim. Choice **C** is incorrect because a judgment by a court that was not competent can ordinarily be challenged on appeal. Choice **D** is incorrect because choice **A** is true.

60. D All defendants must join in a petition for removal such as this one. 28 U.S.C. §1446(b)(2)(A). Hence, choice **B** is correct. In addition, a diversity case may not be removed to federal if any defendant is a citizen of the forum state. 28 U.S.C. §1441(b)(2). State Barn is citizen of Utah. Hence, choice **C** is correct. Choice **A** is incorrect for the reasons stated with respect to choice **C**. Therefore, choice **D** is the correct answer because both choices **B** and **C** are correct, while choice **A** is not.

61. A U.S. district courts have subject matter jurisdiction over federal claims (i.e., claims arising under the Constitution, a treaty, or the laws of the United States). There is no "federal question" because Polly has alluded to a violation of the U.S. Constitution only in the context of anticipating a possible defense that might be raised by Denny. Under the well-pleaded complaint rule, the anticipation of a defense based upon the U.S. Constitution or a federal statute cannot serve as the basis for subject matter jurisdiction in federal court. Moreover, the fact that Denny has raised the defense is irrelevant since jurisdiction must be determined on the face of the complaint. Additionally, as to diversity, the amount in controversy is not satisfied—Polly's claim is for only $3,000 (six months' rent at $500 per month). Choice **B** is incorrect. A defect in subject matter jurisdiction cannot be waived. Choices **C** and **D** are incorrect for the reasons stated in choice **A**.

Erie and Related Doctrines – Answers

62. C Under *Erie Railroad Co. v. Tompkins*, 304 U.S. 64 (1938), a district court sitting in diversity must apply the substantive law that a state court of the forum state would apply to the controversy. This requires that the district court determine the current status of that law. With that in mind, a precedent that is over 50 years old is not necessarily binding. Hence, Choice **A** is not correct. The question is not what the state's high court held in the past; it is what that court would hold today. Choice **B** is incorrect; the legislative intent behind pending legislation is irrelevant. Choice **D** is incorrect. The "arc of the law" in other states is only relevant to the extent it might indicate the direction the forum state courts would take if presented with the issue.

63. D A federal procedural statute must be applied if it is sufficiently broad to control the issue presented and if it is rationally classifiable as procedural. The issue presented is whether removal is proper, which is the precise question §1441 addresses, that is, removability. Moreover, §1441 is rationally classifiable as procedural since it operates to allocate jurisdiction between state and federal courts. Hence, the federal law of removal must be applied. Choice **A** is incorrect. State law cannot alter the federal law of removal. Choice **B** is incorrect. Valid federal law is not subsidiary to state law in diversity cases. Choice **C** is incorrect. The application of valid federal law is not dependent on the federal court's ability to comply with state law.

64. A If a federal rule is sufficiently broad to control the issue presented, is arguably procedural, and does not abridge, enlarge or modify a substantive right, the rule must be applied regardless of state law to the contrary. Rule 8(a)(2) creates the pleading standard to be applied in civil actions filed in federal courts; as such it satisfies each of the foregoing standard. That is to say that it is sufficiently broad to control the issue presented (i.e., the standard of pleading to be followed), it is arguably procedural in that it pertains to the method for instituting a lawsuit in federal court, and it does not in any fashion alter the *substantive* legal standards of to be applied. Choice **B** is an incorrect (overstatement) of the controlling principles. Choice **C** is premised on an incorrect legal principle. As to choice **D**, which is also incorrect, the "abridge, enlarge or modify" qualification pertains to "substantive" rights, not "substantial" rights.

65. D A state claim that is not enforceable as a matter of state law, cannot be filed in a federal court sitting in diversity. *Guaranty Trust Co. v. York*, 326 U.S. 99 (1945). Choice **A** is incorrect. There is no federal statute of limitations for state-law claims. Choice **B** is incorrect to the extent that it ignores the State A report-filing prerequisite. Choice **C** is incorrect since the time to file the report has expired as a matter of State A law.

66. C A district court cannot ignore an applicable constitutional standard, regardless of state law to the contrary. Choice **A** describes the standard applicable to federal judge-made procedural principles such as the doctrine of forum non conveniens. It has no bearing on the scope or applicability of a constitutional standard. Choice **B** states the standard applicable to formal federal rules promulgated pursuant to the Rules Enabling Act. It too has not bearing on the scope or applicability of a constitutional standard. Choice **D** is wrong for the same reason as is choice **A**.

67. C Although federal preclusion law determines the preclusive effect of a federal judgment, in diversity cases that federal law will usually incorporate the law of the state in which the federal court sits. *Semtek Int'l Inc. v. Lockheed Martin Corp.*, 531 U.S. 497 (2001). Hence, the question of whether the State X court should grant the motion is dependent on the preclusion law of State Y—the forum state in the original federal court proceeding. Choice **A** is incorrect. The *Semtek* Court interpreted FRCP 41(b) as having no bearing on the scope of claim preclusion. Choices **B** and **D** are incorrect. Although federal courts sitting in diversity apply a federal preclusion standard, that standard is not uniform as noted in the explanation for choice **C**.

68. A FRCP 14(a) is designed to permit the joinder of third parties under a theory of indemnity. This is a procedural device that promotes the efficient resolution of the overall controversy. The rule does not facially or as applied here abridge, enlarge, or modify the standards for indemnity; rather, it pertains only to filing of such claims against absent third parties. Choice **B** is incorrect. FRCP 14(a) specifically applies to the circumstances presented. Choice **C** is incorrect; so long as the rule does not abridge, enlarge, or modify the state substantive claim, it is valid and must be applied. Choice **D** is incorrect. The rule does not modify the substantive claim in any fashion.

69. C There is no conflict between the affidavit-of-merit requirement and the federal rule since the federal rule addresses only experts who will testify at trial. **A** is an incorrect statement of the law. Choice **B** is incorrect since there is no conflict between the federal rule and the state law. Choice **D** is incorrect for the reasons given in Choice **C**.

70. **A** To be outcome determinative under *Hanna v. Plumer*, 380 U.S. 460 (1965), the difference in outcomes between the application of state law and federal common law must be such that the difference would lead to forum shopping and the inequitable administration of the laws. That would occur, for example, if application of the federal standard enlarged the state-law claim. That is not the case here, for it is not even clear if which party will be advantaged by the federal practice. Choice **B** is incorrect for the preceding reasons. Choices **C** and **D** misstate the law.

71. **A** The FRCP must be followed if the rule at issue conforms to the standards imposed by the Rules Enabling Act ("REA"). Choice **A** correctly describes those standards. Moreover, FRCP 8(a)(2) is consistent with the requirements of the REA, for it can be rationally classified as procedural (it defines part of the process for commencing a lawsuit) and it does not abridge, enlarge, or modify any state substantive right, the state "particularity" requirement being no more than procedural rule applicable in state courts. Hence, Choice **A** is correct. Choice **B** misstates the law. State policy cannot trump a valid federal rule. Choice **C** is incorrect; it confuses "substantial" with "substantive." Choice **D** is partially correct, but still the validity of the rule must be tested against the two-part standard imposed by the REA, as described and correctly applied in choice **A**.

Pleadings and Discovery—Answers

72. **A** In all averments of fraud or mistake, the circumstances constituting fraud or mistake shall be stated with particularity. FRCP 9(b). While FRCP 8(a)(2) requires only "a short and plain statement of the claim showing that the pleader is entitled to relief," FRCP 9(b) imposes a particularity requirement on allegations of fraud. Choice **B** is incorrect because the assertion of a fraud constitutes an exception to the general rules for pleading in federal court. Choice **C** is incorrect because the manner of pleading prescribed by the FRCP controls in the event of a conflict with an otherwise applicable state rule of pleading. Choice **D** is incorrect because choice **A** is true.

73. **B** This choice describes the correct legal standard. Moreover, given the nature of Plaintiff's claims, the matters requested are reasonably calculated to lead to admissible evidence. Choice **A** is incorrect as there is no such admissibility standard on discovery. Choices **C** and **D** are both incorrect as nothing in the request appears to seek confidential communications between the defendant and its attorney; nor does the request appear to include work product.

74. **D** is correct. This is consistent with the standard adopted by the U.S. Supreme Court in *Seattle Times Co. v. Rhinehart*, 467 U.S. 20 (1984). Choice **A** is incorrect, given the rule in *Seattle Times*. Choice **B** is incorrect. The First Amendment limits the district court's discretion. Choice **C** is incorrect. The public has no such broad-based right.

75. **B** The requested privilege is not one recognized under federal law and given the strong presumption against the creation of new privileges is unlikely to be so recognized. In addition, Choice **B** is superior to all the other choices since each of them is plainly incorrect. Choice **A** is incorrect to the extent that it purports to cover the assertion of a privilege in a federal question case. Federal courts recognize state privileges only on questions of state law. *See* Federal Rule of Evidence 501. **C** is incorrect; the presumption goes the other way. Choice **D** is incorrect; federal courts are empowered to recognize new privileges. *See*, for example, *Jaffee v. Redmond*, 518 U.S. 1 (1996) (recognizing psychotherapist-patient privilege).

76. **A** Corporate counsel's interview with Hi-Lo is protected since it was undertaken in the context of advice to be given to the client, that is, the corporation. *See Upjohn Company v. United States*, 449 U.S. 383 (1981). Choice **B** arrives at the correct conclusion, but Hi-Lo status as

a non-party is irrelevant. Choice **C** is incorrect for the reasons given in choice **A**. Choice **D** misstates the law as established in *Upjohn*.

77. **B** It is a common practice in personal injury suits to employ the services of an investigator to assist the attorney. Those services fall within the scope of the work-product doctrine. Choice **A** is incorrect to the extent that the interrogatory seeks work product. Choice **C** is incorrect. This compound interrogatory will count as more than one interrogatory. Choice **D** is incorrect. There is no such rule.

78. **A** This is the standard adopted by the U.S. Supreme Court and would not be satisfied by merely showing that the engineer thought the car was moving just prior to the accident. *See Schlagenhauf v. Holder*, 379 U.S. 104 (1964). Choice **B** is incorrect. Satisfaction of discovery relevance is not sufficient to establish the "good cause" standards of FRCP 35. Choice **C** is incorrect; state law is irrelevant. Choice **D** is incorrect; there is no such merger principle. In any event, such a merger would be inconsistent with the rule established in *Schlagenhauf*.

79. **C** A party may ordinarily obtain discovery of documents and other tangible items prepared in anticipation of litigation or for trial, (1) by or for another party, or (2) by or for that other party's representative (including her attorney), only upon a showing that (1) the party seeking such discovery has a substantial need for the items, and (2) she is unable, without undue hardship, to obtain the equivalent thereof by other means. FRCP 26(b)(3)(A). Choice **A** is incorrect because, even if the report satisfies the discovery relevance standard, it would only be discoverable under the standards described above. Choice **B** is incorrect since the report is not a confidential communication between Delta and its attorney. Choice **D** is incorrect given the standards of FRCP 26(b)(3)(A), as discussed in choice **C**.

80. **B** FRCP 26(b)(3)(B) provides that under such circumstances the district court "must protect against disclosure of the mental impressions, conclusions, opinions, or legal theories of a party's attorney . . . ." Choice **A** is incorrect since there is a less drastic alternative as described in choice **B**. Choice **C** is incorrect; there is no such rule. Choice **D** is incorrect; while the annotations may indeed constitute opinion work product, that fact alone does not taint the entire report.

81. **A** The discovery request is relevant to plaintiff's claim since it is reasonably calculated to disclose the nature of the electrical defect, if

any, in the model line. Choice **B** misstates the law; admissibility at trial is not the standard. Choices **C** and **D** are incorrect for the reason given in choice **A**.

82. **B** Under the FRCP, a pleading must contain a short and plain statement of the claim showing the pleader is entitled to relief. FRCP 8(a). Phil's complaint is certainly minimal, but there is enough there to give Dowd notice that Phil believes Dowd is liable for the injuries Phil incurred in the accident. Notice pleading requires no more than this. See Form 11 (Complaint for Negligence), FRCP Appendix of Forms. Choice **A** is incorrect because a complaint will not be dismissed for the reasons just given. Choice **C** is incorrect because under the FRCP it is not necessary for a plaintiff to articulate the precise legal theory upon which relief is sought. Choice **D** is incorrect for the same reason that choice **A** is incorrect.

83. **C** A party may set forth two or more claims alternatively. FRCP 8(d)(3). Since the FRCP specifically authorizes separate claims, regardless of consistency, a complaint setting forth two different theories for recovery is permissible. In this instance, the inconsistency may be explainable by Phil's inability to recollect the exact circumstances of the accident. Choice **B** is incorrect because the Appendix of Forms permits a simple allegation of negligence. See Form 11 (Complaint for Negligence), FRCP Appendix of Forms. Choices **A** and **D** are incorrect because federal pleadings may contain inconsistent claims or defenses.

84. **B** Where evidence is objected to at trial on the grounds that it is not within the pleadings, a court "should freely permit an amendment [to the pleadings] when doing so will aid in presenting the merits and the objecting party fails to satisfy the court that the evidence would prejudice that party's action or defense on the merits." FRCP 15(b)(1). Although Danielle failed to raise anticipatory repudiation as a defense, she could be permitted by the court to amend her pleadings at trial to conform to the evidence that she wishes to introduce. Choice **A** is incorrect because there is no such *per se* rule. Choice **C** is incorrect because amendments to pleadings may be made after trial has commenced. Choice **D** is incorrect because the admission of evidence outside the pleadings is discretionary.

85. **C** When the mental or physical condition of a party is in controversy, the court may order that party to submit to a physical or mental examination by a physician. Such an order will be made only upon

motion, for good cause shown, and prior notice to the person to be examined and all other parties. FRCP 35. Since Wanda is not a party to the action, an eye examination of her by P cannot be ordered under any circumstances. The other options are all incorrect for the reason just stated, that is, Wanda is not a party and therefore is not required to undergo a medical examination under any circumstances.

86. **C** A party must disclose without waiting for a discovery request any insurance policy under which any person carrying on an insurance business may be liable to satisfy part or all of a judgment. FRCP 26(a)(1)(A)(iv). Thus, the insured party must disclose the insurance policy even if it would not be admissible at trial. The other choices are incorrect because choice **C** correctly states the law.

87. **B** Opinions of experts retained by counsel in anticipation of litigation who are not to be called as witnesses are discoverable only "upon a showing of exceptional circumstances" (where the party would otherwise be unable to obtain the same facts or opinions by other means). FRCP 26(b)(4)(B). Thus, the economist's opinion is not discoverable because there are no indications that the other party was unable to access the facts or opinions through other means. Choice **A** is incorrect because Choice **B** is true. Choice **C** is incorrect since the time at which an expert forms his opinion is irrelevant to its discoverability. Choice **D** is incorrect. An expert's opinion is not automatically privileged and there is no indication as to why this expert opinion would be privileged.

88. **C** FRCP 26(a)(1)(A)(ii) requires that a party disclose "a copy—or description by category and location—of all documents, electronically stored information, and tangible things that the disclosing party has in its possession, custody, or control and may use to support its claims or defenses, unless the use would be solely for impeachment." If these materials would be used to support D's defense, D was required to disclose them in the manner described above. There is no indication of any privilege here, so choice **A** is wrong. Choice **B** is incorrect for the reasons stated above. Choice **D** is incorrect as it overstates the rule. D need only disclose those materials relevant to its claim or defense not to anything relevant to a disputed fact.

89. **D** A party may discover experts retained by counsel who will not be called at trial only upon a showing of exceptional circumstances (e.g., that it is impossible for the moving party to obtain these facts or opinions by another means). FRCP 26(b)(4)(B). Since there is

no indication of such circumstances here, P may not discover the identities and opinions of D's retained experts. Thus choice **A** is false. Choice **B** is incorrect because it states the law prior to the 1993 amendments to the FRCP. As explained above, the current standard is much narrower. Choice **C** is a misstatement of the law since evidence need only be discovery relevant, not admissible, to be discoverable. FRCP 26(b)(1).

90. **A** A party must supplement its initial mandatory disclosures if it discovers they are no longer complete or accurate. FRCP 26(e)(1). Thus, the existence of a new witness who may have discoverable information regarding disputed facts would have to be disclosed by D. Choices **B**, **C**, and **D** are all incorrect because they fail to recognize this mandatory requirement to supplement initial disclosure.

Joinder of Claims and Parties—Answers

91. C This is a statutory interpleader action, which requires minimal diversity between any two claimants and $500 or more in controversy. 28 U.S.C. §1335. Both are satisfied here. Sam and Dave are citizens of Texas and New York, respectively, and the amount in controversy is $7,000. Choice **A** is incorrect; there is no such requirement. Choice **B** is partially correct—§1332's amount in controversy is not satisfied—but ultimately wrong since the bank can rely on §1335. Choice **D** is incorrect; while venue would be improper under the interpleader venue statute, §1397, it would be proper under §1391(a)(2) since the property that is the subject of the action is located in Missouri.

92. B This is a proper use of a counterclaim in interpleader. Given that the stakeholder and the claimants are completely diverse and that the amount in controversy (exceeds $75,000) is satisfied, there is an independent basis of jurisdiction over the counterclaim. Moreover, the federal rules specifically allow this. Federal Rules of Civil Procedure 13(h) & 22(a)(2). In addition, the counterclaim falls within the court's supplemental jurisdiction under 28 U.S.C. §1367(a) since the counterclaim arises out of a common nucleus of operative facts with Plaintiff's claim against Bank. Nothing in §1367(b) forecloses the exercise of jurisdiction over this claim. Choice **A** is wrong; Krooke was a required party since he any the Bank might suffer prejudice in the absence of his joinder. Choice **C** is incorrect; while the standards of §1335 would not be satisfied here, both §1332 and §1367 are satisfied as noted above. Choice **D** is incorrect; while the joinder of Krooke as a defendant may not have been feasible, the suit need not be dismissed since the availability of interpleader permits the court to shape the relief in a manner that eliminates any potential prejudice to the Bank or Krooke.

93. A FRCP 18(a) allows a party asserting a claim to join "as many claims as it has against an opposing party." Choice **B** is incorrect; there is no such rule. Choice **C** is incorrect; the rules of aggregation allow a party to aggregate unrelated claims against a single defendant. Choice **D** is incorrect; the federal rules impose no such requirement.

94. C Under this emerging rule (adopted by three federal circuits), the counterclaim would be treated as permissive—not arising out of the same transaction as the plaintiff's claim—but nonetheless within the district court's supplemental jurisdiction—satisfying the common nucleus of operative facts test. Hence, the district court would have discretion to entertain the claim under 28 U.S.C. §1367(c). Choice **A** is incorrect; the exercise of supplemental jurisdiction is always discretionary. Choice **B** is incorrect; the majority of federal courts would require an independent basis of jurisdiction over the counterclaim. Choice **D** is incorrect given the minority rule described above.

95. **B** A minority of federal courts will not permit a plaintiff to file a crossclaim against a co-plaintiff in the absence of a counterclaim filed against the plaintiffs by the defendant. Choice **A** is incorrect. A majority of federal courts would allow Waylon to file the crossclaim against Willie. Choices **C** and **D** are both incorrect statements of the law.

96. **C** The claim asserted by Waylon would likely be treated as an evasion of the complete diversity rule under *Owen Equipment and Erection Co. v. Kroger*, 437 U.S. 365 (1978), thus running afoul of the limitations imposed by 28 U.S.C. §1367(b). Choice **A** is incorrect. Waylon's claim is premised on state law and he and Willie are from the same state. Choice **B** is incorrect The complete diversity rule does not apply to claims between co-parties. Choice **D** is incorrect since §1367(b) precludes the exercise of supplemental jurisdiction over this claim.

97. **D** Let's eliminate the incorrect answers before explaining why choice **D** is correct. Choice **A** is incorrect since there is no stake at issue; nor are there adverse claimants to a stake. Choice **B** is incorrect. FRCP 13(h) allows the joinder of additional parties to a counterclaim regardless of the compulsory or permissive nature of that claim. Choice **C** is incorrect since Rocky is a defendant and §1367(b) imposes no limits on joinder of parties by a defendant. That leaves us with choice **D** as the only option. The "may" is key. Given the theory of complete-diversity contamination announced by the Supreme Court in *Exxon Mobil Corp. v. Allapattah Services, Inc.*, 545 U.S. 546 (2005), it may be the case that permissive counterclaims, like original claims, will be subject to this same principle.

98. **A** This is not a proper impleader since Rocky is not seeking any form of indemnity from Pierre. Choice **B** is false given the absence of a claim for indemnity. Choice **C** is false. A defendant may file an impleader under FRCP 14. Choice **D** is false for the same reason as choice **B**.

99. **C** is correct; this is a classic example of *Kroger* evasion and not permitted by §1367(b)—see the answer to question 6, *supra*. Choice **A** is an incorrect statement of the law A plaintiff can file alternative claims of liability. Choice **B** is descriptively accurate as far as the transactional relationship goes, but incorrect given the *Kroger* evasion. Choice **D** is incorrect. The rules would allow this, but jurisdictional statutes would not—again, due to the *Kroger* evasion principle. *See Owen Equipment and Erection Co. v. Kroger*, 437 U.S. 365 (1978).

100. **C** In separate lawsuits brought by Myra and Aaron, the Bank might be required to delivery the proceeds of the account to both plaintiffs. Choice **A** is incorrect. Myra would be brought into the lawsuit because of her claim of ownership over the account and as a consequence of the potential double liability of the Bank. Choice **B** is not correct. The Bank would not be subject to inconsistent obligations, but to potential double liability. An "inconsistent obligation" requires a party to both do something and to refrain from doing that same thing. Choice **D** is incorrect. An absent party's status as a required party has nothing to do with whether diversity would be destroyed.

101. **C** FRCP 22(a)(2) allows a defendant to file a counterclaim in interpleader and 13(h) permits the joinder of Myra to that counterclaim. In addition, the interpleader satisfies both §1332 and §1367. Choices **A** and **B** are incorrect. Myra's presence as a defendant—regardless of the reason—would destroy complete diversity. Choice **D** is incorrect. Although the standards of statutory interpleader are not satisfied—the claimants are both from the same state—the standards of rule interpleader are satisfied—complete diversity between stakeholder and claimants and amount in controversy in excess of $75,000. As noted above, supplemental jurisdiction over the interpleader would also be satisfied.

102. **D** Choices **A**, **B** and **C** are incorrect. Choice **A** is incorrect because diversity requires that no plaintiff and no defendant be citizens of the same state. The fact that the plaintiffs are from the same state is irrelevant. Choice **B** is incorrect because plaintiffs are not "compelled" to join their actions simply because their claims arise out of the same transaction or series of transactions. Their joinder is permissive. Finally, Choice **C** is incorrect because D's motion probably would be denied (rather than granted) if the conditions described in Choice **C** are satisfied.

103. **D** Denny's claim is a compulsory counterclaim under the standards of FRCP 13(a)'s "same transaction" test. Moreover, his claim arises out of a common nucleus of operative facts with the plaintiffs' jurisdictionally sufficient claims, thus falling within the court's supplemental jurisdiction under 28 U.S.C. §1367(a). Choices **A** and **C** are incorrect. The claim is compulsory. Choice **B** is incorrect. There is no requirement that there be an independent basis of jurisdiction over a compulsory counterclaim.

104. **D** FRCP 13(g) allows Carmella to file her transactionally related crossclaim. FRCP 18(a) allows Carmella to join her unrelated contract claim to her negligence claim. Choice **A** is incorrect. The negligence claim is not a counterclaim. It is a crossclaim. Choice **B** is incorrect. Crossclaims are permissive. Choice **C** is incorrect for the reasons given in choice **D**.

105. **C** The factually related counterclaim, permitted by FRCP 13, would fall within the court's supplemental jurisdiction, and FRCP 13(h), relying on Rule 20(a)(2), would permit the joinder of Shaker to that claim. Section 1367(b) would impose no limits on the exercise of supplemental jurisdiction over the claim against Shaker. Choice **A** is incorrect. Shaker is not a party, much less a co-party. Choice **B** is incorrect. Hank is not seeking indemnification from Shaker for the claim filed against him by Fire. Choice **D** is incorrect. Hank is not a stakeholder entitled to file an interpleader.

106. **C** Section 1367(b) limits a plaintiff's ability to file a claim against party joined under FRCP 14, 19, 20 or 24 when doing so "would be inconsistent with the jurisdictional requirements of §1332." That "inconsistency" is premised on the law of §1332 as that law stood prior to the adoption of §1367. If prior to the adoption of §1367, a plaintiff impleader of a nondiverse party was permissible, it must have been the case that doing so was *consistent* with the jurisdictional standards of §1332. If that is so, nothing in §1367 renders such joinders *inconsistent* with those standards. Choice **A** is incorrect. FRCP 14(b) allows a plaintiff against whom a claim has been asserted to file an impleader. Choice **B** is incorrect. There is no such rule. Rather, §1367(b) imposes specified limits on a plaintiff's ability to do so. Choice **D** is incorrect for the reasons given in choice **C**.

107. **B** Section 1367(b) precludes the exercise of supplemental jurisdiction over claims by plaintiffs against persons joined pursuant to FRCP 14, 19, 20 or 24 when doing so would be "inconsistent with

the jurisdictional requirements of §1332." Carol's claims both fail under this standard since she has filed them against parties joined pursuant to FRCP 20 and since her claims fail to satisfy the amount in controversy requirement—that is, they are inconsistent with the jurisdictional standards of §1332. Choice **A** is incorrect. Carol's claim are part of the "same case or controversy" as Bob's claims against Ted and Alice, both which are jurisdictional sufficient claims. Choices **C** and **D** are incorrect for the reasons given in choice **B**.

108. **A** Bette should be allowed to intervene. She has an interest in that may be impaired by the board's decision not to appeal and it is clear that no party is adequately representing that interest. Choice **B** is incorrect. The facts indicate that Bette acted promptly once she realized that her interest was no longer adequately represented. Choice **C** misstates the law. There is no such rule. Choice **D** also misstates the law. It is precisely under such circumstances when a party is more likely to be allowed to interevene.

109. **C** There is no adversity among the claimants since the policy limit exceeds the claimants' collective claims. Choice **A** is incorrect. Under the modern law of interpleader, a stakeholder may also be a claimant. Choice **B** is incorrect. The fact that the stakeholder is a claimant does not, in itself, establish the propriety of interpleader. Choice **D** is incorrect since, as pointed out in choice **C**, the claimants are not adverse to one another and interpleader is improper.

110. **C** Statutory interpleader—that is, interpleader under §1335— requires minimal diversity among the claimants. While the estate and Carol are both from State Y, Larry is from State X. Hence, if he is also a claimant, minimal diversity will be satisfied. Choice **A** is incorrect. Rule interpleader requires satisfaction of §1332 and the amount in controversy is not satisfied here (just shy of $75,000). Choice **B** is incorrect. If Larry is not a claimant, minimal diversity will not be satisfied. Choice **D** is wrong because choice **C** is right.

111. **D** This is a proper subject of interpleader since Speedy is faced with adverse claimants to the same stake. Under the rules, Speedy may file a counterclaim in interpleader against Tina—FRCP 13(a) & 22(a)(2)—and may join Oscar to that claim—FRCP 13(h). Subject matter jurisdiction would be satisfied under both §1332(a)(2) and §1367. Choices **A** and **B** are incorrect. For the reasons given in choice **D**, the motion should be denied. Choice **C**

is incorrect since in the absence of Oscar, Speedy could be subject to double liability.

112. **A** In the absence of Local 901, the Coal Company could be subjected to inconsistent obligations, for the Virginia court might order the company to deny seniority to the Orrville miners while a court in Ohio might enforce the grievance decision and order the Coal Company to preserve the seniority of those workers. Choice **B** is incorrect. Local 901 is not required to intervene and if they refuse to intervene, the potential harm will be to the Coal Company, not to Local 901 or its members. Choice **C** is incorrect. Given the potential prejudice to the Coal Company, the district court could not in equity and good conscience proceed without them. Choice **D** is also incorrect for reasons stated in both choices **A** and **C**.

113. **C** There are four prerequisites to a class action: (1) the class must be so large that joinder of all members is not feasible, (2) the claims or defenses of the representatives must be typical of the class they seek to represent, (3) there must be common questions of law and fact to the class, and (4) the representative must fairly and adequately represent the interests of the class. FRCP 23(a). Since there is the possibility that many potential members of the class (all public college and university students in State X) would not be desirous of challenging the flag desecration statute, the defendants' strongest argument for denying certification of the class probably would be on this ground. Choice **A** is incorrect because the class probably would be sufficiently numerous (there are ordinarily thousands of college students within each state). Choice **B** is incorrect because there is no amount in controversy requirement with respect to the assertion of a federal claim. Choice **D** is incorrect because plaintiffs' claim probably would be characterized as a FRCP 23(b)(2) class action, and notice is expressly mandated only with respect to a FRCP 23(b)(3) action. Additionally, even if due process considerations mandated reasonable notice, it probably would not be impossible to notify the class because persons matriculating at a college presumably disclose their names and addresses to the institution. Finally, acceptable notice might be possible through college newspapers and a variety of other methods.

114. **B** If a trial court refuses to certify the class, its finding is not a final order, and therefore, an immediate appeal may not be taken. The case must be tried as a nonclass action, and only after a judgment is rendered can the correctness of the trial court's refusal to grant

certification be reviewed. The result in choice **B** is required as a consequence of the holding in *Coopers & Lybrand v. Livesay*, 437 U.S. 463 (1978). Choice **A** is incorrect because the "death knell" doctrine was specifically rejected in the *Coopers* decision. Choice **C** is incorrect because the opposite is true (the party seeking class certification must try the case on the merits before he can appeal the trial judge's refusal to permit the class action). Choice **D** is incorrect because the existing parties may litigate the case, even though certification of the class has been refused.

115. **D** FRCP 14(a)(3) allows a plaintiff to "assert against a third-party defendant any claim arising out of the transaction or occurrence that is the subject matter of the plaintiff's claim against the third-party plaintiff." Since Pam's claim against Insureall does not arise out of the same transaction or occurrence as her claim against Dr. Dumb, the rule does not allow her to file it; nor would any other rule permit the filing of this claim. For these reasons, choice **A** is incorrect. Choice **B** is also incorrect. Even though Pam's claim against Insureall would satisfy §1332, her claim must also satisfy a rule, which it does not. Choice **C** is incorrect. Dr. Dumb's claim against Insureall would fall within the court's supplemental jurisdiction.

116. **D** While FRCP 18(a) would permit Polly to join these unrelated claims in a single civil action, each claim must also satisfy the district court's subject matter jurisdiction. Polly's "rear-ended" claim is premised exclusively on state law. Since both Polly and Don are citizens of Nevada, diversity is not satisfied as to that claim. Nor is supplemental jurisdiction satisfied since the federal-securities claim and the state-law claim do not form part of the same constitutional case or controversy (i.e., they do not arise out of a common nucleus of operative fact). Hence, the state-law claim must be dismissed. Choice **A** correctly states the liberal joinder standard of FRCP 18(a), but fails to attend to the jurisdictional defect noted above. Choice **B** is incorrect since there is no "common nucleus" between the federal and state claims. Choice **C** provides an inaccurate description of scope of the federal rules.

117. **D** Since the separate claims asserted by Art and Bob arise out of a common nucleus of operative facts (the accident), they form part of the same constitutional case or controversy within the meaning of 28 U.S.C. §1367(a). Art's claim satisfies the requirements of §1332(a)(1) and Bob's claim, therefore, presumptively falls within the court's supplemental jurisdiction. Moreover, even though this

is a diversity case, nothing in §1367(b) limits the exercise of supplemental jurisdiction over Bob's claim. Hence, the district court has the power to hear Bob's claim. Section 1367(c), however, gives the district court the discretion to retain or dismiss that claim. For the reasons given, Choices **A** and **B** are incorrect. Choice **C** is also incorrect since it is premised a duty to exercise supplemental jurisdiction ("must") rather than on discretion.

118. **A** A U.S. district court cannot exercise supplemental jurisdiction over a claim by a plaintiff against a nondiverse defendant. *Exxon Mobil Corp. v. Allapattah Services, Inc.*, 545 U.S. 546 (2005). Choice **B** is incorrect. FRCP 20(a)(1) (same transaction and common question of law or fact) would allow Art and Bob to join together as plaintiffs. Choices **C** and **D** are wrong. Under the rule in *Exxon Mobil*, jurisdiction cannot, under any circumstances, be exercised over Bob's claim.

119. **D** A person who is not a party should be joined as a required party where failure to do so will leave any party to the action subject to a substantial risk of incurring multiple liability for a single obligation. Z is a required party because a judgment in favor of Y could subject X to multiple liability or even inconsistent judgments should Z later sue X. There is a potential problem here, however, since Z and X are from the same state. Hence, if Z is joined as a plaintiff, complete diversity will be destroyed and, under the terms of §1367(b), supplemental jurisdiction would not be available. However, this problem is easily avoided if the court orders X to interplead Y and Z in a counterclaim against Y, combining FRCP 13 and 22(a)(2). Under the standards of §1335, jurisdiction would be established because Z and Y (the claimants) are from different states and the amount in controversy—the value of the vehicle—exceeds the $500 minimum requirement. In addition, since this claim is transactionally related to Y's claim against X, supplemental jurisdiction will be satisfied as well, there being no limit imposed by §1367(b) on this type of joinder by a defendant. Choice **A** is incorrect since Z can be brought into the case as explained above. Choice **B** is incorrect since, as explained above, Z is a required party. Choice **C** is incorrect since joinder is possible through the device of interpleader.

120. **A** A crossclaim may be asserted against a co-party if the cause of action arises out of the transaction or occurrence that is the subject matter of the original action. FRCP 13(g). Since Emily's crossclaim

against Wallace arises from the accident, it may be asserted in this action. Although Emily and Wallace are both citizens of Maine, the court may exercise supplemental jurisdiction over a crossclaim filed by one codefendant against another. Choice **B** is incorrect because crossclaims are not compulsory under the FRCP. Thus, an action is not barred if no crossclaim is made in the original lawsuit. Choice **C** is incorrect for the reason given in choice **A**. Choice **D** is incorrect because Wallace has filed no claim against Emily. Had he done so, her claim would have been a counterclaim.

121. **B** Since CC might have an indemnity-type claim against BB, impleader would be appropriate. FRCP 14(a). Subject matter jurisdiction is not a consideration because supplemental jurisdiction would extend to such an impleader regardless of the citizenship of the relevant parties—rendering choice **C** incorrect. Choice **A** is incorrect because, while BB arguably has an interest in the *Mary v. CC* lawsuit, it is not clear how that interest would be impaired by the pending lawsuit. Relatedly, any judgment obtained by Mary against CC would have no collateral estoppel or *res judicata* effect in a subsequent action by CC against BB. Choice **D** is incorrect because, CC's counterclaim being permissive in nature, the "amount in controversy" requirement would not be satisfied.

Adjudication – Answers

122. **A** Basil met his burden of production by introducing sufficient
material reducible to admissible evidence that, if not rebutted,
would require the court grant him a judgment as a matter of law.
Choice **B** is incorrect. Basil's affidavit is reducible to admissible
evidence, for Basil can testify to the alleged facts at trial. Choice
C is incorrect. Sybil's response does not refute the fact that she
failed to deliver the novel as of the date specified in the contract.
In essence, her response is nonresponsive. Choice **D** is incorrect.
Since Basil met his burden of production (see choice **A**), the burden of production shifted to Sybil.

123. **D** On the assumption that the statute of limitations is tolled only
by service of process, Sybil has met her burden by introducing
sufficient material reducible to admissible evidence that, if not
rebutted, would require the court to rule in her favor. Choice **A**
misstates the law. Basil need only respond if Sybil meets her burden of production. Choice **B** misstates the law. A party with the
burden of persuasion at trial may properly file a motion for summary judgment. Choice **C** misstates the law. Sybil's cross-motion
for summary judgment need not be responsive to Basil's motion
for summary judgment.

124. **A** Bianca failed to meet her burden of production by not responding to the affidavit of her immediate supervisor. As a consequence,
there is no genuine dispute on Qualex's fired-for-cause defense.
Choice **B** is incorrect. While Qualex would have the burden of persuasion at trial on its defense, the affidavit of the supervisor was
sufficient to shift the burden of production to Bianca. Choice **C** is
incorrect. While Bianca did meet her burden of production on this
issue, that does not alter the fact that she failed to meet her burden
of production on the critical fired-for-cause defense. Choice **D** is
incorrect. A for-cause termination would be a complete defense to
Bianca's claim.

125. **D** Bianca provided sufficient factual matter, including the admission, to support each of the elements of her *prima facie* case. The
summary judgment is only partial, however, since Qualex is still
entitled to defend if it had a bona fide nondiscriminatory basis
for terminating Bianca's employment. Choice **B** is incorrect since
Qualex did not file a motion for summary judgment and since
Bianca has not been given an opportunity to respond to the

affidavit filed by Qualex. *See* FRCP 56(f). Choice **C** is incorrect. The failure to respond to the Request for Admission will be treated as an admission.

126. **C** This is the precise standard for entry of default under FRCP 55(a). Choice **A** is incorrect; a defendant's failure to respond does not entitle the plaintiff to a summary judgment. Choice **B** is incorrect; a failure to respond under these circumstances will not trigger sanctions under FRCP 11. Choice **D** is incorrect; there is no such rule.

127. **C** This is a correct statement of the law. *See* FRCP 60(b)(1) and 60(c) (1). Choice **A** is incorrect. A judgment can be rescinded if procured through fraud, but that is not the only basis on which rescission can be granted. See FRCP 60(b)(1)-(6). Choice **B** is incorrect. Only a party who has appeared is entitled to a 7-day notice. FRCP 55(b) (2). Choice **D** is incorrect for the reasons previously given.

128. **B** Default judgments that are constitutionally or procedurally defective are subject to collateral attack. Under FRCP 4 (which has been enacted in State X), there is no provision for service by first class mail. Hence, P failed to comply with the rule. See FRCP 4(e)(2). Since P failed to properly effectuate service of process, the State X judgment was subject to collateral attack. Choice **A** is incorrect because, despite actual receipt of the documents by D, he was not served in accordance with applicable law. Choice **C** is incorrect because, while a default judgment is usually deemed to be "on the merits," that principle only applies to a valid default judgment. Choice **D** is incorrect for the reasons stated above.

129. **C** In U.S. district courts, the judge *may* conduct the voir dire examination. FRCP 47(a). Bias or prejudice of a potential juror against one of the parties is usually a proper subject for inquiry at the voir dire. The defendant's question with respect to prejudice against corporations was therefore an appropriate inquiry, and the judge's refusal to ask that question was error. Choice **B** is incorrect because the fact that a party may exercise peremptory challenges does not detract from the court's failure to inquire about a general prejudice against corporations. Choice **A** is incorrect because any question regarding a juror's ability to reach a fair and impartial verdict is appropriate at the voir dire. Questions in this context need bear no relationship to the factual issues that will be contested at trial. Choice **D** is incorrect because the judge may use her

discretion in determining whether questions that counsel requests are appropriate.

130. C A plaintiff who accepts a remittitur in federal court may not challenge the trial court's ruling on appeal. By accepting the remittitur, and thereby avoiding the delay and cost of a new trial, the plaintiff is deemed to have relinquished her right to appeal the court's order. If Paul was dissatisfied with the remittitur, he should have appealed the court's order on the basis that the judge had abused his discretion (i.e., there was no good faith basis for reducing the verdict by the given amount). The fact that Paul agreed to the reduction "under protest" is irrelevant. Choice **A** is incorrect because the Seventh Amendment argument is overcome by the fact that the plaintiff is considered to have agreed to the remittitur. Choice **B** is incorrect because, whether the trial court abused its discretion or not in ordering a new trial, Paul waived his right to review the court's order by accepting the decreased sum. Choice **D** is incorrect because the Seventh Amendment is applicable to damage issues.

131. B The parties in a federal civil case may stipulate to a jury of fewer than 12 persons, but unless the parties otherwise agree, the verdict in a federal civil trial must be unanimous. FRCP 48(b). Since one of the jurors voted in favor of Defendant, the ruling was defective. Choice **A** is incorrect because the parties stipulated to a jury of fewer than 12 persons. Choice **C** is incorrect because the fact that a verdict fails to exceed $75,000 is irrelevant (the "amount in controversy" requirement is measured only at the time the action is filed). Choice **D** is incorrect because any lack of personal jurisdiction over Defendant appears to have been waived when Defendant failed to assert this alleged defect at the time of pleading. FRCP 12(h)(1).

132. A Under the Seventh Amendment, the right to a jury trial exists as to any issue that pertains to a legal remedy. An action seeking money damages to remedy a trespass is a "legal" claim. Thus, Delbert would be entitled to a jury trial with respect to all issues pertaining to this action. Choice **C** is incorrect because the "clean-up doctrine" (which allows a federal court to determine legal issues that were "incidental" to a primarily equitable claim) has been repudiated. *Dairy Queen, Inc. v. Wood,* 369 U.S. 469 (1962). Choice **B** is incorrect because in federal court, each party is entitled to a jury trial with respect to any legal issue (regardless of the "primary" relief that the plaintiff is seeking). Choice **D** is incorrect because the tort of trespass existed in 1791 (when the Seventh Amendment was ratified) and therefore would constitute a "suit at common law."

133. **C** A motion for a judgment as a matter of law may be granted only where there is no sufficient legal basis for any other judgment. Since it is entirely possible that a jury could conclude that Joan's physical problems were the consequence of the infection (rather than the inadvertent application of an acidic substance by Dr. Jekyll), a judgment as a matter of law would not be appropriate. Choice **A** is incorrect because the fact that Dr. Jekyll admitted that the perforium bottle was located near a container holding an acidic substance would not preclude the jury from reasonably concluding that he had used the correct bottle. Choice **B** is incorrect because it cannot be said that there was no sufficient legal basis for concluding that Dr. Brown was not negligent. Choice **D** is incorrect because choice **C** is true.

134. **A** A motion for a judgment as a matter of law may be granted only where there is no legally sufficient basis for any other judgment. Since a jury could reasonably conclude that Dr. Jekyll inadvertently applied an acidic substance to Joan's ear, a judgment as a matter of law in favor of Dr. Jekyll would be inappropriate. Thus, the trial court's judgment should be reversed and a new trial ordered. Choice **B** is incorrect because, as described in the answer to the preceding question, a jury could reasonably find that Dr. Jekyll was not at fault. Choice **C** is incorrect because a jury could reasonably render a verdict for Joan. Choice **D** is incorrect because choice **A** is true.

135. **D** A motion for a judgment as a matter of law made prior to the submission of the case to the jury is a prerequisite for a JNOV, the latter operating a renewal of the prior motion. FRCP 50(b). FRCP 50(b). Since Dr. Jekyll did not make a motion for a judgment as a matter of law at the close of the evidence, a JNOV cannot be granted. Since the trial court denied the motion for a new trial and Dr. Jekyll did not appeal that decision, the jury verdict must be reinstated. Choice **A** is incorrect because a motion for a new trial may be joined with a JNOV motion. Choice **C** is incorrect because Dr. Jekyll did not appeal the district court's denial of his motion for a new trial. Thus, a new trial cannot be ordered. Choice **B** is

incorrect because no motion for a judgment as a matter of law was made, so the JNOV cannot be sustained.

136. **A** While CC introduced sufficient proof for a fact finder to determine that it had warned Paul not to work near the scaffolding (i.e., the supervisor had told Paul it looked "unsafe"), Mary had to produce proof adequate for a fact finder to conclude that CC otherwise. Her proof indicated only that Paul was apprehensive about working near the scaffolding. Choice **B** is incorrect because the evidence introduced by Mary does not pertain to CC's alleged failure to warn of the danger. Since Mary (as the plaintiff) would have the burden of proof on this issue, a verdict must be directed for CC. Choice **C** is incorrect because, under these circumstances, the court is obliged to direct a verdict in favor of CC. Choice **D** is incorrect because CC introduced enough evidence to rebut the presumption against it (i.e., for a jury to conclude it had inspected the scaffolding).

137. **D** A finding cannot be set aside if there is substantial evidence to support it. Since CC introduced enough evidence to support the court's findings, the court's factual determination and corresponding judgment could not be set aside. Choice **A** is incorrect since CC introduced substantial evidence to support his factual contention that it had warned Paul. Choices **B** and **C** are incorrect because a judgment may not be set aside when there is substantial evidence to support it.

138. **C** Where the jury's answers to written questions are inconsistent with a general verdict rendered by the jury, the judge may (1) enter a verdict in accordance with the answers to the interrogatories, (2) return the answers to the jury for further consideration and verdict, or (3) order a new trial. FRCP 49(b)(3). Choice **A** is incorrect given the above options. Choice **B** is incorrect, for, as noted above, the judge has other options. Choice **D** is incorrect. This is, in fact, one of the options available to the court.

Claim and Issue Preclusion – Answers

139. C The 2000 damage claim is precluded—same claim, same parties, and a final, valid judgment on the merits. The 2002 claim is not precluded since the different timeframe renders the claims different, that is, not the same claims. Choices **A**, **B** and **D** are incorrect for the reasons given with respect to choice **C**—that is, the doctrine of claim preclusion applies to one but not the other claim.

140. B Darla lost her negligence crossclaim against Rita based on the jury finding that Darla was guilty of contributory negligence. The second lawsuit involves the same parties (Rita and Darla), the same issue—Darla's negligence—and that issue was litigated, decided, and necessary to the judgment in the first case. Hence, Darla should be precluded denying her negligence. Choice **A** is incorrect; the finding that Rita was negligent was not necessary to the judgment entered in the previous case. Erase that decision from the final judgment and the judgment remains the same. Choice **C** is incorrect for the same reason. Choice **D** is incorrect, since Darla's denial of negligence should be precluded.

141. A Each of the elements of preclusion is satisfied. Although Holmes was not a party, he is entitled to benefit from the judgment in favor of his employer under a theory of privity premised on the law of vicarious liability. Some courts might describe this as a form of non-mutual defensive estoppel. Choice **B** is incorrect; while Holmes was not technically a party, he still may benefit from the judgment in favor of his employer for the reasons given above. Choice **C** is incorrect; there is no intervention requirement in this context. Choice **D** is incorrect; Holmes's benefit derives not from the hospital's representative capacity but from the law of vicarious liability.

142. B The privity relationship described in the previous answer, only applies if the employer prevails. Choice **A** is incorrect. As a non-party, Holmes is not bound by the judgment against his employer. Choice **C** is an incorrect application of the mutuality principle. Since Holmes was not a party, there was no mutuality. Choice **D** is incorrect; there is no such rule.

143. C The general rule is that person not a party to case cannot be bound by the judgment in that case. Matt was not a party to the first litigation; nor does he fall into any of the limited exceptions to the general rule. Choice **A** is incorrect because Bill could sue Matt for indemnity. Choice **B** is incorrect. Nothing in the law of preclusion prevents Joan from filing separate lawsuits against different defendants. Finally, choice **D** is incorrect because Joan's claim against Bill for personal injuries would barred in most jurisdictions since her property and personal injury claims arise out of the same transaction or occurrence.

144. **A** The California court must apply the law of preclusion that the U.S. district court would apply, that is, federal preclusion law. However, since the U.S. district court was sitting in diversity, under *Semtek Int'l Inc. v. Lockheed Martin Corp.*, 531 U.S. 497 (2001), the U.S. district would borrow the preclusion law of the state in which it sits, that is, California. Under California's primary rights approach to preclusion the breach of contract and defamation claims represent the invasion of different primary rights. Given the rule in *Semtek*, both choices **B** and **C** rely on the incorrect standard. Choice **D** states an incorrect proposition of law.

145. **C** The trial court's rulings are "alternative" in the sense that either ground standing alone would fully support the judgment. Under §27 of the Restatement (Second) of Judgments, neither ground will be deemed binding unless affirmed on appeal. Choice **A** describes a minority approach to this question, but not the approach endorsed by the Restatement (Second). Choice **B** misstates the law. Choice **D** describes the approach taken by the first Restatement, which, as the explanation for choice **C** provides, has been superseded.

146. **A** In order to prevail, the jury was required to find (at least implicitly) that B had reached majority and that there was no fraud. Hence, both findings were necessary to the judgment, that is, both were implicit in the judgment. Choice **B** is incorrect; there was no need to appeal since these are not alternative findings. Choice **C** is incorrect; a specific finding is not required when the decision of the issue is implicit in the judgment. Choice **D** is incorrect since both findings were necessary to the judgment, that is, these findings were not alternative to one another.

147. **C** is correct. Since the standard of proof in the criminal proceeding is higher than the standard of proof in the civil proceeding, a failure to satisfy the criminal standard cannot preclude litigation under the lower civil standard. Choice **A** is incorrect since it states the rule too broadly. If Martha had lost in the criminal proceeding, issues decided against her in that proceeding could be precluded

in subsequent civil proceeding. Choice **B** is incorrect; it's just the opposite and explained in choice **C**. Choice **D** correctly describes the standards for nonmutual, offensive issue preclusion, but overlooks the problem created by the different standards of proof (as noted in choice **C**).

148. **C** A judgment in an FRCP 23(b)(2) class action is binding on the entire class. X would be bound by the determination that there was insufficient proof that D had not read the exams. FRCP 23(c)(3). This issue is critical for both injunctive relief and monetary damages. Choice **A** is incorrect because a judgment rendered by a court that lacked subject matter is generally entitled to full faith and credit. Choice **B** is incorrect because there was diversity between the named plaintiff and the defendant. Choice **D** is incorrect because choice **C** is true.

149. **C** Where the precise issue was actually litigated in a prior action by the party against whom issue preclusion is asserted, and that issue was essential to the decision rendered in the prior lawsuit, issue preclusion will usually be permitted. If Demosthenes prevailed, Aristotle would probably be able to assert nonmutual collateral estoppel against Plato. Alternatively, Aristotle can be seen as being in privity with Demosthenes and entitled to the benefits (but not the burdens) of any judgment issued in the *Plato v. Demosthenes* action. Choice **A** is incorrect since Aristotle was not a party to the *Plato v. Demosthenes* actions. Choice **B** is incorrect for the reasons given in choice **C**, that is, Aristotle may benefit from a judgment in *Plato v. Demosthenes*. Choice **D** is incorrect because choice **C** is true.

150. **C** Since C was neither a party to the *A v. B* lawsuit nor in privity with a party to that suit, C cannot be bound by that judgment. The application of collateral estoppel here would violate C's due process rights. Choice **A** is incorrect. The court would have no such discretion given that C was not a party. Choice **B** is incorrect because (1) a different claim is involved (C's rights of recovery, rather than A's), and (2) A and C were not in privity. Choice **D** is incorrect because collateral estoppel may not constitutionally be applied under any circumstances.

Table of References to the Federal Rules of Civil Procedure

Table of References to
Title 28, United States Code

Index

References are to the number of the question raising the issue. "E" indicates an Essay Question; "M" indicates a Multiple-Choice Question.